FUNDAMENTALS OF
ARCHITECTURAL DESIGN

Paul
Ross
Wallach

PUBLISHED BY a-tec — Textbooks & Curriculum

Published and Distributed by:
Tech Ed Concepts, Inc.
32 Commercial Street
Concord, NH 03301
800.338.2238
www.tecedu.com

Chief Architect® is a registered trademark of Chief Architect, Inc.
6500 N. Mineral Drive, Coeur d'Alene, ID 83815

Printed in the United Stated of America

10 9 8 7 6 5 4 3 2 1

ISBN Number: 0-538-30006-X

Wallach, Paul Ross
Fundamentals of Architectural Design/Paul Ross Wallach

ABOUT THE AUTHOR

Paul Ross Wallach brings more than 40 years of classroom teaching experience including junior high school, high school, and community college levels to the writing of this unique text. In addition to his teaching experience, he has worked extensively in the development of educational programs and texts. Through these experiences, he has built a unique talent for showing students, through practical illustrations, how architectural designing and drafting is done.

PREFACE

Fundamentals of Architectural Design is intended for use as an introductory, basic text. This text makes it possible for students to learn basic drafting skills through architectural drafting principles and techniques. This text is concise while covering all the basic skills and knowledge necessary for residential design.

Part I provides an introduction to architecture and the need for architectural plans.
Part II covers building sites, including the orientation of structures on their sites.
Part III introduces the student to the design process used in planning a house.
Part IV introduces the student to fundamental drafting skills. Content stresses elementary drafting skills, techniques, and background information for the preparation of architectural drawings.
Part V explains the practices and procedures necessary for the preparation of specific types of architectural plans.
Part VI presents two complete set of working drawing plans. One set has a series of blueprint reading questions which may be used as homework or testing.

ORGANIZATION

Each part is divided into a series of units. The units are sequenced to provide only the basic information necessary to complete simple architectural plans and designs. Presentations and examples are carefully prepared to relate to the student's environment. New terms are defined in context at first use. All units are extensively illustrated. The illustrations are captioned with questions relating to text content.

FEATURES

The vocabulary level has been computer-analyzed to assure that readability is at or below student grade levels. In addition, large, clear type has been set in readable-width columns. Further, there is a close integration between the text and some 300 illustrations.

• The technical portions of the text are presented for ready learnability. All technical terms are defined when introduced. Once defined, the terms are consciously repeated for reinforcement. New terms are also listed in a Vocabulary Checklist at the end of each unit. For additional reinforcement, a glossary is provided.

PREFACE

FEATURES cont...

- A simplified, professionally drawn set of architectural plans is used as an instructional model. These plans may be used for student practice in such skill areas as print reading, design analysis, and drawing practice.

- The book is designed as an aid to student career exploration. Units within the book deal specifically with architecture, drafting, and architectural-related occupations. In addition, discussions cover such topics as the relationship of architects and clients, and livability of homes.

- This book is technologically current. To illustrate, topics covered include the framing of homes for passive and active solar systems, and metric standards of measurement.

- At the end of each unit, there is a complete set of review activities that can be assigned to meet student needs. Included are a listing of vocabulary terms, a series of content-related review questions, and a section entitled "Your Architectural Scrapbook." The architectural scrapbook provides a unique opportunity to promote student understanding and learning. Students are instructed to build a scrapbook of clippings and drawings that they prepare themselves. The scrapbook activities are designed to help students relate their learning experiences about architecture to their own environments and everyday encounters. As scrapbook-building instructions are followed, students build personal references that can be used to reinforce the learning that has taken place through reading and classroom practice.

ACKNOWLEDGMENTS

The author expresses his appreciation to Wendy Talcott, President of Home Planners, Inc., for use of many of her firm's home plans and renderings.

- * Wine Creek Road Residence, Firm: Siegel & Strain Architects Photo © JD Peterson, 2003 AIA COTE, Top 10 winner.
- * Hidden Villa Hostel & Summer Camp, Firm: Arkin Tilt Architects, Photo © Ed Caldwell 2003 AIA COTE, Top 10 winner.

CONTENTS

CONTENTS

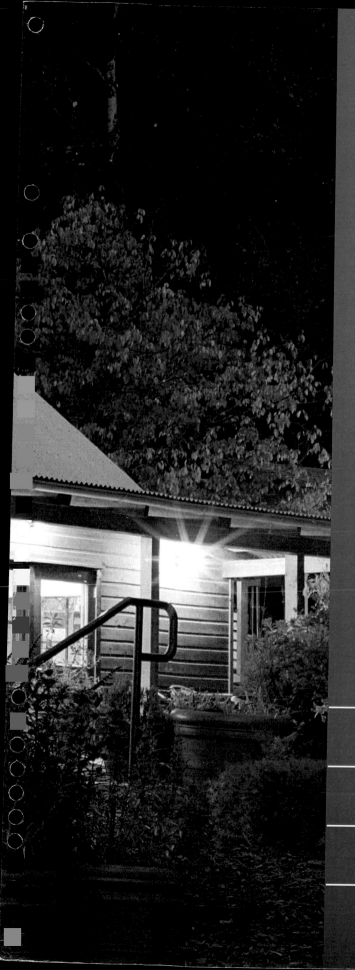

PART I

An Introduction to Architecture

The Story of Architecture

Architectural Styles

Forms in Architecture

Architects and Builders

PART I

AN INTRODUCTION TO ARCHITECTURE

SOME DEFINITIONS

Architecture is both an art and a science. It is an art because architects create new ideas and new places for people to live and work. Architecture is also a science because architects work closely with the sciences. The designs and materials used in buildings must follow scientific principles. The job of the *architect* is to design structures. The architect may also be in charge of supervising the building of these structures.

Architectural drafting is the preparation of special drawings of buildings. These drawings show how buildings are constructed. The drawings must show the size of all parts and segments of a structure. A *drafter* is a person who prepares the working drawings. These drawings show the size and details of buildings designed by the architects or designers.

YOU AND ARCHITECTURE

No matter what you do in school or after you graduate, architecture will be a part of your life. You may want to go on to a career in architecture or architectural drafting. You may also find yourself in work that requires the use and reading of architectural drawings. This would be the case if you went into the fields of construction or real estate.

Your knowledge of architecture and drafting will be helpful even if you don't use this information at work. You will have to live somewhere. Knowledge of the design and construction of buildings will make you a better consumer. You will be able to use your knowledge in selecting places to live. You will also be able to do a better job of remodeling or decorating your home.

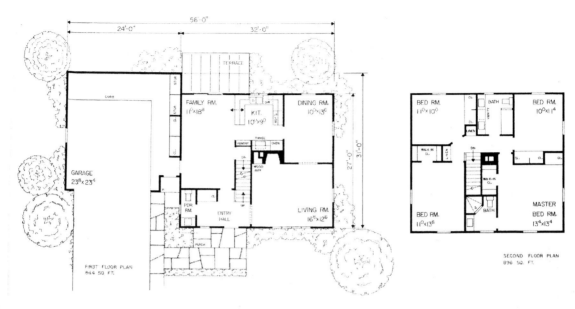

YOUR LEARNING JOB

Part I of this book helps to build your understanding of architecture. It covers:
- The history and development of architecture
- Shapes and styles used in architectural design
- The job of the architect, the architectural drafter, and the builders with whom these people work.

Your knowledge about these subjects will be developed in reading the units within Part I of the text. You will also learn from the questions you answer and the activities you complete as you work through this text.

The work you do in Part I will give you the understanding necessary to move ahead in this book. As you continue your study, you will learn how to perform architectural drafting yourself.

UNIT 1
THE STORY OF ARCHITECTURE

THE NEED FOR SHELTER

All living creatures need shelter. This need applies to birds, animals, insects, and people. **Figure 1-1** shows a number of shelters built or used by animals. Notice that some of these shelters are natural. That is, they are found in nature. Natural shelters can be caves, crevices in rocks, or boughs (sheltering formations) of trees.

Other creatures build shelters from materials that are found in nature. A bird's nest is an example. Most animals are born with instincts that determine the kinds of shelters they find or build. An instinct is a natural desire or drive to do something . Most creatures have both a need for shelter and an instinct that controls the kind of shelter they build or use. Usually , each species of bird, insect, or animal builds a specific type of shelter. A species is a specific kind of creature. Each species has its own specific instinct about shelter. There are few variations. For example, if you found two different beehives, one might be larger than the other. But their designs would be basically the same. This is also true for birds. Each type of bird builds one type of nest. The only variations might be in the location or materials available when the shelters are put together.

People are the exception. Only humans have developed creative skills for designing and building different shelters. People create a variety of shelters used for different purposes. These structures are used for living, working, religion, government, and recreation. The designing of these shelters is the job of the architect. All of

Figure 1-1. All living creatures follow instincts to find or build shelters. *What is an instinct?*

these structures go beyond the basic need for shelter. A modern home like the example in **Figure 1-2** does much more than protect people from the weather. People use their homes for entertainment, for hobbies, for study, and for many other activities. All of these home uses go beyond the function of basic shelter.

Figure 1-2. Humans have expanded their design and building of structures beyond basic needs for shelter. *What purposes other than shelter are served by a modern home?*

PRIMITIVE ARCHITECTURE

Design in human shelters is a recent development in human history. Prehistoric people were not builders. The term *prehistoric* identifies people who lived before human events were recorded. Their instincts drove them to find food, water, warmth, and safety. These are the same instincts that drive animals to seek shelter. So, prehistoric people lived in natural caves or burrows (dug out spaces) in the ground as shown in **Figure 1-3**. This type of cave provided only the most basic warmth and shelter. With these basic needs met, prehistoric humans had little need to build or design better structures.

Figure 1-3. Prehistoric Living quarters provided only basic shelter and warmth. *What did people look for in selecting natural shelters?*

As populations expanded, more people had to share available food and water. It became necessary for humans to travel further to find their food and water. As they traveled, it became necessary for people to find new shelters. But this was not always possible. This brought about the primitive period of human development. *Primitive* means early, or beginning. Primitive shelters were simple and basic, limited by the materials and tools developed in these early times.

Primitive humans built shelters from available materials. Some of these structures are illustrated in **Figure 1-4**. Early humans approached the building of structures in much the same way as some animals. For example, some shelters were built from available sticks, twigs, mud, and grass. This is basically the same approach used by beavers.

Some groups of primitive people found that they had to travel in search of food and water. People who wander widely and regularly are called *nomads*. Because they traveled so much, nomads didn't have time to build permanent shelters. So, nomadic people developed shelters that they could carry with them. An example of a

Figure 1-4. The first shelters built by humans were made from available materials. *What are some reasons for building shelters instead of looking for natural shelters?*

primitive nomad movable shelter is shown in **Figure 1-5**. These are simple structures that use materials that are easily carried, such as poles and animal skins. With these, people could travel all day, then put up shelters at night to protect themselves from the weather.

Eventually, groups of these primitive people found large supplies of food and water in safe locations. The nomads could then live in one location for longer periods of time. This led to the building of a more permanent type of structure-a shelter that could not be moved. Some early types of permanent homes are shown in **Figure 1-6**. Note that, during this stage of development, people began to use stones as a building material.

TOOLS AND HUMAN-MADE MATERIALS

Two important characteristics of humans played important roles in the improvement of shelters:

1. Humans have brains that are superior to those of other creatures. Brains enable people to invent new methods and to learn from experience. Thus, early people began to develop structures that would be more comfortable and more useful. They began to want more than basic warmth and shelter from their structures.

2. Humans are equipped with a unique tool for building structures. Only people have hands in which thumbs oppose four fingers. This is known as the prehensile hand. With their prehensile hands, people discovered that they could make and use tools to improve upon natural materials.

Figure 1-5. Nomadic people created shelters that they could carry with them as they traveled. *Why did people travel as a regular part of their lives?*

Figure 1-6. The first permanent shelters built by primitive humans were made from natural materials. *Why did people begin to build permanent shelters?*

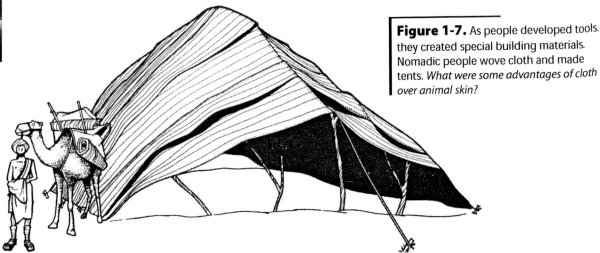

Figure 1-7. As people developed tools. they created special building materials. Nomadic people wove cloth and made tents. *What were some advantages of cloth over animal skin?*

The combination of hand and brain was applied to create tools. The tools were used to cut materials and to fit them together for better structures. Eventually, nomadic people learned to weave cloth. They then developed structures that were larger and lighter than those made from natural materials. Tents like those shown in **Figure 1-7** became the traveling homes of nomads. Later, people living in permanent homes learned to form bricks from clay. These were dried in the sun or by fire. With bricks, people were able to construct the types of homes shown in **Figure 1-8**.

As the quality of tools improved, humans were also able to cut and move large stones. Structures grew larger and more permanent because they could resist climate and other natural forces, such as wind. Structures made from brick and stone were also safer. Occupants were protected against animals and other natural enemies.

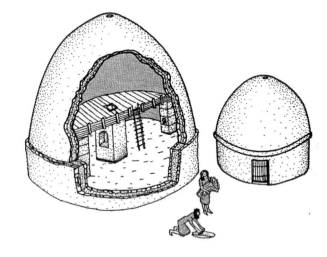

Figure 1-8. Tools were used to create bricks that were dried in the sun or by fire. These bricks were used to build permanent structures. *What special advantages over animals did humans have for creating tools and designed structures?*

Part I—An Introduction to Architecture

HISTORIC DEVELOPMENT

As buildings grew larger, the need for structural design increased. With bigger buildings, more cooperation between workers was necessary. The need to provide materials for use in building also became more complicated. To meet these developing needs, the art and science of architectural design was born.

People moved into communities. They found they could protect themselves better and improve their lives by living in groups. This changed their needs for buildings. Specialized buildings began to appear. One type of structure that developed was a building devoted to religion. Example of religious structures in the Middle East are shown in **Figure 1-9**.

Later, people began to develop buildings for use by government. The Mediterranean countries, particularly Greece and Rome, were leaders in this development. An example of a Greek structure used for both government and religion is shown in **Figure 1-10**.

Buildings that served as centers for both religion and government were also built by early settlers of Central America. Examples of their architecture are seen in **Figure 1-11**.

Still other types of governmental and religious buildings were constructed in the Far East, or Orient. An example is shown in **Figure 1-12**.

Figure 1-9. Social buildings for religion were constructed. These structures are examples of religious buildings in the Middle East. *Why was architecture necessary for creating buildings of this type?*

Figure 1-10. Governments began to construct buildings for their own use. These buildings are examples from the Mediterranean area, Greece and Rome. *What purpose do such structures serve beyond basic shelter?*

Figure 1-11. Elaborate buildings that combined governmental and religious uses were constructed in Central America. *Look at the shapes of these buildings. Find a basic difference between these shapes and the Greek and Roman structures.*

Notice the differences in the designs of buildings in **Figures 1-10**, **1-11**, and **1-12**. These buildings were created by people in different parts of the world. The people of each region developed a style of architecture to meet their own needs. Architectural styles in each region were influenced by many factors. These factors included climate and the types of materials available. Other influences on architecture were the wealth of the people and the role of religion in their lives.

Europe led the way in the development of towns and cities with large buildings. Many of these structures were designed specifically as centers where people worked. These buildings were used for commerce (business) and for manufacturing.

The growing needs of people led to designs known as *modern architecture*. Modern architecture does not refer to a single style or type of building. Instead, modern architecture is *functional*. This means the designs are tailored to the uses of the buildings. Styles and types of architecture are discussed further in Unit 2.

Figure 1-12. This is an example of the religious and governmental buildings constructed in the Far East. *How do the Far East designs differ from those of the Greek and Roman buildings?*

As business and manufacturing were concentrated in cities, new classes of people arose. People successful in business gathered large sums of money. With wealth they could afford homes that were larger, more comfortable, and often more highly decorated, or ornate. These types of homes are called *mansions*. As cities in Europe became crowded, it became necessary for people to spread out again. Populations shifted to places like America. Early settlers in America had basic skills in and knowledge about architecture. But they did not have the same materials as they had used for building in Europe. The structures in America thus reflected the materials and tools available in the new land. One example is a building constructed from trees in the plentiful forests of the New World. This was known as the *log cabin*, as seen in **Figure 1-13**.

Figure 1-13. In America, people constructed buildings with tools and materials available to them. The log cabin is a prime example of architecture at work in the American colonies. *Why were log cabins practical?*

A PERIOD OF RAPID CHANGE

The last 50 years has been a time of great change in building materials and designs. More change has occurred in the last 50 years than in the previous 50 million years.

Some of the most important of these changes include:

- Entirely new materials have been developed, including aluminum, plastics, and protective coatings.

- Older materials produced in new, improved forms have become available. New methods have been developed for making building materials from these older materials. Included are wood, glass, and metals. These materials can now be put together in lighter, larger shapes.

- Modern engineering techniques have made it possible to use these new and improved materials in different ways.

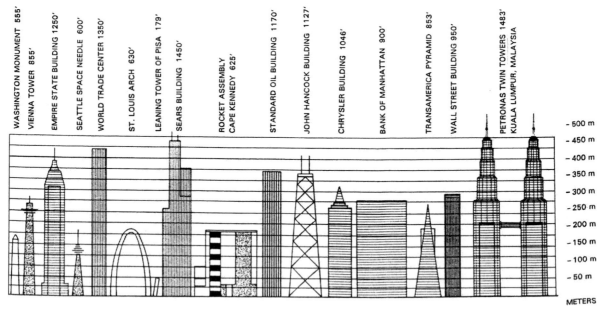

WASHINGTON MONUMENT 555'
VIENNA TOWER 855'
EMPIRE STATE BUILDING 1250'
SEATTLE SPACE NEEDLE 600'
WORLD TRADE CENTER 1350'
ST. LOUIS ARCH 630'
LEANING TOWER OF PISA 179'
SEARS BUILDING 1450'
ROCKET ASSEMBLY CAPE KENNEDY 625'
STANDARD OIL BUILDING 1170'
JOHN HANCOCK BUILDING 1127'
CHRYSLER BUILDING 1046'
BANK OF MANHATTAN 900'
TRANSAMERICA PYRAMID 853'
WALL STREET BUILDING 950'
PETRONAS TWIN TOWERS 1483' KUALA LUMPUR, MALAYSIA

- 500 m
- 450 m
- 400 m
- 350 m
- 300 m
- 250 m
- 200 m
- 150 m
- 100 m
- 50 m

METERS

With these new and improved materials, it is possible to construct buildings that have almost no limits in size and shape. **Figure 1-14** shows some structures of modern design.

Advanced methods of engineering have made it possible to build structures in new shapes. Some of these modern designs were previously impossible. As one example of the kinds of structures possible today, see **Figure 1-15**.

Figure 1-14. New, modern materials and advanced engineering methods are making it possible to construct buildings in shapes that would have been impossible previously. *What features of these buildings rely on modern engineering methods?*

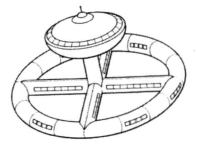

Figure 1-15. The architecture of tomorrow holds unlimited potential. *What special designs are necessary to provide shelter for humans living in outer space?*

UNIT 1 ACTIVITIES

VOCABULARY CHECKLIST

1. architecture
2. architect
3. drafter
4. prehistoric
5. primitive
6. nomads
7. modern architecture
8. mansion

REVIEW QUESTIONS

1. What kinds of shelter did prehistoric humans first seek?
2. In addition to shelter, what were the main concerns of primitive humans?
3. Why did primitive people become nomads?
4. Why did nomads begin building permanent shelters?
5. How did the form of the human hand contribute to changes in the design of structures?
6. How did architectural styles change as people moved into communities?
7. What were the main factors that led to the development of modern architecture?

YOUR ARCHITECTURAL SCRAPBOOK

As a personal project, develop an architectural scrapbook. Building a scrapbook will help make you aware of architecture and drafting methods. As you read through each unit of this book, keep your eyes open for matching illustrations. Copy or cut out these illustrations from newspapers, magazines, or other materials that can be cut up and paste them in your scrapbook. If you find a picture in a book, draw a copy or photocopy the page. Finding these illustrations will take some searching. This type of searching is known as research. Research is an important part of learning.

Organize your scrapbook by units, to match your learning experiences. The scrapbook is for you, and your learning. It will help you remember and build upon the ideas and information you gain from this book-and from your class. Be sure to label each of your illustrations as you insert them. A couple of words will do. Start each section on a new page.

1. Start your scrapbook with illustrations of shelters found in nature.
2. Find illustrations showing architecture that is at least 2,000 years old.
3. Add pictures showing architecture of the Middle Ages.
4. Draw or find illustrations showing early American architecture.
5. Add examples showing modern architecture in the design of houses and large buildings.
6. Can you think of other illustrations of architecture of interest to you? If so, add illustrations.

CAD ACTIVITIES

After reading Unit 1, refer to Chapter 1 in the *Chief Architect Tutorials* and practice:

- Logging on.
- Moving
- Selecting objects.
- Stretching
- Deleting
- Rotating

UNIT 2
ARCHITECTURAL STYLES

TYPES OF ARCHITECTURAL STYLES

An *architectural style* is defined as a set of structural design features that makes one type of building different from others.

An accurate description of modern architectural styles is difficult to determine because:

- Each geographical area will develop its own various designs within its architectural style?
- New building materials will affect the design.
- Advancements in building techniques will change the characteristics of a building.
- Personal tastes will change the building's style.
- The mixing of various architectural styles creates a new, eclectic style.

The pure architectural style begins with its early historic development. Regardless of the basis for the identification of an architectural style, there are few structures that are pure examples of a specific style because of the constant flux of design changes. An example is how Colonial architecture has changed.

- Early Colonial - Original design.
- Classical Colonial - Adaptations of ancient and classical building forms.
- Traditional Colonial - Adaptations of an older style of architecture with modernizing features.
- Contemporary Colonial - Clean modern lines with lots of glass and open style floor plan.

An architectural style of a building may incorporate a few or many of the typical characteristics of a particular style and may also borrow characteristics from different styles (eclectic). This often makes it difficult to classify structures as a true architectural style. Based on their characteristics, homes are usually said to follow one of two major architectural styles. These styles are:

- Traditional
- Contemporary

Traditional refers to customs or habits (traditions) established in the past. Traditional architecture, therefore, is usually related to a period of history. An architectural tradition may also be connected with a specific geographic area. For example, there are styles

connected with New England, as well as with the southern and western parts of the United States. Some traditional styles of architecture are based on Greek and Roman designs. You saw examples of these styles in Unit 1.

Contemporary style is current; they are not related to history or tradition. They are part of the times and customs of the period in which they are built. Contemporary styles, however, also vary with areas or regions.

You can identify the architectural style of a building from a number of its features. These features, or characteristics, include:

- Shape of the structure.
- Roof design.
- Chimney style.
- Exterior (outside) building materials, including siding, windows, doors, or trim.

These features and how they are used in different styles of architecture are covered later in this unit.

FORMAL AND INFORMAL DESIGN

Home styles can also be described as formal or informal.

Formal design in architecture means that buildings follow set patterns. These patterns relate both to the appearance of a building and to its uses. For example, one formal feature might be columns taken from Greek or Roman designs. Another formal feature might be an enclosed kitchen in a separate room with its own door. Floor plans for formal homes are usually balanced. This balance of structural features is known as *symmetrical design*. As an example, see **Figure 2-1**. Note the way this plan is designed as a series of separate rooms. The dining room, front entry area, and living room are all enclosed individually.

Informal homes are usually built for people who prefer modern lifestyles. Most informal homes are of contemporary design. They tend to have features such as open kitchens and breakfast bars, as shown in **Figure 2-2**. This home contains many open areas without walls. The openness of the dining room, kitchen, living room, and family room are typical of informal homes. The overall floor plan is in a nonsymmetrical, or rambling, style.

Externally, informal homes are usually adapted to their surroundings. The homes are designed to fit in with the features of the land and with the natural or landscaped foliage.

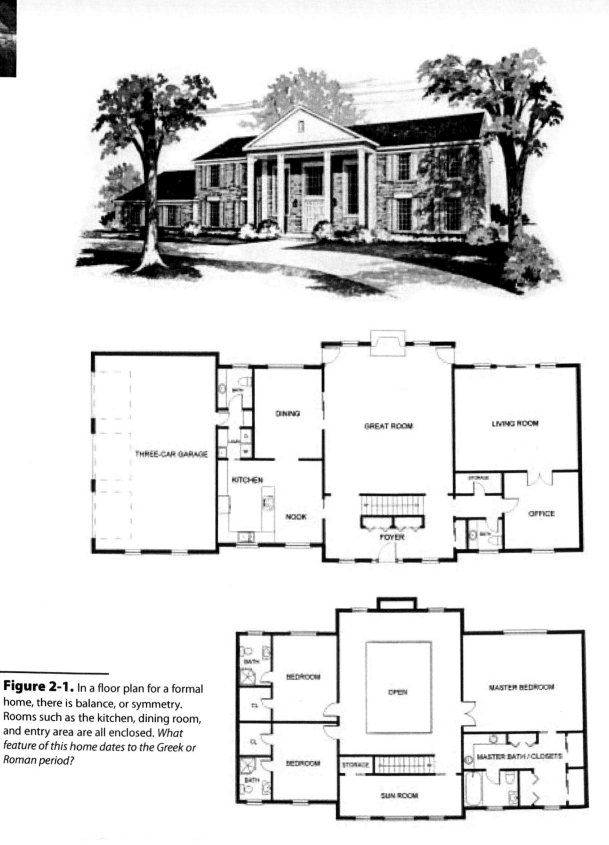

Figure 2-1. In a floor plan for a formal home, there is balance, or symmetry. Rooms such as the kitchen, dining room, and entry area are all enclosed. *What feature of this home dates to the Greek or Roman period?*

Figure 2-2. An informal home has an open floor plan. There are no dividing walls between the kitchen, dining area, and family room. *Is the floor plan of this home designed in a specific pattern or is it irregular?*

TRADITIONAL STYLES

Many individual styles make up traditional design. Most of these styles were developed around the building materials of certain areas or periods of history. A number of these classic, traditional home styles have become popular in this country. Their popularity is due chiefly to appearance. Modern building materials have been adapted to fit these traditional designs. Some popular traditional styles include:

English Tudor

This style is characterized by exposed, heavy timbers on outside walls. *Timbers* are wide, heavy beams of lumber. Between the timbers, several siding materials can be used. These include stucco, brick, or stone. *Stucco* is a cement-type material spread on a frame. The frame is usually made from wood and wire to hold the stucco.

Windows in these homes are tall and narrow. They frequently contain diamond-shaped panes of glass. High, decorative chimneys are used; built on outside walls. Most chimney pots are exposed to outside view. *Chimney pots* are the ends of pipes that carry the smoke into the air.

The roof of an English Tudor home is quite steep. Typically, there is at least one gable facing the street. A *gable* is a pointed section of a roof that slopes steeply.

Tudor floor plans are usually informal, as shown in **Figure 2-3**. The Tudor design was developed in England in the 1400s.

French Mansard

This style of architecture was developed by Francois Mansard, a Frenchman, in the eighteenth century. Homes built in this style have a roof that has a double slope on all sides. The top slope is almost flat, while the bottom slope is very steep. Dormers usually thrust out from the slanting sides of the second floor exterior. A *dormer* is a window with a framework that extends from the side of a building, as shown in **Figure 2-4**.

The outside of a Mansard home typically is finished in brick, with quoins at the corners. *Quoins* are stone surfaces that cover corners of buildings. Windows and doors usually have full-length shutters. *Shutters* are wooden panels mounted beside windows. The original purpose of shutters was to protect windows from bad weather. Old-fashion shutters could swing shut and be locked to cover windows. On modern homes, shutters are usually for decoration. The roof of a Mansard home usually has cedar shingles.

A Mansard floor plan frequently contains a double-sized fireplace. The layout of the floor plan is symmetrical and formal. Many Mansard homes have large entry areas inside the front door. There are often curved staircases leading to the second floor.

STEEP GABLE ROOF   LARGE CHIMNEY/POTS

HEAVY TIMBERS

BRICK/STUCCO SIDING

TALL WINDOWS/SMALL WINDOW PANES

MASTER BEDROOM

BATH

CL.

FAMILY ROOM

KITCHEN

BATH

LAUN.

TWO-CAR GARAGE

BEDROOM

BEDROOM

ENTRY

LIVING ROOM

Figure 2-3. The most noticeable characteristic of an English Tudor home is the use of large timbers on exterior walls. Gables are also typical features. *What are gables and where are they located on this home?*

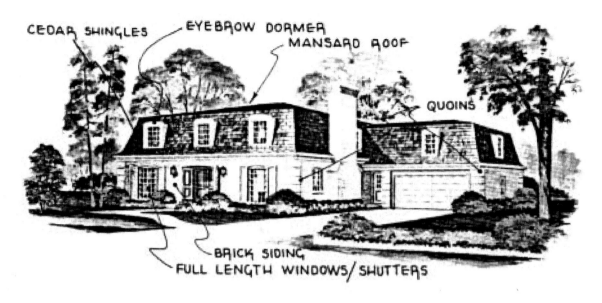

CEDAR SHINGLES
EYEBROW DORMER
MANSARD ROOF
QUOINS
BRICK SIDING
FULL LENGTH WINDOWS/SHUTTERS

DINING

KITCHEN

BREAKFAST

STOR

GARAGE

MECH

BATH

CL

LIVING ROOM

CL

FAMILY ROOM

ENTRY

Figure 2-4. French Mansard homes are characterized by roofs that slope at the second floor. Second-story windows usually have dormers. *What are dormers and where are they located on this home?*

BEDROOM

CL CL

BEDROOM

STORAGE / STUDIO

CL

CL

HALL

BATH

MASTER BEDROOM

CL

BATH

BEDROOM

French Provincial

The name French Provincial comes from the fact that this style was developed in the provinces of France. In the French countryside, the weather, particularly in winter, can be severe. For this reason, the main feature of this style of architecture became a high-pitched, or steeply sloped, roof. Snow and rain could then easily run off.

The roof style used on French Provincial homes is known as a hip roof. A *hip roof* is a roof with both ends and sides that slope. This can be seen in **Figure 2-5**.

Other features frequently found on French Provincial homes include large chimneys and shutters for doors and windows. In addition; there are often quoins at the corners, brick siding, and curved lintels over windows and doors. A *lintel* is a support beam over an opening in a wall.

Early American

Early American settlers were greatly influenced by English styles of architecture. However, conditions made it necessary to change the styles of their homes. The early settlers had little time to build homes. Also, it was necessary to use materials and tools that were available locally. Thus, early homes built in America were relatively simple.

Figure 2-6 shows a modern home built on Early American design principles. In homes of this style, the floor plan is usually rectangular and balanced. The exterior walls of Early American homes were often plain and covered with wood siding.

Another design feature is the simple gable. Windows of early homes were usually double-hung with shutters. A *double hung window* is a window with two separate frames. These frames are mounted in separate tracks. This makes it possible to open the top and bottom of a window separately. Windows are opened or closed by sliding them up or down in their tracks.

The floor plan of Early American homes had a story and a half of living area. That is, the second story was smaller than the first. There was usually a large fireplace in the center of the structure.

American Colonial

Later, an American style known as colonial was developed. This style was more elaborate than the original early American style. Additional features included vertical trim boards at corners and simple columns on the sides of the front doors. A modern home built in the American Colonial style is shown in **Figure 2-7**.

Variations of colonial architecture were introduced in the Dutch and German (Deutsch) colonies in America. The style became known as Dutch Colonial. This design was similar to earlier colonial homes. However, there were some differences. Brick or stone siding, wood shake shingles, and double-pitched (Gambrel) roofs were used. A modern home built in this style is shown in **Figure 2-8**.

Figure 2-5. A main feature of a French Provincial home is a high-pitched, sloping hip roof. There are usually shuttered doors and windows. *What is a hip roof?*

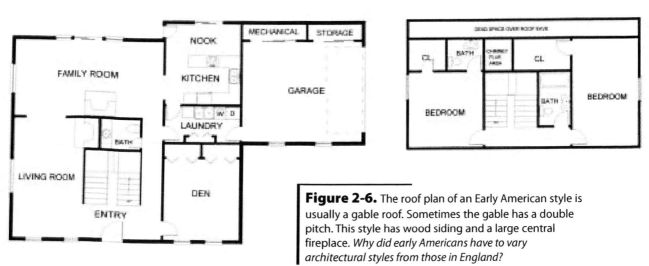

Figure 2-6. The roof plan of an Early American style is usually a gable roof. Sometimes the gable has a double pitch. This style has wood siding and a large central fireplace. *Why did early Americans have to vary architectural styles from those in England?*

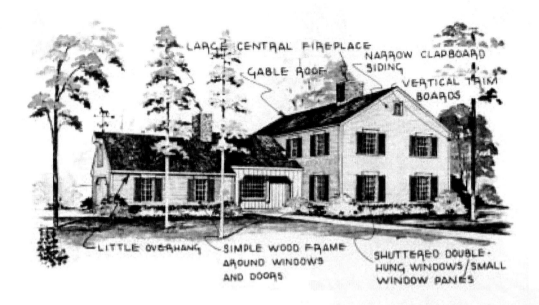

LARGE CENTRAL FIREPLACE

GABLE ROOF

NARROW CLAPBOARD SIDING

VERTICAL TRIM BOARDS

LITTLE OVERHANG

SIMPLE WOOD FRAME AROUND WINDOWS AND DOORS

SHUTTERED DOUBLE-HUNG WINDOWS / SMALL WINDOW PANES

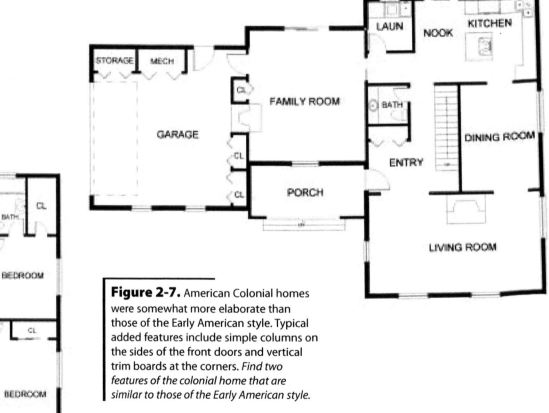

Figure 2-7. American Colonial homes were somewhat more elaborate than those of the Early American style. Typical added features include simple columns on the sides of the front doors and vertical trim boards at the corners. *Find two features of the colonial home that are similar to those of the Early American style.*

WOOD FRAMED WINDOWS AND DOORS
LARGE CENTRAL CHIMNEY
DOOR COLUMNS
DOUBLE-PITCHED ROOF
DORMERS
CENTERED ENTRY
FLAT FACADE
SHUTTERED DOUBLE-HUNG WINDOWS
LITTLE ROOF OVERHANG
NARROW WOOD SIDING
VERTICAL TRIM

Figure 2-8. The Dutch Colonial home has a double-pitched roof. Other features include shuttered, double-hung windows. *What is the meaning of double-pitched?*

The Gambrel roof is named after its designer. It is double-pitched. This means portions of the roof slant at two different angles. Another example of a modern Dutch Colonial formally designed home is shown in **Figure 2-9**.

Another form of colonial architecture developed in the South. Southern Colonial homes became the centers of life on large plantations. These structures were much larger than Early American or other colonial homes. They included full-sized second floors. Also, two-story columns supported extended roofs. These roofs covered large porches, known as *verandas*. See **Figure 2-10**.

Southern homes, although larger, had most of the other features of colonial homes. However, a major feature was added to the interior. At the center of a typical two-story structure, most southern homes had a large spiral staircase. This was the main access from the large entry area to the second floor. Many Southern Colonial features are borrowed from other architectural styles such as the Greek pediment as shown in **Figure 2-11**.

Western Ranch

Another change in architectural style took place as Americans built homes in the west. On the frontiers, large tracts of land were available. To match these areas, architects developed the Western Ranch style of home.

Ranch-style homes are usually informal and spread out. They are generally built on one level. The areas in which these homes are built have mild, relatively warm winters. A steep sloped roof is therefore unnecessary. Instead, ranch homes use low-pitched gable roofs. These roofs have large *overhangs*. This means that the roof extends past the outer wall of the house. The overhang protects the house from the hot summer sun. Also, because of the mild climate, ranch homes usually have large "picture" windows. Large outdoor patios or courtyards are often included in these home designs. See **Figure 2-12**.

Exterior materials of Western Ranch homes include local woods or stone. Roofs are often shake shingles. Interior designs are often rustic or country style and include exposed wooden beams.

Western Adobe

An excellent example of how homes are adapted to their surroundings can be seen in the Western Adobe style. *Adobe* is a type of soil found in the West with a high clay content. Wet adobe material can be formed into bricks or spread on walls. When dry, the material provides excellent protection against sun, wind, and rain. This style of architecture is also referred to as Southwest Spanish or Mexican.

A Western Adobe home is similar to a ranch home. It is usually built on one level and spread out. However, a Western Adobe home frequently has a U-shaped floor plan and a courtyard, as shown in **Figure 2-13**.

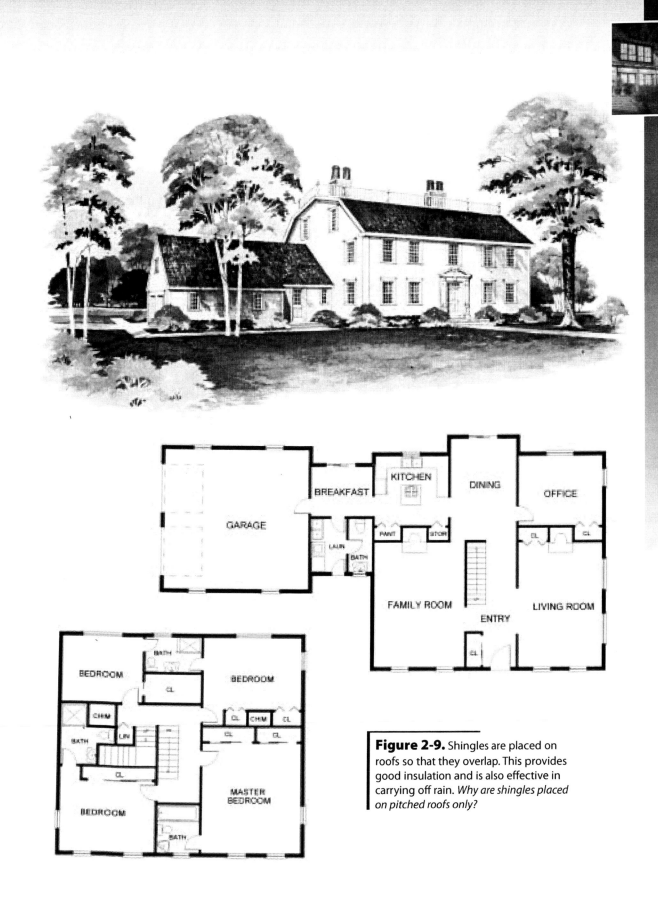

Figure 2-9. Shingles are placed on roofs so that they overlap. This provides good insulation and is also effective in carrying off rain. *Why are shingles placed on pitched roofs only?*

Figure 2-10. Southern Colonial homes retained many established colonial features but added a second story and a large porch supported by columns. *What is the porch of a Southern Colonial home called?*

VERTICAL TRIM — LARGE CHIMNEY — SHUTTERED DOUBLE HUNG WINDOWS/SMALL PANES — EAVE ORNAMENTATION — WOOD SIDING — PEDIMENTS — FRAME AROUND WINDOWS AND DOORS DETAILED TRIM — CENTERED ENTRY FLANKED BY COLUMNS

Figure 2-11. Many Southern Colonial features are included in modern traditional homes that have two-story designs. Some of these are identified in this drawing. *What are double-hung windows and how do they work?*

Figure 2-12. The Western Ranch style of home is informal and has an irregular floor plan. The style developed partly because of the larger land tracts available for building in the West. *What is the main reason for the wide roof overhang on many ranch homes?*

LOW PITCH GABLE ROOF
TILE ROOF
LONG FRONT PORCH
ARCHWAYS
ARCHES
ROUGH PLASTER
COURTYARD
LONG WINDOWS/ IRON GRILLS

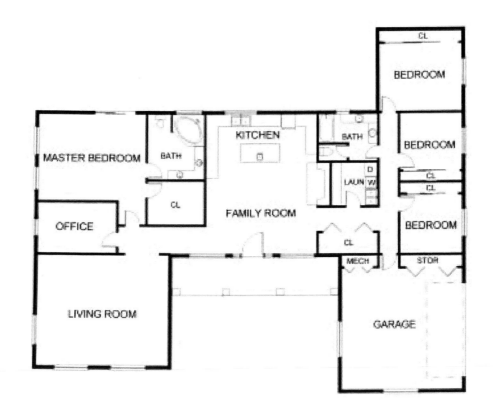

Figure 2-13. The Western Adobe home, like the Ranch, is built on one level and is spread out. Windows and doors usually have rounded arches. *Many adobe homes have tile roofs. Where does the adobe home get its name?*

Outside hardware for Western Adobe homes, including gates and window grills, is usually made of wrought iron. Most homes of this type have low roofs covered with tile. *Wrought iron* is a decorative metal used for railings, grills, fences, and furniture. Interiors are finished with beams and archways. Windows and doors often have arched tops.

CONTEMPORARY STYLE

Many of the needs and demands of modern homeowners are met by contemporary style homes. Contemporary means "now." Contemporary homes are thought of as being part of modern architecture.

Some forces that have been behind the development of contemporary architecture include:

- Lighter, stronger building materials became available. These made it possible to build styles that were impossible with traditional materials.

- More people than ever before earned enough money to own their own homes. The trend toward home ownership was encouraged by government programs that supported time-purchase plans for homes. As mortgages (home loans) were easier to obtain, the demand for homes grew.

- A combination of wartime shortages and rapid population growth created a housing shortage. There was a need to build more houses in shorter-than-usual time spans. The materials and methods of modern architecture helped to meet these challenges.

- Costs have increased rapidly in recent times. Contemporary architecture saves money by simplifying the structure of homes.

The term contemporary doesn't identify any one specific type or style of architecture. Many contemporary homes borrow some of their features from traditional styles. The main goal of modern design has been to appeal to the needs of growing numbers of homeowners.

For example, look at the contemporary home in **Figure 2-14**. This house has a gabled roof, but the sides of the roof are not equal. This style of roof is called *salt box*. Also, there is a courtyard borrowed from the Western Adobe style. However, this home does not fit into any single traditional style; it is contemporary.

Another feature common to many contemporary homes is the split-level design that is fitted to the shape of the land. When a house is built on a hillside, it is possible to have separate levels. Different areas, or sections, of the home, used for different purposes, can be on separate levels. For example, look at the home in **Figure 2-15**. This hillside building has two different levels that permit entry into different areas of the house.

Fundamentals of Architectural Design

NATURAL BUILDING MATERIALS

INFORMAL PLAN
SIMPLE DESIGN

Figure 2-14. Contemporary-style homes are usually informal and are built to fit in with their surroundings. Open-space design is used in the interior living areas. *Why do most contemporary homes of the type shown have large windows?*

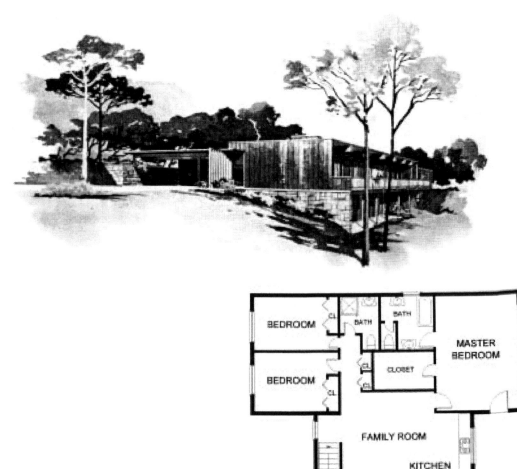

Figure 2-15. This home has many features typical of contemporary structures. Included are split-level design adapted to a hillside, a carport, and a flat roof. *Why does a split-level design fit particularly well in a hillside location?*

Other common features for contemporary homes, particularly in warm sections of the country, are flat roofs and carports. Flat roofs are possible because there is no worry about runoff of snow. Carports are possible because vehicles are not exposed to extreme cold. It is only necessary to protect homeowners from rain as they go from their cars to the buildings.

Contemporary styles vary from one part of the country to another. However, most contemporary homes share certain features. They use natural materials and include a feeling for the surrounding area within the home. Large windows provide beautiful views of the surrounding areas. Homes are designed to fit into their environments. An *environment* includes all natural and human-made materials and conditions that affect the lives of people.

UNIT 2 ACTIVITIES

VOCABULARY CHECKLIST

1. architectural style
2. traditional style
3. contemporary style
4. formal design
5. symmetrical design
6. informal style
7. timber

8. stucco
9. chimney pot
10. gable
11. dormer
12. quoin
13. shutters
14. hip roof

15. lintel
16. double-hung window
17. shingles
18. veranda
19. adobe
20. environment

REVIEW QUESTIONS

1. What is meant by traditional architectural style?
2. What is meant by contemporary architectural style?
3. How is formal design different from informal design?
4. Name three types of traditional architectural designs.
5. How do ranch and adobe style homes reflect the principle of using local materials for home construction?

YOUR ARCHITECTURAL SCRAPBOOK

1. Add one example of each style of architecture discussed in this unit. Locate several pictures or draw your own.
2. Identify and add examples of two or more styles of architecture not described in this unit.
3. Draw various styles of architecture with a CAD system. Print hard copies and place them in your scrapbook.

CAD ACTIVITIES

After reading Unit 2, refer to Chapter 2 in the *Chief Architect Tutorials* and practice:

- Walls
- Naming rooms
- Windows
- Doors

- Saving a drawing file.
- Opening a drawing file.
- Design a small floor plan and save it to a disk.

UNIT 3
FORMS IN ARCHITECTURE

THE FLOOR PLAN

The basic shape, or outline, of a building's walls and its interior walls is known as its *floor plan*. A floor plan is a two-dimensional bird's eye view that shows how much area, or space, a structure has.

Floor plans of buildings are set up in a variety of geometric shapes. The word *geometric* refers to certain types of shapes. These floor plans follow straight lines, triangles, squares, or circles. Geometric shapes can also be a combination of these basic forms. Several basic geometric forms are shown in **Figure 3-1**.

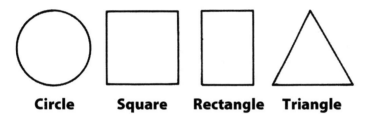

Circle   Square   Rectangle   Triangle

Figure 3-1. Geometric designs are formed from regular lines and shapes. A number of shapes are used in floor plans for buildings. *Why is it hard to determine the floor plan of a house when you are standing in front of the building?*

In buildings, each kind of geometric shape has advantages and disadvantages. The type of design chosen depends on the desires of the people who occupy a building. It should be made clear to the occupants that an irregular designed floor plan will increase the building costs significantly. The more irregular the design, the higher the construction costs will be. The design should satisfy the occupant's needs and meet their budgetary requirements.

The lowest cost floor plan designs have rooms with right angles. A *right angle* has a 90-degree (90°) measurement. A drawing of right angle walls is shown in **Figure 3-2**. Buildings with right angles are less expensive to build than those with other shapes. Rooms built in circles or with different angles are more expensive to build because extra work is involved. When walls meet at right angles with flat surfaces they can be easily fitted together.

Figure 3-2. A right angle occurs when crossing lines form a square (90°) corner. Buildings with floor plans that use right angles cost less to build than structures with unusually shaped rooms. *Why does it cost more if rooms have unusual angles or circles?*

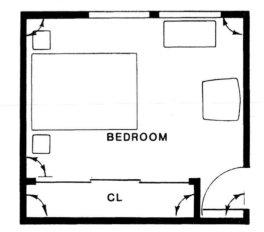

BEDROOM

CL

Geometric Forms

Floor plans for houses follow a series of geometric shapes. Some of the most popular shapes include:

- Rectangular
- Square
- Round
- Hexagonal
- Octagonal

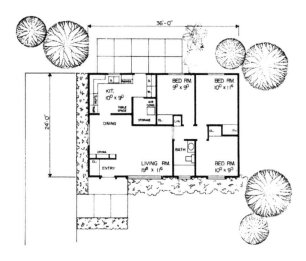

Figure 3-3. A rectangle is formed by two sets of parallel lines. A rectangular shape has four right angles. *What are parallel lines?*

Rectangular Floor Plans

A *rectangle* is a shape created with two sets of straight, parallel lines and four right angles, as shown in **Figure 3-3**. *Parallel lines* run in the same direction and are always the same distance from each other. In a rectangle, both lines in each parallel set are the same length.

A rectangle provides the most practical geometric form for a building or room and is the most cost effective. The rectangle enables the designer to use space well. There is no wasted space in a rectangular room. This is part of the reason why structures with rectangular floor plans are the least costly to build. A pleasing rectangular ratio for overall floor plans and single rooms is 3:5. This is the ratio of a post card. **Figure 3-4** is an example of a basic rectangular floor plan. Note the efficient design. There is no wasted space.

Figure 3-4. A rectangular house makes the best use of space. It is also the least costly to build. *Give one reason why a rectangular house costs less to build than houses with unusual shapes.*

Square Floor Plans

A *square* is a rectangle with four sides of equal length. There are four right angles in a square. The two sets of straight lines are parallel.

A square house and floor plan are illustrated in **Figure 3-5**. A square floor plan, like a rectangular design, is easy to construct. This helps to keep costs down. However, it is more difficult to plan efficient use of space in a square area than in a rectangular one. This is especially true for larger structures. The square floor plan is best for a small building.

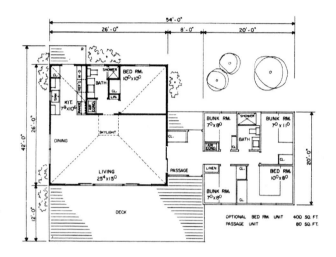

Figure 3-5. A square house, like a rectangular one, is easy and comparatively inexpensive to build. *Which sides of a square are equal in length?*

Square units also work well in buildings designed to be expanded, or made larger. Notice in **Figure 3-6**, how a combination of squares works well for a home plan. This kind of floor plan is said to have clusters. *Clusters* are groups of objects or areas kept together for a single purpose. For example, note that one cluster in Figure 3-6 is for the living area; the others are for bedrooms.

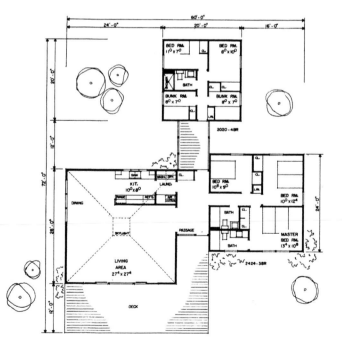

Figure 3-6. Square floor plans work well in cluster designs. Cluster-type houses are easy to expand when a family needs more room. *What is a cluster?*

Round Floor Plans

A house with a round floor plan is built in the shape of a circle. The circular shape means that the house has a central area, as shown in **Figure 3-7**. Usually, this is used for an area which a family shares. This central living area is then surrounded by wedge-shaped rooms. It is best not to design vertical and horizontal walls for a round floor plan. The design will have too many irregular room corners.

Outside rooms in round homes usually have a lot of window area. This is because there is more outside wall space in relation to the room areas. To bring daylight and fresh air into central areas, skylights are used. *Skylights* are windows placed on the roof.

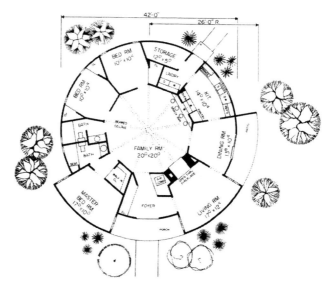

Figure 3-7. Houses with round floor plans usually have central areas for family use. Other rooms are built in wedge or pie shapes around the outside of the structure. *What problems can arise in furnishing pie-shaped rooms?*

Although they can be interesting, round houses are expensive to build. Walls meet each other at unusual angles. This means that costly construction is necessary. Special, expensive construction techniques are also needed for roofs and foundations. In addition, it can be difficult to fit ordinary furniture into pie shaped rooms.

Hexagonal and Octagonal Floor Plans

Structures with six sides are called *hexagonal*. See **Figure 3-8**. Structures with eight sides are called *octagonal*. See **Figure 3-9**.

Hexagonal and octagonal plans are very similar to round plans. However, hexagonal and octagonal structures have straight lines on the outside walls. This makes it somewhat easier to use standard furniture and building materials. However, the unusual angles of all the walls mean that construction costs will be higher.

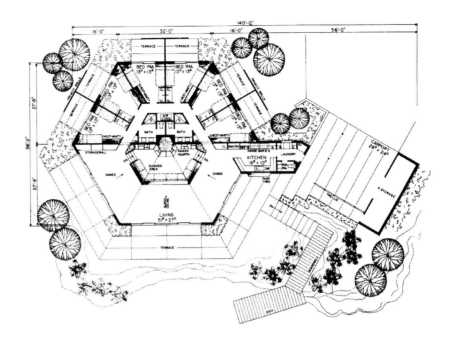

Figure 3-8.
A hexagonal house has a design similar to a round structure. The difference is that the outside walls are formed by a series of lines. *How many sides does a hexagonal house have?*

Figure 3-9.
An octagonal house has pie-shaped rooms around a central area. The floor plan for this shape is also similar that of a round building. *How many sides does an octagon have?*

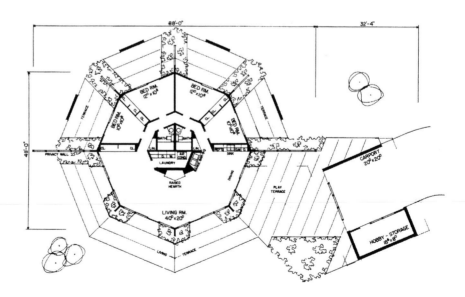

Irregular Floor Plans

Some floor plans do not fit any single geometric form. These plans may use a combination of forms. They are known as *irregular floor plans*. As an example, look at the house in **Figure 3-10**. This home has many comfortable features. It is designed with squares, rectangles, and triangles. *Triangle* shapes get their name from having three angles with three straight lines that meet.

Irregular floor plans are often used to design a home to a specific building site. Building sites often have odd shapes or contours that will effect the final design of a home. *Contours* are land formations that rise and fall. Another reason for using an irregular floor plan may be the view from a specific site. If there is a beautiful view, the owners may want to design the house so that it can be seen from most rooms. The home's design may be spread out to take advantage of the view.

Sometimes irregular floor plans are used because of building conditions. For example, it may be impossible to dig a foundation deep enough to support a two-story structure. To provide enough living space on one floor, an irregular floor plan may be necessary. Irregular shapes are usually more expensive to build than rectangular or square structures. However, extra costs can be kept down if the irregular floor plan uses a combination of rectangles and squares. Note that the home in **Figure 3-10** uses some square and rectangular areas.

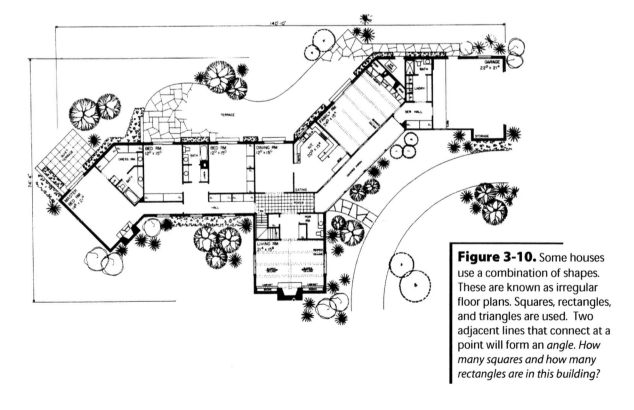

Figure 3-10. Some houses use a combination of shapes. These are known as irregular floor plans. Squares, rectangles, and triangles are used. Two adjacent lines that connect at a point will form an *angle. How many squares and how many rectangles are in this building?*

Another consideration is that a plan like the one in **Figure 3-10** creates a large amount of outside wall space. This provides light, airy living areas. Occupants can also enjoy a view from all rooms. However, this outside wall space adds costs for heating or air conditioning.

Figure 3-11 shows an irregular floor plan that keeps building costs down. This design uses only squares and rectangles. An interesting feature of this home is that it has an atrium. An *atrium* is an open area in the center of a building. The atrium in the floor plan in **Figure 3-11** is surrounded by squares and rectangles.

Figure 3-11.
Costs are lower if irregular floor plans use only rectangles and squares. This structure has a series of rectangles and squares built around an atrium. *What is an atrium?*

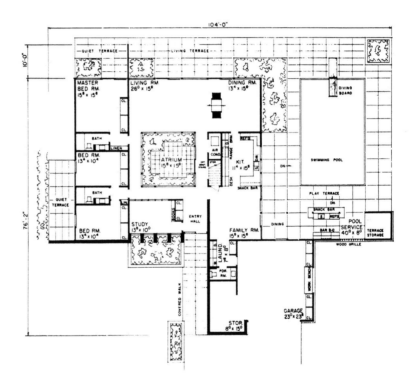

UNIT 3 ACTIVITIES

VOCABULARY CHECKLIST

1. floor plan
2. geometric
3. right angle
4. rectangle
5. parallel lines

6. square
7. skylight
8. clusters
9. hexagonal
10. octagonal

11. irregular floor plans
12. triangle
13. contours
14. angle
15. atrium

REVIEW QUESTIONS

1. Which geometric type of floor plan is least expensive to build?
2. Why is a round house relatively expensive to build?
3. What is the difference between a hexagon and an octagon?
4. Why do heat and air conditioning cost more if a building has a lot of outside wall space?
5. What are living-area clusters within a floor plan?
6. What is a skylight?
7. Which geometric shapes have right angles?

YOUR ARCHITECTURAL SCRAPBOOK

1. Find or draw examples of all of the geometric shapes covered in this unit.
2. Find as many additional geometric shapes as you can and add them to your scrapbook.
3. Design several irregular floor plans with a CAD system. Make hard copies and place them into your scrapbook.

CAD ACTIVITIES

After reading Unit 3, refer to Chapter 3 in the *Chief Architect Tutorials* and practice:

- Placing cabinets.
- Placing furniture.
- Placing appliances.
- Placing fixtures.
- Place all the items into the floor plan that you have saved.

UNIT 4
ARCHITECTS AND BUILDERS

THE DESIGNER-BUILDER TEAM

An architect designs buildings to serve certain purposes. These purposes may involve the needs for residential design, business offices, medical facilities, and factories. The architect is required to design efficient and attractive structures. The responsibilities of an architect often extend beyond the development of the designs and drawings for a building. Many architects are actively involved in coordinating or supervising the building of a structure.

Each architect, in effect, decides how much involvement he or she will have in a building project. No matter how much an architect does, however, few individuals complete building projects by themselves. There are isolated situations in which people design and build their own small homes. Aside from such cases, the development of a modern building is a team effort. Architects start these efforts by designing structures. Other key people involved in creating buildings include:

- Landscape architects
- Architectural drafters
- Engineers
- Contractors
- Trade specialists
- Interior designers

This unit introduces you to the roles and responsibilities of these members of the building development team.

ARCHITECTS

A successful architect needs many skills. An architect must have the combined talents of an artist, engineer, builder, planner, and manager. With these skills and knowledge, architects can design many types of structures. The architect usually completes his or her designs with a computer-aided drafting (CAD) system using an architectural software program. Two excellent architectural programs are *Chief Architect* and *DataCAD*.

The work of the architect usually begins with a series of client conferences. For larger structures, architects often work with officers or managers of the companies that will own or use the buildings. Often, an architect and his or her clients discuss designs using a CAD system. This enables the architect to make very fast drawings for the clients to review while they are reviewing the design. During client conferences, architects ask for and listen to explanations about how a building will be used. The types of people who will occupy a building and the activities they will carry out must be known. The needs of clients provide the basic purposes for which architects design structures.

In addition to designing floor plans, architects must also have considerable technical knowledge. Client needs must be met with such support functions as electrical, air conditioning, and plumbing service.

For some projects, particularly small structures such as private homes, the architect personally prepares a full set of plans. On larger jobs, however, specialized help may be needed to complete the job. Such projects might include factories, office buildings, or large apartment structures. On these jobs, the architect may need design help from specialists. These specialists can include landscape architects, architectural drafters, engineers, contractors, trade specialists, and interior designers.

LANDSCAPE ARCHITECTS

The external environment of a building site is the interest of a *landscape architect*. These specialists deal with all outside areas around a building. They plan plantings, roads, parking areas, and uses of the land.

ARCHITECTURAL DRAFTERS

Architectural drafters prepare the drawings and plans that communicate the basic design of the architect. Their plans and drawings convey information to the persons who will actually construct, or build, the structure. The documents prepared by drafters are the floor plans, site plans, elevations, foundation plans, floor, wall, and roof framing plans, and all the required construction details needed for the correct construction.

An experienced architectural drafter often assists with the actual design of a structure or works in tandem with an architect on a building project.

ENGINEERS

Civil engineers design roads, bridges, and water and utility systems.

Air conditioning engineers design heating, ventilating, and air conditioning systems.

Acoustical engineers design equipment and systems to control sound within a structure. Their specialties include insulation and noise control of machines in factories. In auditoriums or meeting rooms, they are consulted about sound systems.

Mechanical engineers design a variety of ducts to carry air, plumbing, and other support systems that require the support of mechanical parts to operate.

Structural engineers use calculations to insure the structures components will make building safe under all conditions.

OTHER SPECIALISTS

Estimators examine architectural drawings to determine construction costs. Their job is to figure out the building construction cost after an architect has completed the design and working drawings.

Specification writers add important details to architectural plans. The specifications they prepare are documents listing the specific materials and instructions needed to construct the building.

Surveyors prepare the survey plans and plot plans for the building site. Their drawings define specific units of land. Survey plans are used as guides by architects and landscape architects. These plans are also legal documents. They establish ownership of land.

CONTRACTORS

Actual construction is the responsibility of a contractor. The *contractor* handles all the materials and provides all of the services needed to complete construction. Often, segments of a construction job are assigned to subcontractors. These are the trade specialists who provide specialized construction services. *Subcontractors* usually handle one type of work such as carpentry, plumbing, heating, ventilating, air conditioning, masonry, electrical, and landscaping.

TRADE SPECIALISTS

Carpenters complete wood frames for buildings (rough carpentry). They also complete all the finish carpentry in the structure. This includes paneling, cabinets, and trim.

Masons work with cement, stone, and ceramic materials.

Electricians install electrical outlets and lighting fixtures.

HVAC specialists work on heating, ventilating, and air conditioning.

Other skilled specialists include **painters, wallpaper hangers, landscapers, drywall specialists,** and **roofers.**

In construction, there are also unskilled workers. These individuals work largely as an apprentice or a helper for the trade specialists.

INTERIOR DESIGNERS

The selection of colors, furnishings, surface covers, lighting systems, and decorations for the inside of a house is the responsibility of the *interior designer*. An interior designer is usually hired by the owners or occupants of a residence. Close cooperation must exist between the people who will live in a home and the interior designer. In effect, it is the job of the interior designer to turn a building into a livable home. For large commercial structures, the interior designer and architect usually work closely together with the final design.

UNIT 4 ACTIVITIES

VOCABULARY CHECKLIST

1. landscape architect
2. architectural drafter
3. structural engineer
4. air conditioning engineer
5. civil engineer
6. acoustical engineer
7. mechanical engineer
8. estimator
9. specification writer
10. surveyor
11. contractor
12. subcontractor
13. carpenter
14. mason
15. electrician
16. HVAC specialist
17. interior designer

REVIEW QUESTIONS

1. Why are conferences between architects and clients important?
2. What are some of the management responsibilities undertaken by architects?
3. What is the role of an architectural drafter?
4. How do architects and architectural drafters work together?
5. Why are the people who work together on the design of a building called a design team?

YOUR ARCHITECTURAL SCRAPBOOK

1. Prepare a list of trade specialties involved in building construction. Add this to your scrapbook.
2. Find pictures of famous homes or homes designed by famous architects. Include these in your scrapbook.
3. Find pictures of well-known commercial buildings or buildings created by famous architects. Add pictures of these to your scrapbook.

CAD ACTIVITIES

After reading Unit 4, refer to Chapter 4 in the *Chief Architect Tutorials* and practice:

- Screen management.
- Automatic dimensioning.
- Dimension the floor plan that you have saved.

PART II

The Site

Building Codes

Orientation

PART II

THE SITE

THE STARTING POINT

The planning for a structure cannot begin until the building site is thoroughly examined. A *building site*, in architectural terms, is an area of land available for construction. A building site may be a single lot, a series of lots, or subdivision. A *subdivision* is a large tract of land that is being developed.

All the facets of a building site must be carefully studied before a building is designed. Features of a site studied by an architect include:

- Terrain (Slopes, drainage, vegetation, and soil makeup.)
- Zoning laws (Ordinances controlling the structures that can be built in specific areas.)
- Orientation to natural elements (The design considering the sun, wind, terrain and view.)

All of these factors must be understood and considered carefully before starting the design process.

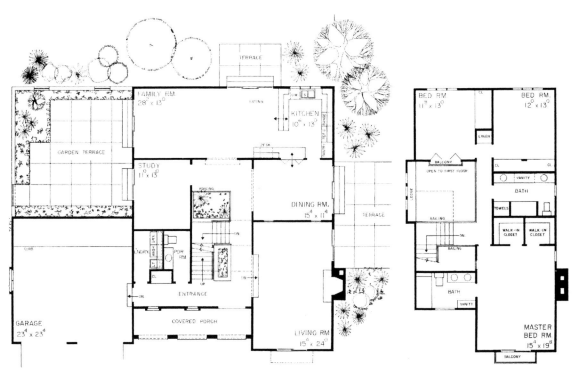

Part II has information to help you understand the importance of the zoning ordinances and how they affect the structure's design. You will also learn basic information about how structures are located on building sites. The next two units discuss:

- The effect of zoning laws on architectural design.
- The orientation of buildings on sites.

This study of zoning ordinances and structure orientation will help you with learning the first steps of design. When you complete the study of these units, you will have a better understanding of architectural planning and design.

UNIT 5
BUILDING CODES

PURPOSE OF BUILDING CODES

Local laws that set standards for structural design within a community are called *zoning ordinances* and *building codes*. All construction in an area must meet the requirements of the zoning and building codes. Some of the design and construction features covered by building codes include:

- Qualifications of persons who can design buildings.
- Structural designs.
- Site sizes for specific types of buildings.
- Types, sizes, installation of building materials.

ZONING ORDINANCES

A major area covered by building codes is the zoning ordinance. Zoning ordinances are designed to keep different types of construction in a community separated. For example, a factory or an airport in the center of a residential area is undesirable. In most cities or towns, separate areas are set aside for specific uses. Examples include commercial, industrial, or residential zones. These areas are established and protected by zoning laws. Another zoning ordinance is minimum size of the building site. Minimum site sizes will vary according to use. That is, different size sites may be required for residential, commercial, and industrial buildings. Maximum land coverage for a typical city home is about 35 percent.

One of the first things an architect must do in designing a building is to check the zoning codes. The intended use of the building has to be within the limits of zoning laws. Also, the size of the lot must be large enough to meet the minimum requirements.

PROPERTY LINES

Once it has been determined that zoning ordinances can be met, the architect turns attention to the building site. The next planning step is to prepare the plot plan drawing that shows the shape and size of the lot.

The line delineating the outside of the lot area is the *property line*. A drawing with property lines in place is shown in **Figure 5-1**.

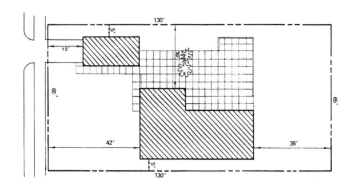

Figure 5-1. A starting point for the development of plans for a building is the preparation of a dimensioned drawing showing property lines. *What does the word "dimensioned" mean in reference to a lot drawing?*

DRAWING PLOT PLANS

A typical scale drawing for a city size plot plan may be 1/8 inch = 1 foot or 1 inch = 10 feet. For large parcels of land a smaller scale must be used such as 1 inch = 20 feet or 1 inch = 30 feet. An example of a scaled site plan is shown in **Figure 5-1**.

The plot plan's drawing is a legal document. It may become part of the deed to the property. A *deed* is a document of ownership for the property. When *dimensioned drawings* are prepared by licensed surveyors, they are known as *survey drawings*.

SETBACKS

Zoning laws also control how close a building can be located from the property lines of a lot. This distance is known as a *setback*. Building codes specify setbacks according to the front, side, and back of the building site. An example of setbacks is shown in **Figure 5-2**. Setbacks differ according to the use of the property. Different rules apply for residential, commercial, or industrial use.

The setbacks are drawn parallel to the property line on a drawing. This line delineates the area in which construction can take place. The line marking off usable area is known as the *building line*. The area within this line is the *buildable area*.

The buildable area will always have the same shape as the lot because the setback lines are always parallel to the property lines. If a lot has an irregular shape, the buildable area will also have the same irregular shape. See **Figure 5-3**.

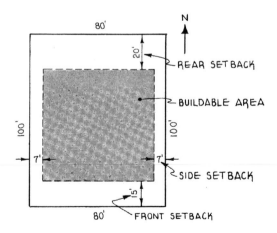

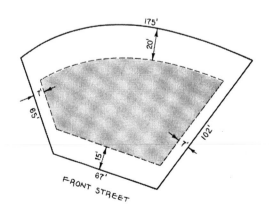

Figure 5-2. The area within setbacks required by the zoning laws is called the buildable area of a lot. *Are setbacks the same for all lots within a city or do they vary with use? Why?*

Figure 5-3. The buildable area always follows the shape of a lot. Irregular-shaped lots have irregular buildable areas. *How are setbacks determined on irregular-shaped lots?*

Zoning ordinances will specify that only a certain percentage of the site can be used for structures. For example, a typical rule is 35 percent of the site's area may be used for construction. The architect has to consider such rules in planning structures on a lot. **Figure 5-4** illustrates how this may be accomplished.

DAYLIGHT PLANE

Many communities have restrictions on how much space the upper levels of a home may consume. This zoning ordinance is called the daylight plane. It eliminates the possibility that a next door neighbor may build a large structure that will screen a view or block the sun light. There are various procedures to calculate the daylight plane. One method is to draw an elevation envelope that the structure must not extend beyond as shown in **Figure 5-5.**

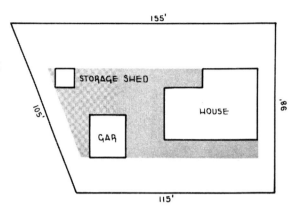

Figure 5-4. In many areas, there are restrictions about the percentage of buildable area that can be used for actual structures. A typical limit is 35 percent. *What uses do you think residents of a house could make of the area on which building is not permitted?*

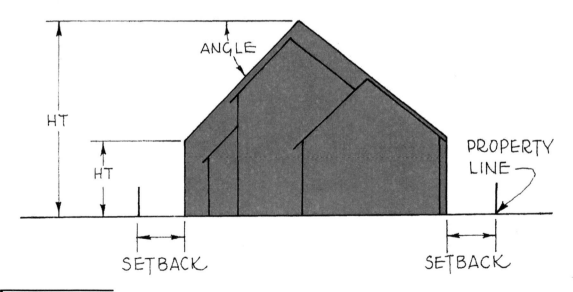

Figure 5-5. The daylight plane limits the size and height of a structure. *What is the purpose for the daylight plane ordinance?*

UNIT 5 ACTIVITIES

VOCABULARY CHECKLIST

1. building site
2. subdivision
3. building code
4. zoning ordinance

5. property line
6. deed
7. survey drawings
8. setback

9. building line
10. buildable area

REVIEW QUESTIONS

1. What factors in building plans may be affected by zoning laws?
2. What is a setback?
3. Why are property lines drawn first in planning a building?
4. Why are setbacks drawn before the building is positioned on a drawing?
5. What is the buildable area of a lot?

YOUR ARCHITECTURAL SCRAPBOOK

1. Call or visit your city hall or an office of the building or zoning department in your area. Ask for a copy of the local building code. Study this and add it to your scrapbook.
2. Draw a plot plan with a CAD system. Make a hard copy and place it in your scrapbook.

CAD ACTIVITIES

After reading Unit 5, refer to Chapter 5 in the *Chief Architect Tutorials* and practice:

• Activating your floor plan and check for errors.
• Changing defaults.
• Creating a window and door schedule.
• Creating a material list.

UNIT 6
ORIENTATION

PURPOSE OF BUILDING CODES

The position of a building on its site is its architectural orientation. In this context, the word *orientation* means positioning or location.

The orientation of a building is an important concern of the architect. Some of the factors considered in orienting a building include:

- View
- Noise
- Wind or breeze
- Sun

View

The view enjoyed from a home is often one of its main environmental benefits. Certainly, one of the goals of home design is to produce the best possible views available. The living area of the home will usually be placed so that it faces the best possible view. This principle is illustrated in **Figure 6-1**.

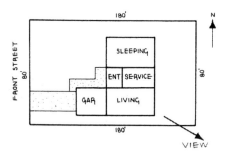

Figure 6-1. The living area of a home is usually oriented toward the best available view. *Why is view important as a factor in the orientation of a home?*

Noise

An architect designing a home always checks noise levels in the area. A study is made to find the source of the greatest amount of noise. The goal is to orient the home so that its occupants will be disturbed by as little noise as possible. In general, people are affected most by noise when they sleep. Thus, it is usually best to orient sleeping areas away from the source of noise.

The position of the living areas is always important. Noise can occur at any time of day. For example, suppose noise in the area of a site occurs mostly in the daytime. It would then be best to orient the home so the living areas were away from the noise. The orientation of the sleeping areas would be less important in this case.

If possible, the service area of the home should be oriented to buffer noise. That is, the service area is placed toward the noise. This protects the living and sleeping areas.

Landscaping can also be used to cut the effects of noise. **Figure 6-2** shows the orientation of a home to minimize the effects of noise.

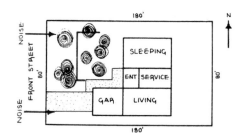

Figure 6-2. Both living and sleeping areas of a home may have to be oriented to minimize the effects of noise. In this drawing, note the positions of trees on the site. *What is the importance of these trees in relation to noise levels within the home?*

Wind or Breeze

Another orientation factor is the direction of wind or breeze patterns that normally cross the site. The season or time of day of these winds or breezes must also be determined.

The architect should take advantage of breezes for the comfort of the home occupants. At the same time, orientation should limit any undesirable effects from strong winds. The home in **Figure 6-3** has been positioned for best use of wind and breeze patterns.

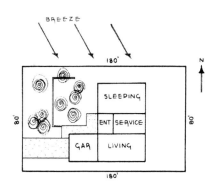

Figure 6-3. Breezes can be advantages and winds can cause problems in the orientation of a home. Normal seasons and times of day during which breezes and winds blow should be considered in designing a building. In this design, the idea is to bring cool, fresh air to sleeping areas. *During what time of day do you think the breezes normally occur?*

Sun

The path of the sun is one of the most important orientation concerns for homes. For example, consider the normal path of the sun in the northern hemisphere (northern half of the earth). The sun rises in the east, moves across the southern sky, and sets in the west.

The architect must consider the path of the sun in locating rooms within a house. In the morning, the sun has not yet heated the home. In the afternoon, the sun builds heat. For most of the year, this warmth is desirable in indoor and outdoor living areas. By late afternoon, the heat of the sun builds to levels that might become uncomfortable. Therefore, it is desirable to protect the home from the afternoon sun as much as possible. **Figure 6-4** illustrates the relationship of a home's orientation to sunshine.

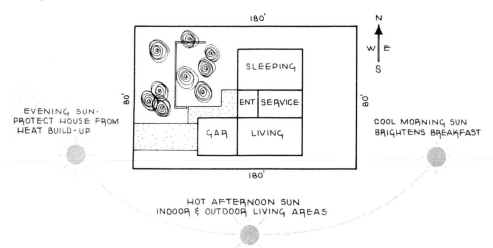

Figure 6-4. The path of the sun can be the most important factor in determining the orientation of a home. This drawing covers the positions of the sun and the effects of the sun's heat on a home. *What are the benefits to the occupants from the position indicated in this drawing?*

ORIENTING THE STRUCTURE

In considering these four orientation factors: view, noise, breeze or wind, and the sun, the architect must decide their importance. It is usually not possible to orient a structure to take advantage of all four factors. Instead, it is necessary to make trade-offs. An orientation should be chosen that posseses as many advantages as possible.

Figure 6-5 shows a home designed with excellent orientation to its site. This home has protection from noise and the afternoon sun. The view, the morning sun, and the breeze are used to the best advantage. Note the role of landscaping in relation to orientation.

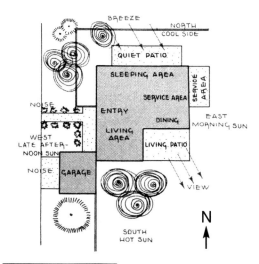

Figure 6-5. Trade-offs must be established to balance the factors affecting the orientation of a home. *How does landscaping help in the orientation of this home?*

SOLAR ENERGY

In temperate zones, the cost of heating a home in winter is a major expense. *Temperate zones* are areas of the earth with seasonal climates. These areas are hot in summer and cold in winter. Homes should be designed to keep heating costs as low as possible. Heating costs are minimized by designing homes to take advantage of the sun's heat. There are two different approaches for adding the heat of the sun, or *solar energy*, to work in homes.

- Active solar systems
- Passive solar systems

Active Solar Systems

Solar systems that collect the sun's heat outside the building, store it, and distribute warmth with a mechanical system are called *active solar systems*.

There are four basic parts to an active solar system.

1. Collectors
2. Storage
3. Distribution
4. Control.

Special panels that collect the heat of the sun, or *solar collectors* are mounted outside the building. These panels are usually set on a roof facing south, as shown in **Figure 6-6**. Many pipes or passages containing air or liquid make up the panels. The air or liquid is heated by the rays of the sun.

Figure 6-6. In active solar systems, the sun's heat is collected through use of solar panels mounted outside the house. These panels face south. *Why are solar collectors oriented toward the south?*

The air or liquid heated by the sun is stored within the system. During cool times of the day, the heat is distributed through the home. An active system also needs some methods to keep temperatures from being too hot or too cold. For example, there may be several cloudy or stormy winter days on which the sun does not shine. To deal with such problems, these systems often include conventional heaters using natural gas or electricity. Such devices are called *auxiliary heaters*. They are used when the solar system does not keep up with the needs of the home.

Figure 6-7 diagrams active solar systems that provide heat through the use of air and liquid.

Figure 6-7.
Active solar systems store the sun's heat by warming air or water. This heat is then pumped through pipes to heat the home. *Why do the systems in this illustration have auxiliary heaters?*

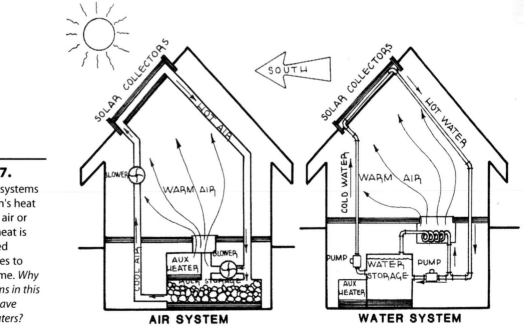

AIR SYSTEM

WATER SYSTEM

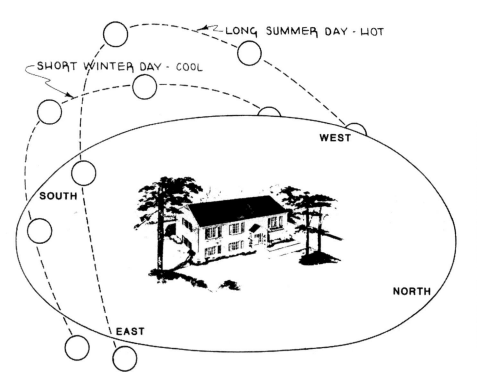

LONG SUMMER DAY - HOT

SHORT WINTER DAY - COOL

WEST

SOUTH

NORTH

EAST

Figure 6-8.
During long summer days, the path of the sun is high. During short winter days, the sun is lower in the sky. Passive solar systems are designed to take advantage of these positions of the sun. *What are the main differences between active and passive solar systems?*

Passive Solar Systems

Passive solar systems make it is possible for homes to capture solar heat through the home's orientation and its construction features. There are no mechanical parts in passive solar systems.

Passive solar homes are designed to capture solar energy and to keep heat losses to a minimum in winter. In summer, the same homes keep the hot summer heat out. These designs are worked out through an understanding of the paths of the sun. In the summer, the path of the sun is high in the sky, therefore the summer days are long. In the winter, the sun is lower in the sky, therefore the days are short. **Figure 6-8** illustrates these differences in patterns of exposure to the sun. Houses can be designed around these pathways of the sun. Most of the sun's heat is kept out in summer. Most of the sun's warmth is admitted to the home during winter.

One important design factor for passive solar systems is building orientation. The building should be positioned to receive as much sunshine as possible during cold months. Many other features can help to heat a building in winter and to cool it in summer. Some of these design features are described below.

- *Insulation* is installed to repel heat in the summer and to keep heat inside the home in the winter. Insulation materials have properties that block the flow of heat. The use and effects of insulation are illustrated in **Figure 6-9**. Insulation should be placed between the rafters, ceiling joists, wall studs, and floor joists.

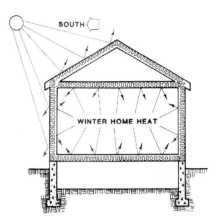

Figure 6-9. Insulation is used to keep heat out in summer. In winter, the same insulation saves heat within the building. *What are the sources of heat in summer and winter?*

- Landscaping plans use deciduous trees on the south side of the home. *Deciduous trees* are those that grow leaves in summer and lose them in winter. Thus, deciduous trees provide shade in summer. In winter, when the leaves are gone, they allow the sun's rays to heat the home. This landscaping pattern is illustrated in Figure **6-10**.

- Vents are built in the attic or ceilings of the upper floor. This makes it possible for warm air to be forced out in summer. Warm air rises to the top of any space. With the vents opened in summer, the warm air rises out of the building. In winter, the vents are closed to keep the warm air in the building. See **Figure 6-11**.

Home Planners, Inc.

Figure 6-10.
Landscape planning is important to passive solar systems. Deciduous trees are placed on the south side of the home. *Why do deciduous trees provide shade in summer and permit the sun to warm the home in winter?*

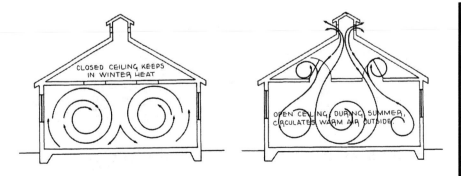

Figure 6-11.
Use of vents in the ceiling or attic gives a home natural air conditioning. In the summer, vents are opened to permit warm air to escape. In the winter, the vents are closed to keep the warm air in the house. *Why does the warm air escape from the house when the vents are open?*

• Buildings are designed with wide roof overhangs. The *overhang* is the part of the roof that extends beyond the side walls. Wide overhangs create shade that protects windows from the high summer sun. This shade reduces heat in the building. In the winter, the sun is lower in the sky. From its lower position, the sun can shine through the

Home Planners, Inc.

Figure 6-12. A wide roof overhang shades windows during the summer. This minimizes the heat that comes into the home from the sun. In winter, the sun's warmth is admitted. The seaonal changes effect the sun's position in the southern sky. *Why does the sun's warmth reach the windows in winter and not in summer?*

windows. The effect of a wide overhang is illustrated in **Figure 6-12**. The use of wide overhangs can also be combined with the positioning of deciduous trees. This makes it possible to use large window areas that are protected in summer but admit the sun's warmth in winter. **Figure 6-13** illustrates this design feature. Large windows are usually used to admit as much sun as possible in winter. **Figure 6-14** demonstrates how architects design the amount of roof overhang that is needed.

Figure 6-13. This home combines the methods of roof overhang and the use of deciduous trees. The overhang reduces sunshine in summer. The trees provide shade in summer and access to the sun in winter. *Why are large windows used on the south side of the house in this design?*

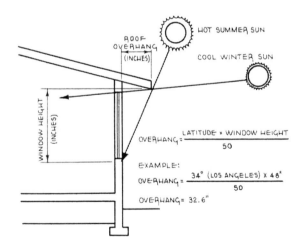

$$OVERHANG = \frac{LATITUDE \times WINDOW\ HEIGHT}{50}$$

EXAMPLE:

$$OVERHANG = \frac{34°\ (LOS\ ANGELES) \times 48"}{50}$$

$$OVERHANG = 32.6"$$

Figure 6-14. This illustration shows how to calculate the proper roof overhang. The formula considers the geographic latitude and height of the window. The geographic latitude determines the angle of the sun's rays. *Why is the height of the window important in this formula?*

- Double-glazing is used on windows. Even though the walls and roof are well insulated, heat can be lost through the windows. *Double-glazing* traps air between two panes of glass. This provides insulation that keeps out heat in summer and retains heat in winter. See **Figure 6-15**.

- *Earth sheltering* can be used for insulation. The home may be built partly underground. Or, earth can be piled around part of the home after construction is completed. The earth traps cool air within the house in summer. In winter, warmth is retained. This method is illustrated in **Figure 6-16**.

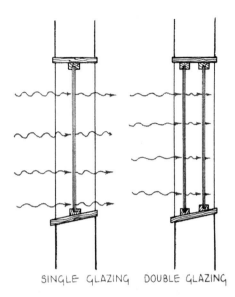

SINGLE GLAZING   DOUBLE GLAZING

Figure 6-15. Double-glazing keeps out more heat than a single pane of glass. The effect is to add to the home's insulation. *How does double-glazing help to keep out heat?*

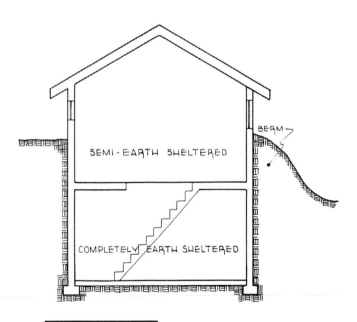

Figure 6-16. In passive solar systems, earth can be used to insulate a building. Warm or cold air is retained in the building, depending upon the season. *How does the use of earth keep a building cool in summer and warm in winter?*

- A structure made from bricks or stone (*masonry*), holds heat longer than most other building materials. Therefore, masonry is used in passive solar systems to collect and store heat within the home. The sun heats the masonry during the day. The warmth is then given off at night. See **Figure 6-17**.

- An excellent passive system is to build a *greenhouse* on the south side of the building. The sun's radiant heat passes through the glass structure to heat the air in the greenhouse. The warmth of the greenhouse can be stored in walls, thick floors, or water- filled containers. Warm air is then used to heat the house. In some systems,

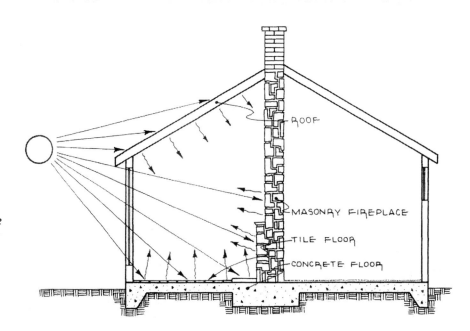

Figure 6-17. Masonry walls within buildings can play important roles in passive solar systems. The sun heats the masonry during the day. At night, the heat is given off to warm the interior. *Why are masonry walls used for this purpose?*

fans are used to circulate the warm air. Use of a greenhouse for winter warmth is shown in **Figure 6-18**. In the summer, the system can be reversed to circulate the warm air outside through the greenhouse roof. This is illustrated in **Figure 6-19**.

- Light colors reflect heat. Dark colors absorb heat. In warm climates, light colored roofs should be placed on homes. In cold climates, dark colors may be used for roofs.

- Heavy curtains can be hung in southern windows. During cold months, they can be drawn back in the daytime to permit the sun's heat to enter. Then, the curtains are closed at night to prevent heat loss. In summer, the curtains are closed to keep out the sun's heat.

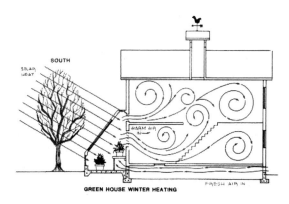

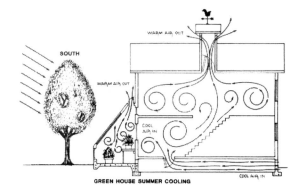

Figure 6-18. Placement of a greenhouse on the southern side of a building can be the basis for a natural heating system. Heat is collected in the greenhouse and distributed through ducts. *Why does a greenhouse collect heat?*

Figure 6-19. A greenhouse system can be used for natural air conditioning in the summer. Warm air is drawn out of the house through the same system that delivers heat in the winter. *Why does the greenhouse in this illustration remain cool in summer?*

UNIT 6 ACTIVITIES

VOCABULARY CHECKLIST

1. orientation
2. temperate zone
3. solar energy
4. active solar system
5. solar collectors

6. auxiliary heaters
7. passive solar system
8. insulation
9. deciduous trees
10. overhang

11. double-glazing
12. earth sheltering
13. masonry
14. greenhouse

REVIEW QUESTIONS

1. Which side of a house is normally the warmest?
2. Which side of a house receives the morning sun?
3. Why are breezes and winds important in orienting a home?
4. What is the name of the solar heating system that uses collector panels?
5. Why are auxiliary heaters often installed in solar-heated homes?

YOUR ARCHITECTURAL SCRAPBOOK

1. Sketch the floor plan of a home and show the factors that might affect its orientation.
2. Sketch a home showing the basic features of an active solar energy system.
3. Sketch a home with some of the passive solar energy features about which you have learned. Label these features on your drawing.
4. List other possible features of passive solar energy systems that might not have been included in your drawing.
5. With a CAD system, design a home with solar panels and a greenhouse. Make a hard copy and place it in your scrapbook.

CAD ACTIVITIES

After reading Unit 6, refer to Chapter 6 in the *Chief Architect Tutorials* and practice:

- Activating your floor plan.
- Going to the **Preferences** drop-down menu and practicing the various modifications that may be made to your drawing and software program.

PART III
The Planning of a House

The Design Process

Room Planning

Exterior House Forms

PART III

THE PLANNING OF A HOUSE

PURPOSE OF HOME PLANNING

The features of a home should meet the living, working, and recreational needs of the occupants. This matching of home design to the needs of people is carried out in a series of steps followed by the architect.

The architect must plan for use of space within the home according to area. The best choice must be made for space to be used for living, sleeping, working, and storage.

Individual rooms must be designed within the areas of the home. These rooms must meet both structural and functional requirements. Structural requirements involve the placement of supporting walls. The soundness of the building depends on these design decisions. The sizes and features of rooms are also important.

The architect must be concerned about the exterior appearance of the home. Exterior features can add greatly to the livability of a home.

All of this planning must be done with the needs of the occupants of the home in mind. Each occupant of a home has his or her own lifestyle and needs. The end result of home planning should be a house that fits the needs and tastes of its users.

Part III contains a series of units that introduce you to these planning steps.

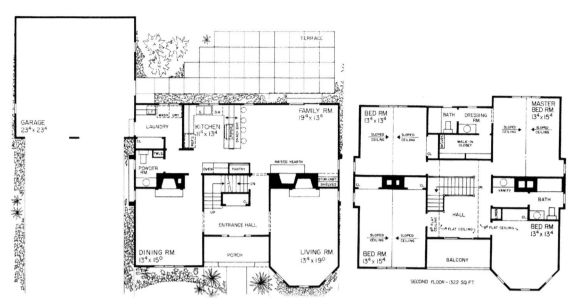

YOUR LEARNING JOB

There are three learning units in Part III. They cover:

- The design process
- Room planning
- Exterior house forms

The reading and work in these units completes your review of the home planning process. With this understanding, you will be ready to build actual drafting skills

UNIT 7
THE DESIGN PROCESS

The architectural *design process* is a series of procedural steps used to design a structure. This process begins with the lifestyles of the occupants, and ends with a set of working drawings

THE DESIGN STEPS

There are many factors that must be considered when designing a home (see **Figure 7-1**.) Using the design process steps shown in **Figure 7-2** will aid in the functional design of a home that meets the needs of the occupants.

The Designing and Planning for:

1. The Family
2. Living Styles
3. Living Needs
4. Furniture Needs
5. Room Sizes
6. Number of Rooms
7. Architectural Styling
8. Zoning Laws
9. Site Considerations
10. Room Orientaion
11. Solar Orientaion
12. Sketching and Planning the Floor Plan

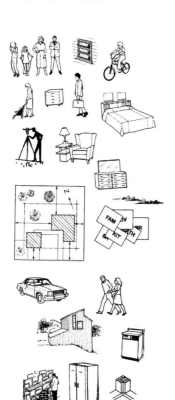

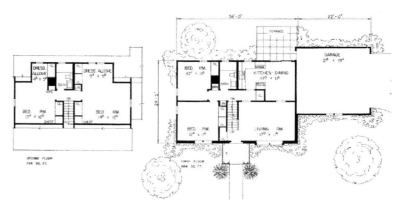

Figure 7-1. The information to properly design a home. *Why is information about occupants listed first?*

```
STEPS IN THE DESIGN PROCESS

1.  DEFINE LIFESTYLES
2.  DEFINE THE PROJECT
3.  DETERMINE WANTS AND NEEDS
4.  ESTABLISH GOALS
5.  STUDY SPACE NEEDS
6.  STUDY SITE CONDITIONS
7.  DEFINE HOME AREAS
8.  PREPARE BUBBLE DIAGRAMS
9.  POSITION ROOMS
10. FLOOR PLAN DESIGN
11. ELEVATION DESIGN
12. WORKING DRAWINGS
13. CONSTRUCTION DOCUMENTS
```

```
LIFESTYLE ACTIVITIES

1.  SWIMMING
2.  TENNIS
3.  PRIVACY
4.  FREE TIME AT HOME
5.  OUTDOOR ENTERTAINING
6.  TWO TEENAGERS IN SCHOOL
7.  TWO ADULTS COMMUTE TO WORK
8.  FREQUENT DINNER GUESTS
9.  MODEL BUILDING HOBBY
10. ONE TEENAGER ON BASKETBALL TEAM
11. ONE TEENAGER ON TRACK TEAM
12. WHOLE FAMILY RUN & JOG
```

Figure 7-2. The steps in the design process follow a logical sequence.

Figure 7-3. The lifestyles and habits of occupants will greatly affect the home's design.

DEFINING LIFESTYLES

The first step in designing a home is to determine the *lifestyles* of the occupants. There must be a list of each occupant's personal habits, occupation, and interests. **Figure 7-3** shows an example of the lifestyles for a family. You must understand how this list will determine the specific design features for their home.

PROJECT DEFINITION

Once a list of the lifestyles is completed, a definition of the design should be prepared as shown in **Figure 7-4**. Information about the building site, architectural style preference, major uses for the home, financial constraints, and potential problems, provide a direction to the design process.

WANTS AND NEEDS

To develop a functional plan, the wants and needs must be listed. A need is a feature the occupants must have. A want is a preferred feature that may be omitted if necessary. Since all needs are absolute, they can be listed in any order. The wants should be ranked in order of importance. This ranking permits the want list to be cut from the bottom up if necessary. **Figure 7-5** shows a list of wants and needs for the occupants.

GOALS AND OBJECTIVES

When the occupants agree on the definition of the project and on the list of wants and needs, the major goals are developed. This is a critical step because this list must be incorporated into the design. **Figure 7-6** shows a set of goals and objectives.

PROJECT DEFINITION

MR & MRS BILL JONES HAVE PURCHASED A CORNER LOT. THE JONES'S HAVE TWO TEENAGE SONS. THEY WANT A HOUSE DESIGNED TO MEET THEIR NEEDS AND TO TAKE THE BEST ADVANTAGE OF A BEAUTIFUL VIEW. THEY WANT THE MORNING SUN IN THE BREAKFAST AREA AND THE SLEEPING AREA AWAY FROM THE FRONT ST. & TRAIN NOISE. THE JONES PREFER CONTEMPORY DESIGN AND MUST KEEP THE BUILDING COSTS <u>UNDER</u> $400,000.

Figure 7-4. The project definition should be stated in writing as part of the contract.

NEEDS AND WANTS

NEEDS

- SEPARATE LIVING & DINING ROOMS
- SEPARATE FAMILY ROOM
- TWO-CAR GARAGE
- EAT-IN KITCHEN
- MASTER BEDROOM SUITE
- TWO TEENAGE BEDROOMS WITH SHARED BATH
- ONE LEVEL DESIGN WITH BASEMENT
- SEPARATE FOYER
- SWIMMING POOL

WANTS

1. TENNIS COURT
2. BASKETBALL HOOP/BACKBOARD
3. 1ST FLOOR LAUNDRY
4. FIREPLACE
5. CATHEDRAL CEILINGS
6. RUNNING PATHS
7. EXERCISE ROOM
8. POWDER ROOM
9. FOURTH BEDROOM
10. HOT TUB
11. SAUNA
12. POOL TABLE IN FAMILY ROOM

Figure 7-5. The design must meet all the stated needs and as many of the wants as possible. *Why are the wants listed in order?*

MAJOR GOALS

1. PLACE HOME ON SITE TO CAPTURE VIEW FROM THE LIVING AREA.
2. POSITION HOUSE TO BAFFLE UNDESIRABLE VIEW AND NOISE.
3. POSITION HOUSE FOR MAXIMUM SOLAR EFFICIENCY.
4. PROVIDE TRAFFIC PATTERNS FOR EFFICIENCY AND PRIVACY.
5. PLAN DINING FACILITIES FOR 8 TO 10 GUESTS.
6. INTEGRATE POOL WITH LIVING AREA
7. PLAN STORAGE FACILITIES IN BASEMENT
8. SAVE EXISTING PLANTS & TREES WITH MINIMUN SITE DESTRUCTION.
9. PLAN LARGE FAMILY ROOM

Figure 7-6. The major goals are guide posts during the design process.

PLANNING STUDIES

The designer must now determine the amount of space needed to meet the goals and objectives. **Figure 7-7** shows a chart to show the uses, and amount of space required, for each occupant.

SPACE STUDY

AREA	USERS	SIZE	NOTES
LIVING ROOM	8-10 ADULTS	280 SQ FT	RELATE TO PATIO, POOL & DINING AREA. CAPTURE BEST VIEW.
DINING ROOM	8-10 ADULTS	200 SQ FT	RELATE TO KITCHEN, PATIO AND LIVING ROOM
FAMILY ROOM	2 ADULTS & 2 TEENAGERS	200 SQ FT	TV, READING, POOL TABLE & MODEL BUILDING
MASTER BEDROOM	2 ADULTS	250 SQ FT	SEPARATE DRESSING AREA & BATH. TV VIEWING
TEEN BEDROOMS	2 TEENS	130 SQ FT PER BR	BUILT-IN DESKS
GUEST BATH	TEENS & GUESTS	60 SQ FT	FULL BATH ACCESS TO TEEN BEDROOMS & LIVING AREA
FOYER	ALL TRAFFIC	100 SQ FT	CENTRAL TRAFFIC ACCESS TO ALL AREAS & BASEMENT - GUEST CLOSET
KITCHEN	ALL OCCUPANTS	230 SQ FT	BREAKFAST AREA, PANTRY
LAUNDRY	ALL OCCUPANTS	100 SQ FT	WASHER, DRYER, SINK, HALF-BATH, STORAGE
GARAGE	TWO-CAR	24' x 24'	STORAGE & WORKSHOP AREA
SWIMMING POOL	ALL OCCUPANTS	18' x 36'	DIVING BRD, ADJACENT PATIO & LIV AREA, CAPTURE VIEW & SUN
PATIOS & DECKS	ALL OCCUPANTS	VARIES	ADJACENT TO POOL & LIV AREA, DINING AREA, CAPTURE VIEW, SPACE TO ENTERTAIN
RECREATION AREAS	ALL OCCUPANTS	VARIES	TENNIS CRT, BASKETBALL BACKBOARD, JOGGING PATHS, TRACK

Figure 7-7. A *space study* is used to record the amount of required space for each room or area.

SITE STUDIES

Before beginning the design, the features of the site must be studied. This will insure that the best features of the site are used for the design. The condition of the soil and the angle of the site's slope determines where the structure may be located. To begin a site study, a base drawing of the property must be prepared showing the property lines, adjacent roads, utility lines, easements, setbacks, and compass direction **(see Figure 7-8)**. The next few site studies are produced with tracing paper or vellum placed over the site's base drawing.

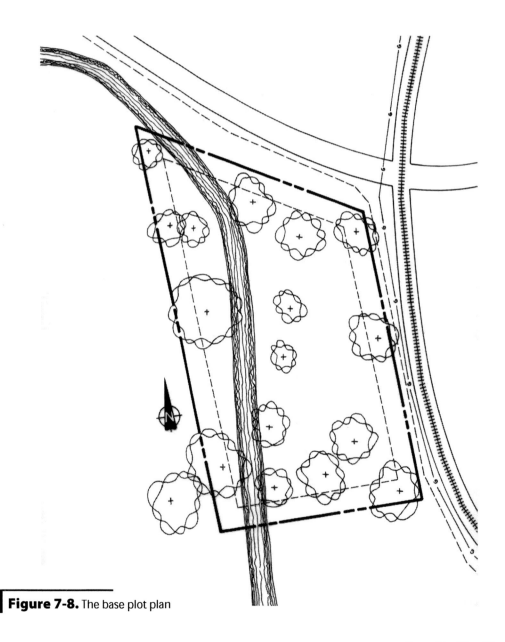

Figure 7-8. The base plot plan

A *soil study* will show the soil's ability to support structural weights. Soils with no organic matter, compacted soil, and/or rock are excellent for structural support. Sandy soil, high organic content soil, and soil with a high silt or clay content range from poor to fair for structural support. To prepare a soil study drawing, as shown in **Figure 7-9**, follow these steps.

1. Classify the soil condition areas as excellent, good, poor, or not suitable for building.

2. Draw an area on the base drawing, with an overlay, on the soil conditions.

3. Shade each area with a different color.

4. Prepare a key to show the soil condition each color represents.

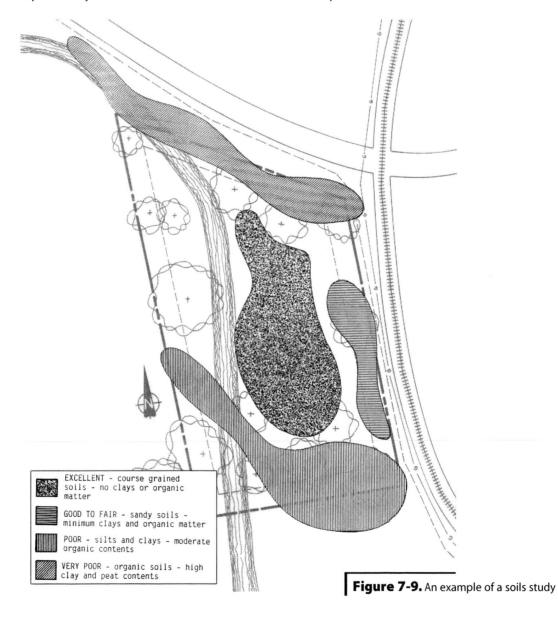

EXCELLENT - course grained soils - no clays or organic matter

GOOD TO FAIR - sandy soils - minimum clays and organic matter

POOR - silts and clays - moderate organic contents

VERY POOR - organic soils - high clay and peat contents

Figure 7-9. An example of a soils study

SLOPE STUDY

The slope of the various areas is critical for planning the placement of the structure. Building on steep slope requires earth moving, special foundation piers, and structural engineering. This significantly increases the cost of building.

To prepare a slope study drawing as shown in **Figure 7-10**, follow these steps on an overlay.

1. Draw the contour lines on an overlay of the base drawing.

2. Identify the building areas with the percent of slope.
   a. Excellent = 0 to 5%
   b. Fair to good = 6% to 10%
   c. Poor to fair = 11% to 25%
   d. Not suitable = over 26%

3. Identify each area with a different color.

4. Prepare a key to represent each color.

5. Note drainage and erosion areas.

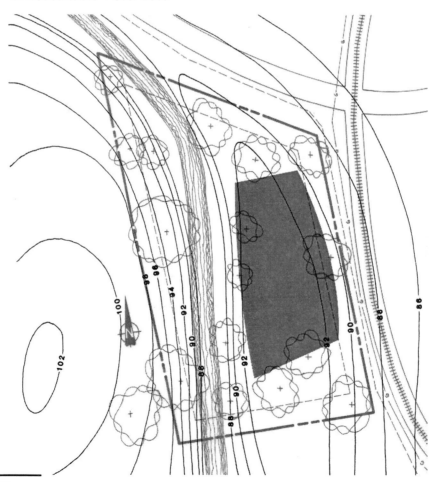

Figure 7-10. A *slope study* shows the flatest area to in which to build.

VISUAL STUDY

Preparing a *visual study*, as shown in **Figure 7-11**, helps the designer use the important site features for the orientation of room placements. To prepare this type of study, follow these steps on an overlay.

1. Locate the best views.
2. Locate the sunrise, afternoon sun, and sunset.
3. Locate the direction of objectionable noises and odors.
4. Show the direction of prevailing breezes.
5. Show landscape features such as plants, water, and rock outcrops.
6. Show wildlife habitats.
7. Locate the private and public areas.

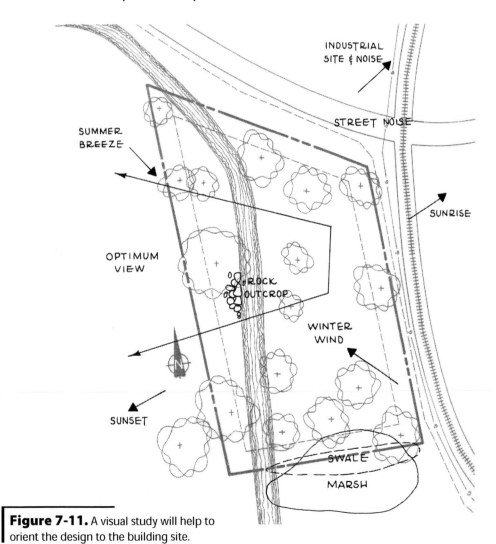

Figure 7-11. A visual study will help to orient the design to the building site.

THE COMBINED SITE STUDY

To finalize the site study, the site overlays should be combined into one study as shown in **Figure 7-12**. To prepare this study, follow these steps.

1. Align the soil and slope overlay studies over the visual study drawing.

2. Place tracing paper over the three drawings and trace an outline from each study which buildable areas are excellent, good, fair, poor, and not acceptable.

3. Color-code each area.

4. Draw the setback lines and color the areas between the setback lines and property as not buildable.

5. Add notes from the studies that will effect the design and location of the house and its rooms.

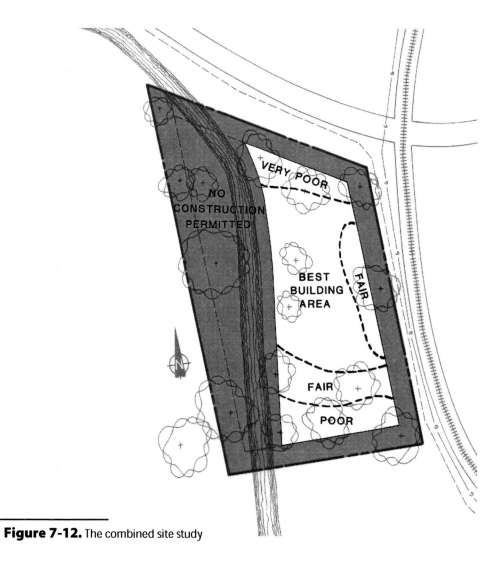

Figure 7-12. The combined site study

FLOOR PLAN DESIGN

After the site studies, the designer will start the preliminary floor plan using only the major room areas. The major areas of a house are:

1. The entry.

2. The *living area* (living room, dining room, family room, den, entry powder room, and miscellaneous rooms such as music and recreation).

3. The *sleeping area* (bedrooms and bathrooms).

4. The *service area* (kitchen, laundry, utility room, garage, workrooms, and storage rooms.)

5. The four areas should be located and sketched as bubbles in the best possible location using the information gathered from the design process **(see Figure 7-13)**.

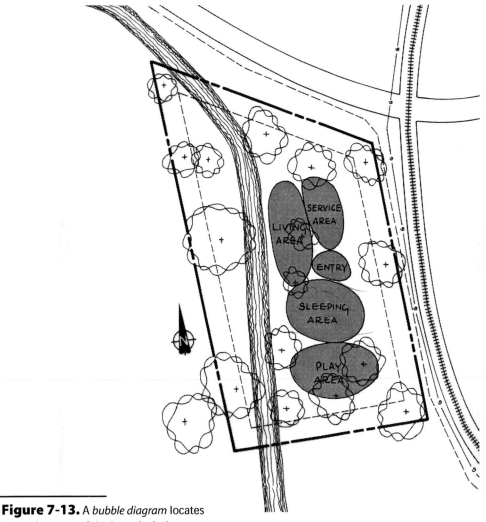

Figure 7-13. A *bubble diagram* locates the major areas of the home's design.

The next design step is to sketch rooms into each bubble as shown in **Figure 7-14**. You will be making many changes with these sketches before the owners, building department, and contractor are satisfied. At this juncture of the design process, design changes are fast, easy, and inexpensive to make.

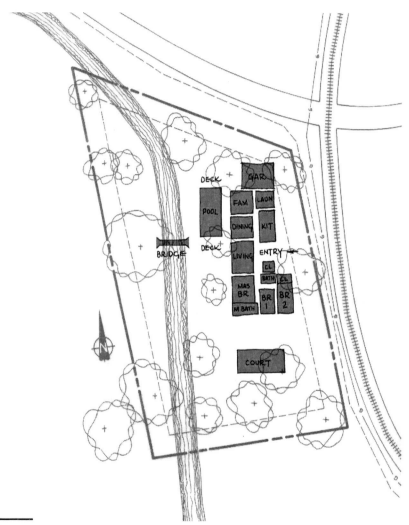

Figure 7-14. Room postioning may be done by sketching or making room templates and positioning them for best arrangement.

Once approved, a scaled floor plan sketch is prepared to check that the square footage of the structure does not exceed the zoning ordinance **(see Figure 7-15)**. When all facets of the design are acceptable, **(Figure 7-16)** the final set of working drawings may be prepared for the building permits and the contractors (See Units 28 and 29 for examples for a full set of working drawings).

Figure 7-15. The finished preliminary floor plan

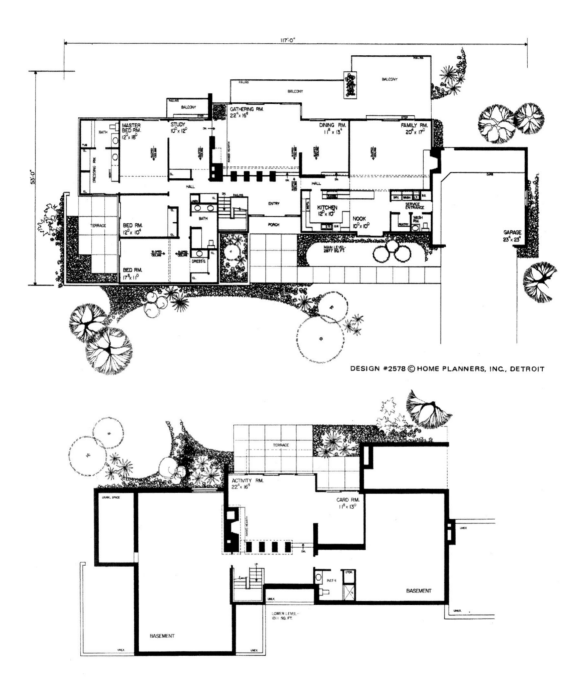

DESIGN #2578 © HOME PLANNERS, INC., DETROIT

Figure 7-16. After the floor is completed a full set of working drawings must be completed to obtain a building permit. *(Floor plan and basement plan shown above).*

Figure 7-17 shows various designs with the entry, living, sleeping and service areas. Also noted are the design features for outdoor areas (**Figure 7-17** and **7-18**).

1. Outdoor areas are adjacent to indoor living areas.
2. Outdoor service areas are adjacent to indoor service areas.
3. Outdoor quiet areas should be adjacent to indoor sleeping areas.
4. Outdoor children areas should be visible from the most often used indoor areas.

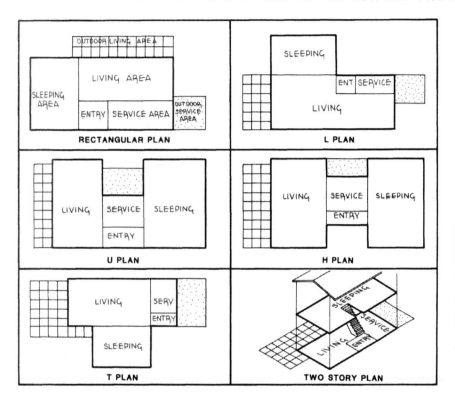

Figure 7-17. This series of designs shows how an entry can be retained to other functional areas of a home. *Why is the entry always adjacent to the three planning areas?*

Figure 7-18. This plan for a home shows how outdoor and indoor areas are related functionally. *What is the relationship between the children's play area and the kitchen?*

The Design Process

UNIT 7 ACTIVITIES

VOCABULARY CHECKLIST

1. design process
2. functional design
3. lifestyle
4 space study

5. soil study
6. slope study
7. visual study
8. living area

9. sleeping area
10. service area
11. bubble diagram

REVIEW QUESTIONS

1. List the steps of the design process.
2. List six lifestyle activities for your family.
3. What is the difference between a design need and a design want?
4. What information does a space study contain?
5. What type of soil should not be used for construction?
6. What is the best type of soil for construction?
7. What is a bubble design?
8. What is required to get a building permit?

YOUR ARCHITECTURAL SCRAPBOOK

Visit your community's zoning department and ask for a copy of the residential zoning and building ordinances. Study the material and add them to your scrapbook.

CAD ACTIVITIES

After reading Unit 7, refer to Chapter 7 in the *Chief Architect Tutorials* and complete:

- Designing a new floor plan using the **House Wizard**.
- Adding the following rooms: living, kitchen/family room, dining room, three bedrooms, 2 ½ baths, office, and a three car garage.

UNIT 8
ROOM PLANNING

REVISIONS DURING THE DESIGN PROCESS

It is usually impossible to think of all of the needs for the occupants of a home in the first draft of plans. Almost always, it is necessary to improve, or revise, the first draft of plans.

One reason for a *plan revision* is that new ideas for home features may be introduced. These ideas result from additional thought about the lifestyles and needs of the occupants. People often have additional ideas once they see the plans for a house.

The architect may also find problems that should be considered. Room sizes may have to be adjusted. The shape of the house may not look right after further study. There may be too much hall space, for example, causing waste of possible living area.

Development of a final plan for a new home requires several steps. The first sketch is based on the information gathered from the building site and the occupants needs and wants. After that, each new sketch improves upon the one before. For example, a first, rough (preliminary) sketch for a home might take the form of the floor plan shown in **Figure 8-1**. Note that this plan gives the sizes (dimensions) of the rooms. Take a moment to study the plan in Figure 8-1. Concentrate on the bedroom cluster and on the entry. Think about any changes you might make if this were your home.

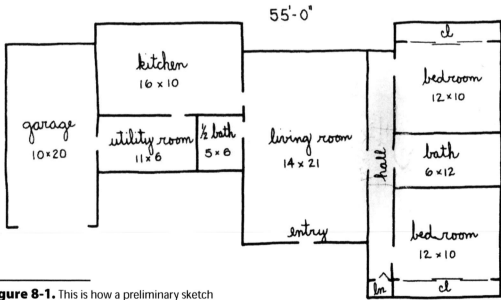

Figure 8-1. This is how a preliminary sketch for the design of a home might take shape. A preliminary sketch serves as a basis for changes that might make the home more comfortable. Look at this plan. *If you had guests who wore coats when they entered, what would you do with them? Does the living room need a closet?*

Now look at the sketch of the same home in **Figure 8-2**. Many sketches should be drawn before reaching the final revisions for the floor plan. The original design had two major design problems: the closet design needed improvement, and there is too much hall area. The purpose of the hall is to provide privacy to people using the bedrooms and bathroom. They can use the sleeping area without interfering with activity in the living room. However, in Figure 8-1, there is too much hall space. Further, the bedroom closets in Figure 8-1 take up too much room space. Also note that space has been added to the living room for a *guest closet*. Study Figure 8-2 for a few moments. Think about further improvements that may be made in this home design.

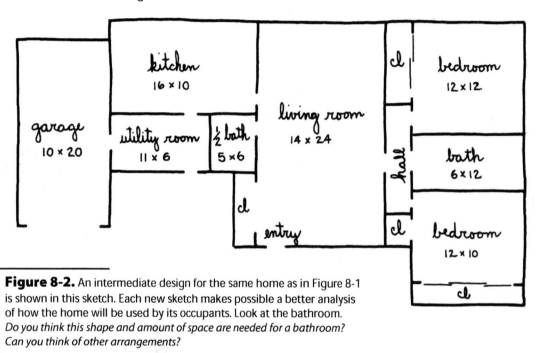

Figure 8-2. An intermediate design for the same home as in Figure 8-1 is shown in this sketch. Each new sketch makes possible a better analysis of how the home will be used by its occupants. Look at the bathroom. *Do you think this shape and amount of space are needed for a bathroom? Can you think of other arrangements?*

A final revision of the floor plan for the same home is shown in **Figure 8-3**. Several important changes have been made.

- The entry has been moved to a location where it is sheltered during bad weather. Taking the entry away from the front of the living room clears the front wall. This wall can now be used for a large window with a view. Furniture could also be placed along the front wall.
- The size of the bathroom has been reduced to provide closets for the bedrooms. The bedrooms now have more floor space.
- The living room now has both a guest closet and a storage closet. A storage closet or entertainment center now uses unneeded space formerly included in the hall. The hall has also given up space for a linen closet.
- The half-bath now opens into the service area rather the living area.

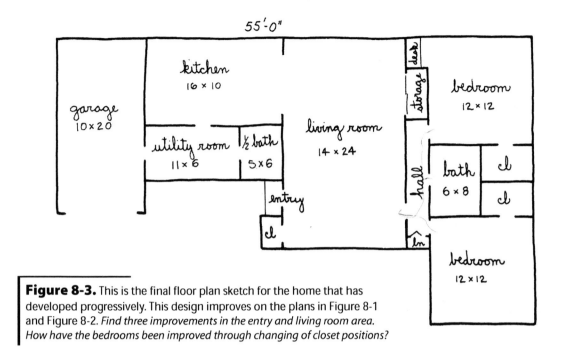

55'-0"

kitchen
16 × 10

garage
10×20

utility room
11×6

½ bath
5×6

living room
14 × 24

storage

desk

bedroom
12×12

hall

bath
6×8

cl

cl

entry

cl

bn

bedroom
12×12

Figure 8-3. This is the final floor plan sketch for the home that has developed progressively. This design improves on the plans in Figure 8-1 and Figure 8-2. *Find three improvements in the entry and living room area. How have the bedrooms been improved through changing of closet positions?*

The design in **Figure 8-3** provides more useful living area than the one in Figure 8-1. This series of sketches illustrates that home design is a progressive process. That is, there are a number of steps, each adding to the next. The process of designing a home uses sketches as a means of putting thoughts on paper. The planning stages often require many more sketches before the plan is finalized. Making changes at this point is simple, quick, and cost-free. Changes can become extremely expensive once construction starts.

ROOM SIZES

One of the factors considered in developing floor plans is the size of rooms. An architect develops knowledge about space needed in different rooms. This space must be large enough so that the occupant's furniture will fit comfortably into the room. There must also be space for people to move around. This is called the *traffic area*. **Figure 8-4** is a list showing typical sizes of rooms, closets, and other spaces for homes. Three sizes are given for small, average, and large rooms.

It is important to match the size of a room with its contents. If the room is too small for its furniture, people won't have room to move around or to live comfortably. See **Figure 8-5**. At the same time, if a room is too large, space is wasted. In a home, space costs money; living area should not be wasted. Too much space can also make a room uncomfortable. It becomes difficult for activities and conversation. It can also be inconvenient to have to walk across a large room to perform simple tasks. For an example of a room that wastes space, see **Figure 8-6**.

Figure 8-4. The table shows typical sizes of rooms and other areas for small, average, and large homes. Look at these figures. *What is the main advantage of using an open design to combine living and dining areas in a small home?*

	TYPICAL ROOM SIZES (FEET)		
BASIC ROOMS	SMALL	AVERAGE	LARGE
1. LIVING ROOM	12 x 18	16 x 20	22 x 28
2. DINING ROOM	10 x 12	12 x 15	15 x 18
3. KITCHEN	8 x 10	10 x 16	12 x 20
4. UTILITY ROOM	6 x 7	6 x 10	8 x 12
5. BEDROOM	10 x 10	12 x 12	14 x 16
6. BATHROOM	5 x 7	7 x 9	9 x 12
ADDITIONAL ROOMS			
7. HALLS	3' WIDE	3'-6" WIDE	3'-9" WIDE
8. GARAGE	10 x 20	20 x 20	22 x 25
9. STORAGE WALL	6" DEEP	12" DEEP	18" DEEP
10. DEN	8 x 10	10 x 12	12 x 16
11. FAMILY ROOM	12 x 15	15 x 18	15 x 22
12. WARDROBE CLOSET	2 x 4	2 x 8	2 x 15
13. ONE ROD WALK-IN CLOSET	4 x 3	4 x 6	4 x 8
14. TWO ROD WALK-IN CLOSET	6 x 4	6 x 6	6 x 8
15. PORCH	6 x 8	8 x 12	12 x 20
16. ENTRY	6 x 6	8 x 10	8 x 15

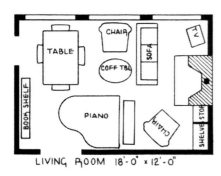

LIVING ROOM 18'-0" x 12'-0"

Figure 8-5. Here is an example of what can happen if too much furniture is crowded into a room. *Find at least two problems with the traffic pattern in this room.*

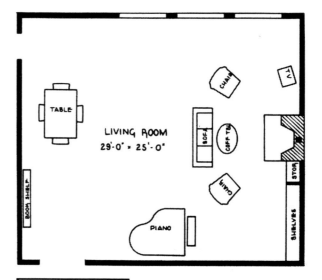

LIVING ROOM 29'-0" x 25'-0"

Figure 8-6. This floor plan has the same furniture as the one in Figure 8-5. However, in this room, space is wasted. Note that this room is almost square in shape. *Would the design be improved it the room were rectangular? Why?*

CONSTRUCTION COSTS

Construction costs are the total of expenses for creating a building. Typical residential construction costs average $125 per square foot. To find the number of *square feet* for a square or rectangular area, multiply one side by the other side. For example, if a room measures 10 feet by 12 feet, it has 120 square feet.

High construction costs provide a good reason to avoid wasting space in designing and building a home. A house should have enough room for comfort. However, oversized houses or rooms are wasteful.

Figure 8-7 illustrates how space that is unnecessary can waste money. This floor plan shows a one-bedroom home measuring 24 feet by 28 feet. At $125 per foot, the construction cost would be $84,000. Adding five feet to the length of the home adds $15,000 in cost. (5 feet times 24 feet = 120 square feet. 120 square feet x $125 = $15,000.) Costs like these make it wise to think carefully about how much space a home really needs.

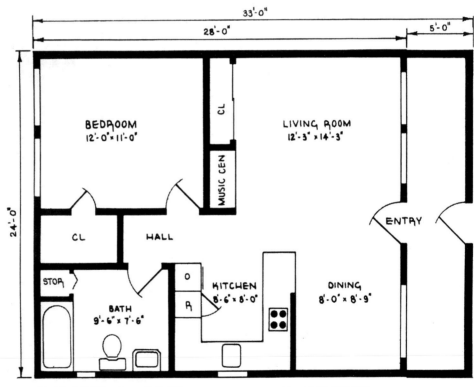

Figure 8-7.
Unneeded space can greatly increase the cost of a home without improving its livability. Adding five feet to the length of this home would increase its cost by $15,000. *Do you think the added space would be worth the extra cost? Why or why not?*

BLDG COST = $125/SQ FT
28' x 24' = 672 SQ FT
672 x 125 = $84,000 HOME COST

5' - 0" ADDITION
5' x 24' = 120 SQ FT ADDITIONAL AREA
120 x 125 = $15,000 ADDITIONAL COST

PLACING FURNITURE

Placement of furniture in rooms is important in the planning of a comfortable, livable home. Traffic and use patterns for each room must be considered. These traffic and use patterns are different for each type of room. A series of drawings illustrates some principles for the placement of furniture and appliances.

Figure 8-8 shows a diagram of a dining room. Space is provided for people to move around the table and to seat themselves. Note placement of the service units such as the china cabinet, serving table, and buffet. They are all close to the head of the table. The person sitting in this position needs to be able to reach these service units. For entertaining large groups, the dining room should be open to the living area so the dining room table can be expanded.

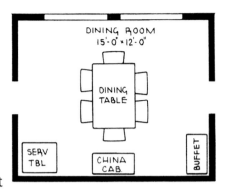

Figure 8-8. Here is a floor plan for a dining room. *Why do you think the serving table, china cabinet, and buffet are all at one end of the room?*

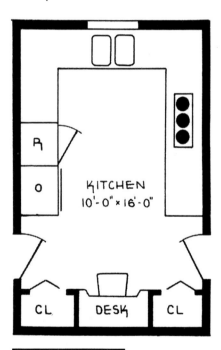

Figure 8-9. This is a floor plan for a kitchen. *Why are all of the cooking or work areas close together?*

Figure 8-9 shows an efficient U-shaped kitchen design. A person working in the kitchen can reach any of the work or cooking areas with just a few steps.

Figure 8-10 shows a design for a utility room. It is equipped with a water heater, laundry tub, washer, and dryer. All of this equipment is placed along an outside wall of the building. This makes it easier to bring in services or to vent equipment. The water heater must be vented to the outside of the home. It is also desirable to be able to expel the damp, hot air, and lint from the clothes dryer to the outside. In addition, it is often easier to make plumbing connections on the outside wall. All of these considerations will affect the costs of installing the water heater, tub, washer, and dryer. If the home is in an area that has freezing weather, all plumbing lines must be in the interior walls.

Figure 8-11 shows a design for a typical bedroom. The traffic pattern involves movement around the bed to the places where clothes are stored. People dress in their bedrooms. They must be able to reach closets, bathrooms, and dressers conveniently.

Figure 8-12 shows a family bathroom. This room is designed with two sinks, making it possible for two people to complete their washing routines at the same time. This is an advantage for people who have limited time to prepare for work or school in the morning.

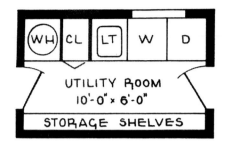

Figure 8-10. An example of a utility room. *Why is it advisable to place the clothes dryer adjacent to an outside wall?*

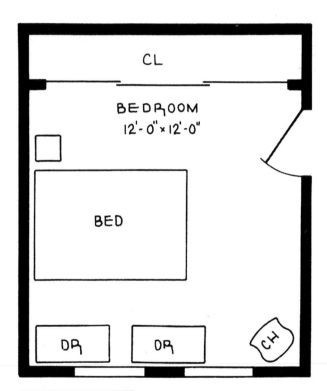

Figure 8-11. A floor plan for an average bedroom is shown here. *Why is it important to provide space for easy access to the closet and dressers?*

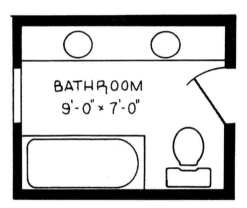

Figure 8-12. This is a floor plan for a typical bathroom. *What is the advantage of having two sinks in a family bathroom?*

Figure 8-13 shows a living room. A *sectional sofa* is placed around a coffee table to provide a convenient place where people can gather and talk. This sofa is made in sections that can be used together or separately. Lamps are provided near the piano and the chairs in which people might want to read.

Figures 8-14 and 8-15 show floor plans for two small comfortable homes of 880 square feet. Both homes have the same overall size. These floor plans illustrate how use of the same amount of space can be varied. People have a variety of tastes and different activities, clothes, cars, foods, etc. Tastes will differ in home design. Certain basic principles apply to home design. Beyond that, however, there are no "rights" or "wrongs." There are only preferences that change with the tastes of the people who will live in the homes.

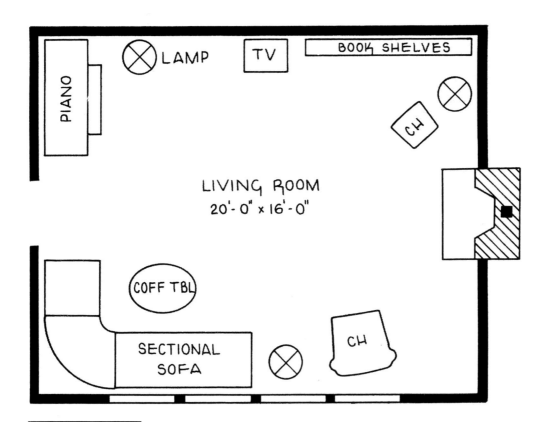

Figure 8-13. Here is a floor plan for a typical living room. *Why is most of the seating provided by a sectional sofa located in one corner of the room?*

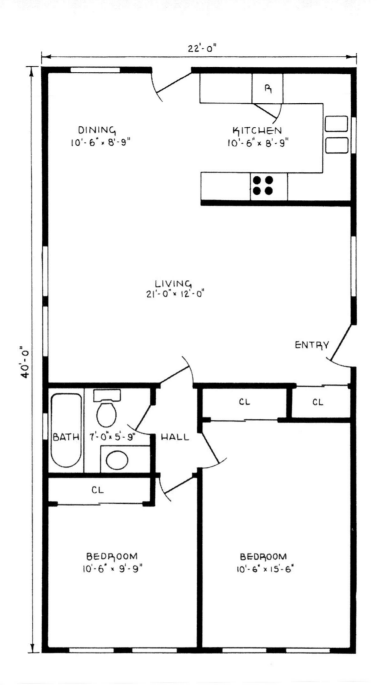

Figure 8-14. A floor plan for a rectangular home is shown here. *Why does the door leading to the sleeping area open outward into the living room?*

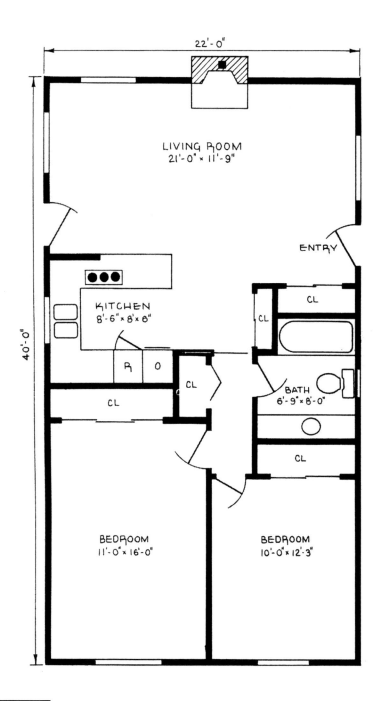

Figure 8-15. This is an alternate floor plan for a rectangular home. Compare this floor plan with the plan in Figure 8-14. *Which home has easier access from the kitchen to the outside?*

UNIT 8 ACTIVITIES

VOCABULARY CHECKLIST

1. plan revision
2. guest closet
3. traffic area
4. construction costs
5. square feet
6. sectional sofa

REVIEW QUESTIONS

1. If construction costs $125 per square foot, what will it cost to build a room measuring 15 feet by 20 feet?
2. Why is it important to provide closet space near a home's entry?
3. Why is a hall often used to separate sleeping and living areas of a home?

YOUR ARCHITECTURAL SCRAPBOOK

1. Draw or cut out pictures of living rooms with two or more floor plans. Add these to your scrapbook.
2. Draw or cut out pictures of two or more kitchens showing different floor plans. Enter notes about the conveniences or potential problems in using each area for food preparation.
3. Draw or cut out pictures of at least two different bedrooms. Make notes on the conveniences or problems in each room.
4. Design a 1,200 square foot home with a CAD system. Make a hard copy and place it in your scrapbook.

CAD ACTIVITIES

After reading Unit 8, refer to Chapter 8 in the *Chief Architect Tutorials* and practice:

- Going to the **Help** drop-down menu, locating and reading information for the drawing commands you are having trouble with.
- Going to the **Default** menu and practice changing the various default controls.

UNIT 9
EXTERIOR HOUSE FORMS

EXTERIOR APPEARANCE FACTORS

The exterior appearance of a house depends on a number of factors. These include:

- Number of levels of the structure.
- Style of the roof.
- Architectural style of the total exterior.

Number of Levels

Every building must be adapted to its site. The ideal shape for a building depends on the contour of the land on which it is built.

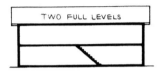

Figure 9-1 shows several basic shapes that can be used for multi-story homes. Think of the reasons why different shapes might be used. For example, two full levels provide living space at a relatively lower cost than a one-story house with the same floor space because there will be less foundation and roof construction. The *foundation* is the structure on which a home rests. A foundation must be anchored in the earth and the house's construction securely fastened to the foundation. It is necessary to pour concrete for the T and slab foundations.

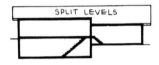

Split-level homes represent a compromise. They are part two-level and part single-level. This can be an interesting way to separate living areas in a home's design. To have a split-level home, the lot should be contoured for the structure or a special foundation must be designed for a flat building site.

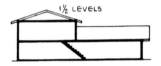

A home design with a combination of one and two-stories reduces the costs for the two-level area. Sometimes a sun deck or porch is built over the single-level area of the home. This can provide an additional outdoor area.

Figure 9-1. Multiple-level designs can have a great effect on the exterior appearance of a home. The use of multiple levels can also affect the cost of building living areas. *How does the use of a double-level design affect the cost of living-area construction?*

A home that has one level with an attic is similar to a two-story home. The roof system acts as the ceiling for the attic room. The shape and pitch of the roof will limit the living area for the attic room. Dormer windows are often added to provide light and more head room.

A home that has one level and a basement provides a different kind of space. Basement areas do not get the light that most people like in living areas. Basements may be dark because they are largely underground. Usually basement space is used for service areas. Many families build recreation rooms in their basements. In appearance, a basement is similar to a one-story home. The main difference is that there are usually small windows at ground level for the basement area.

The architectural style of an *A-frame home* is comparatively inexpensive to build. Its structure consists mainly of straight, simple lines. The living area is reduced by the shape of the full-length roof, however, the straight, long roof lines save construction costs by eliminating the walls. Many A-frame homes are used for recreational purposes.

Roof Styles

The effect on appearance of a number of roof styles is shown in **Figure 9-2**. As you review these styles, think about their effects on the home's design and the additional building costs for unusual roof designs.

A *gable roof* has a pitch on two sides. This is relatively simple to build, since the roof consists of only two straight roof panels.

A *hip roof* is pitched on four sides. It is a very popular roof design for contemporary homes.

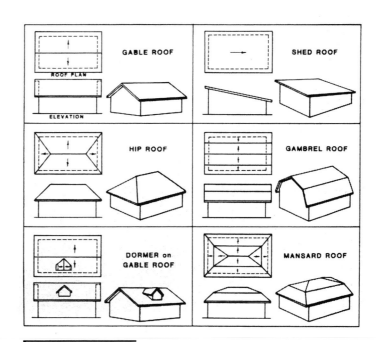

Figure 9-2. Roof styles affect exterior appearances of homes. *What is the purpose of a dormer?*

The illustrations of the gable and hip roofs have no windows in the roof area. However, if living space is to be made from the attic, windows are necessary. A common method of building windows into slanting roofs is with the *dormer window*. An illustration in Figure 9-2 shows a gable dormer in a gable roof.

A *shed roof* is a flat roof that is slanted for runoff of rain and snow. A single flat surface significantly reduces the cost of construction. Shed roofs are popular with modern designs.

A *gambrel roof* is double-pitched, with parts of the roof slanting at two different angles. This design breaks up the long flat surfaces that can detract from the appearance of homes with gable roofs.

A *Mansard roof* is double-pitched at all sides of the structure. In effect, this is like a hip roof with a double-pitch design.

Study these roof styles. Notice how the different styles treat or "break up" the large structural areas of roofs. This is done to add visual interest to the design of a home's exterior.

Total Exterior Effect

The number of levels and roof style are major factors in the appearance of a home. In addition, several other factors can affect exterior appearance. These include:

- Materials used.
- Door styles and types.
- Window styles and types.
- Chimney design.

By altering one or more of these factors, the architect can change the appearance of a home. Even homes with identical floor plans can look different from the outside. **Figure 9-3** illustrates how these factors can be used to change the external appearance of homes. All of the homes in this figure have the same floor plan.

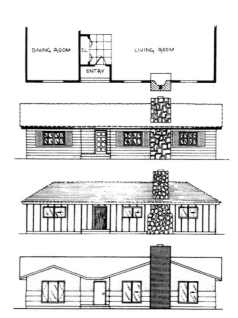

Figure 9-3. Materials used, roof type, types of windows, door style, and chimney design affect exterior appearances of homes. All homes in this illustration have the same basic floor plan. *Which home in this illustration has a hip roof?*

UNIT 9 ACTIVITIES

VOCABULARY CHECKLIST

1. foundation
2. split level home
3. A-frame home
4. gable roof
5. hip roof
6. dormer window
7. shed roof
8. gambrel roof
9. Mansard roof

REVIEW QUESTIONS

1. Why is a house with two full levels more economical to build than a house with the same number of rooms all on one level?
2. How can more outdoor area be added to a home that has one-and-a-half levels?
3. What is the most economical roof to build, and why?

YOUR ARCHITECTURAL SCRAPBOOK

1. Draw or copy a picture of a building with each of these types of roof: gable, hip, shed, gambrel, and Mansard. Add these to your scrapbook.
2. Draw or copy a picture of a building with dormers. Add this to your scrapbook.
3. Use a CAD system to design four elevations for the floor plan you have already drawn. Make a hard copy and place it in your scrapbook.

CAD ACTIVITIES

After reading Unit 9, refer to Chapter 9 in the *Chief Architect Tutorials* and practice:

- Drawing straight walls with the various child tool buttons.
- Add decks, railings, and fences to your floor plan.

PART IV
Basic Drafting Skills

Drafting Equipment and Procedures

The Architect's Scale

Architectural Lettering

Architectural Symbols

Architectural Line Work

Architectural Dimensioning

Sheet Layouts

PART IV

BASIC DRAFTING SKILLS

THE ROLE OF DRAFTING

It is important to design a functional, livable home. Once the home is designed, it is also important to provide construction details to the builder. This is accomplished through a carefully prepared set of working drawings that contain all the data required to build the finished home. The set of working drawing plans must contain:

- Detailed working drawings
- Specifications
- Schedules
- Contract

This information must be complete and accurate. Mistakes or details left out of the plans can result in an incorrectly built home and have major costs for design changes. Therefore, the ability to draw plans is an essential skill in architectural design.

Today, the vast majority of architectural working drawings are drawn with a CAD (computer-aided drafting) system using an architectural software program. However, it may still be necessary to have sketching and manual drafting skills. In the field, the architect may have to make modifications to the plans or produce emergency sketches for the workers.

SECOND FLOOR - 850 SQ. FT.

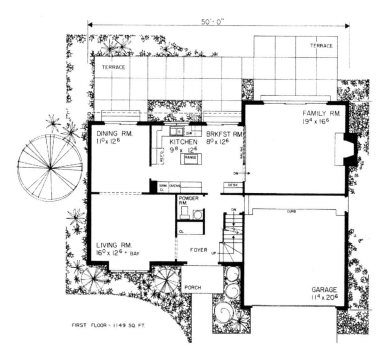

FIRST FLOOR - 1149 SQ. FT.

YOUR LEARNING JOB

There are seven learning units in Part IV. They cover:

- Basic drafting equipment and procedures
- The architect's scale
- Architectural lettering
- Architectural symbols
- Architectural line work
- Architectural dimensioning
- Sheet layouts

UNIT 10
DRAFTING EQUIPMENT AND PROCEDURES

THE ROLE OF DRAFTING

Architectural sketches of floor plans are rough, unfinished drawings. These sketches are important steps in determining the appearance and features of a home before the final plan set is drawn. The final set of working drawings must not be started until the final sketches are approved by the owners, architect/designer, building department, contractor, and the community's design committee.

Before a home can be built, final, *working drawing plans* are needed. These plans must be prepared with great detail. All specific information must be included so contractors can follow the plans while building the structure.

DRAFTING TOOLS

To be sure the necessary accuracy and detail are included, final plans are drawn with the aid of special drafting tools. Some of the key tools used in manual drafting of architectural plans are described and illustrated in this unit.

Drawing Board

The development of accurate manual drawings requires a *drawing board* with a precision drawing surface. The surface must be soft enough so that pencils can easily draw lines. The surface must also be perfectly flat and smooth. There can be no holes or warped places on the board. Any bumps or holes in the surface would throw off the accuracy of drawn lines. It is important for the edge of the board to be straight and smooth for the head of the T-square.

A drawing board is shown in **Figure 10-1**. This drawing board is made from a soft wood such as bass wood, and is sometimes covered with a special vinyl drawing board cover.

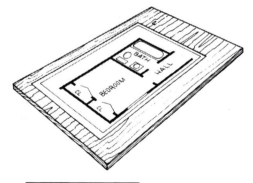

Figure 10-1. It is important to have a flat, smooth surface on which to draw. This is provided by one of the drafter's basic tools, a drawing board. *What problems could arise if the drawing board had holes or bumps?*

T-Square

Straight and accurate drawing of horizontal lines requires a *T-square*. This tool gets its name from the fact that it is shaped like the letter T. The top, or head, of the T-square is placed along the side of the drawing board. The long strip of the T-square is known as the *blade* and is 90 degrees to the head of the T-square. A right-handed drafter works with the head of the T-square against the left side of the drawing board, as shown in **Figure 10-2**. A left-handed person may place the head of the T-square against the right side of the drawing board. To draw lines, a pencil is guided along the top edge of the blade. The T-square is also used to position paper on a drawing board. The edge of the blade is matched with the horizontal edge of the paper.

Triangle

A drafter's *triangle* is a precision tool for drawing lines at specific angles. Angles are measured in degrees. A full circle is the basis for the measurement of degrees. A circle has 360°. A right angle is formed by two lines that mark off one-quarter of a circle, or 90°.

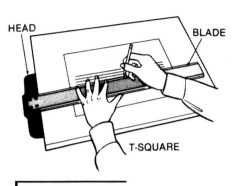

Figure 10-2. An important tool for drawing lines on architectural plans is the T-square. To line up the T-square for use, the head is placed against one side of the drawing board. *What part of the T-square is used for the actual drawing of straight lines?*

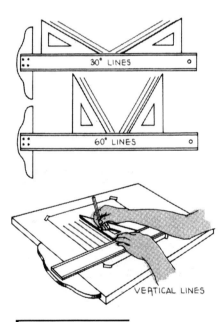

Figure 10-3. To draw lines at angles to lines drawn with a T-square, the drafter uses triangles. This triangle can create lines at 30°, 60°, and 90° angles. *How is a triangle positioned to drawn lines?*

A drafting triangle always has one right angle (90°). This makes it possible to put a triangle against a T-square to draw vertical lines, as illustrated in **Figure 10-3**. The other angles in the triangle in Figure 10-3 are at 30° and 60°. Lines drawn at these angles are also shown in the illustration. The drafter in this drawing is right-handed. The triangle is held firmly against the blade of the T-square with the left hand. A vertical line is drawn by moving a pencil along the edge of the triangle. Obviously, if you are left-handed, you may reverse these procedures.

Another drafting triangle often used by drafters has one 90° angle and two angles of 45°. The lines that can be drawn with this triangle are illustrated in **Figure 10-4**.

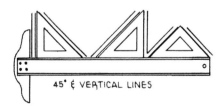

Figure 10-4. This triangle has one angle at 90° and two at 45°. The 45° angle is halfway between the 30° and 60° angles. *What is the angle between a vertical line and a horizontal line?*

Protractor

When it is necessary to draw angles other than 30°, 45°, 60°, or 90°, a *protractor* is used. See **Figure 10-5**. A protractor displays angle markings for a half-circle, or a 180° arc.

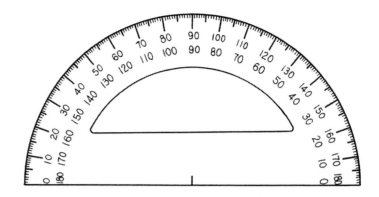

Figure 10-5. A protractor is used to measure angles and to mark points for the drawing of angles at intervals of less than 15°. *What is the total number of degrees spanned by a protractor?*

Compass

To draw arcs or circles on architectural plans, a *compass* is used. See **Figure 10-6**. A compass is a tool with two arms. One arm of a compass has a needle, or shoulder needle. The other arm contains drafting lead.

To draw a circle or arc, first adjust the width, or spread, of the compass. Then place the compass needle at the center of the circle where the two center lines intersect. Rotate the compass to draw the line. This is accomplished by twisting the thumb and forefinger, as shown in **Figure 10-6**. During rotation, lean the outer edge of the compass in the direction of the movement.

The drafting lead in a compass should be sharpened to a chisel point. This will result in a line of even thickness during rotation. The compass lead must be soft (F or HB) so the circle can be drawn with dark object lines.

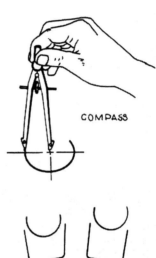

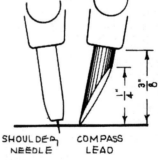

Figure 10-6. A compass is used to draw circles or arcs. After the width of the compass is adjusted, the shoulder needle is anchored on the drawing. Then the compass is rotated to create a circular line. *Into what shape should the lead of a compass be sharpened?*

Divider

A *divider* is a tool used to compare sizes of drawing elements. The ends of a divider are placed on a section of a drawing or against the scale of a ruler. The divider is a tool for comparing sizes, dividing line segments, and measuring distances on drawings. A divider is illustrated in **Figure 10-7.**

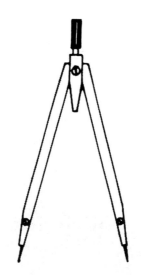

Figure 10-7. A divider is used to compare or measure distances of objects or lines on plans. *Why is a divider a potentially important tool in drafting plans for a home with a symmetrical design?*

Template

When standard symbols are to be drawn repeatedly, templates can be used. A *drafting template* is a flat piece of plastic with standard symbols cut in it. **See Figure 10-8.** These shapes are used as guides for drawing symbols on plans.

Many templates are available for various architectural scales. Templates are also available for a variety of floor plans and elevation systems. Included are doors, windows, plumbing fixtures, electrical devices, and landscape features.

Figure 10-8. Architectural templates are cut-out plastic guides used to draw standard shapes and symbols on plans. *How does use of a template save time and assure accuracy for the drafter?*

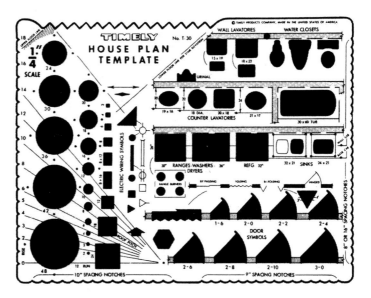

Architectural pencils

For precision in the drawing of lines, *architectural pencils* are made in a number of grades. The grades for the graphite (pencil lead) range from hard to soft. In general, hard pencils draw light lines; soft pencils draw darker and wider lines.

The hardest standard grade for architectural pencils is 9H. The softest pencil is grade 7B. See **Figure 10-9**. In general, a 4H pencil is used for light layout lines and guide lines that are easy to erase. A sharp H pencil is used for thin dark lines (dimension and extension lines, template work, and lettering). A blunted F pencil is used for thick/dark object lines for walls and borders.

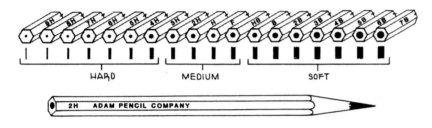

Figure 10-9.
Architectural pencils come in a range of grades. These run from 9H, the hardest, to 7B, the softest. *Why should you always sharpen the end of the pencil opposite the lettering?*

Drafting paper

Drafting papers come in a variety of materials and surfaces. Drawings may be prepared on paper, *vellum*, (a heavy transparent tracing paper) or plastic film. Drafting papers can be purchased in sheets or rolls, as shown in **Figure 10-10**.

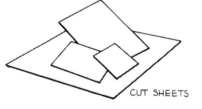

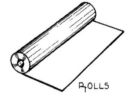

Figure 10-10. Drafting papers come in a variety of materials and surfaces. These include paper, vellum, and plastic film. *How does the surface of drafting paper affect the selection of tools for drawing?*

Drafting tape

As they work, drafters mount and remove plans on their drawing boards frequently. To avoid damage to either the plans or the drawing board, *drafting tape* is used to position and hold paper. As shown in **Figure 10-11**, strips of tape are placed over the corners of plans.

In positioning the drawing paper on the board, a T-square is used to align the paper before it is taped to the board.

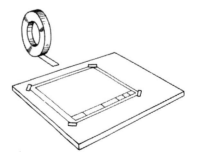

Figure 10-11. Drafting tape is used to hold drafting paper in position on the drawing board. *How does the use of tape avoid damage to the drawing board?*

UNIT 10 ACTIVITIES

VOCABULARY CHECKLIST

1. architectural sketch
2. working drawing plan
3. drawing board
4. T-square
5. blade

6. drafting triangle
7. protractor
8. compass
9. divider
10. drafting template

11. architectural pencils
12. vellum
13. drafting tape

REVIEW QUESTIONS

1. Why does a contractor require construction plans rather than floor plan sketches?
2. What are some of the requirements for a drawing board?
3. What tool is used to position paper and draw horizontal lines?
4. What tools are used for drawing angles?
5. What tool is used to measure angles?
6. What tool is used to draw circles?
7. Why is it best to use drafting tape to position work on a drawing board?
8. Which end of a drawing pencil should you sharpen? Why?

YOUR ARCHITECTURAL SCRAPBOOK

1. Find pictures of the tools discussed in this unit in a catalog of drafting supplies. Cut them out and add them to your scrapbook. Label each tool.
2. Note and enter catalog prices for all of the tools you add to your scrapbook.
3. Draw a series of lines in your scrapbook. If possible, use a T-square, at least one triangle, and a compass. Note the tools used alongside these lines.
4. Research CAD catalogs and list in your scrapbook various architectural software programs.

CAD ACTIVITIES

After reading Unit 10, refer to Chapter 10 in the *Chief Architect Tutorials* and practice:

- Drawing a floor plan with curved walls.
- Drawing curved walls with the various child tool buttons.
- Drawing curved decks, railings, and fences to your plan.

UNIT 11
THE ARCHITECT'S SCALE

SCALED DRAWINGS

In architecture, the term *scale* has two meanings. A scale is a dimension that represents the structure shown in a plan. A scale is also a ruler used in drawing and measuring architectural plans.

The scale units used in architectural drafting are based on foot/inch dimensions. Floor plan drawings are usually drawn to the scale of 1/4" = 1'-0". For a very large plan, a scale of 1/8" = 1'-0" may be used. When drawing a small plan or a single room, scales of 3/8" = 1'-0", 1/2" = 1'-0", 3/4" = 1'-0", or 1" = 1'-0" may be used to fit the size of your drawing format. The need for scaled drawing is obvious; buildings are large and plans must be limited in size.

Today, it is important that drawings be scaled accurately. This requirement was not always so critical. Years ago, building materials were not produced with great precision. For example, when a house was made from wood, the carpenter could trim the edges of boards to make the pieces fit. Today, however, building materials are made to precise measurements. Metal, glass, and wood pieces must be fabricated to exact sizes.

Plans must be just as reliable. Accurate plans will save money because of fewer building errors and lead to quality construction.

STANDARD SCALES

Several standard scales used by architects are illustrated in **Figure 11-1**. These four scales are as follows.

- 1/8" = 1'-0" (one-eighth inch equals one foot)
- 1/4" = 1'-0" (one-quarter inch equals one foot)
- 1/2" = 1'-0" (one-half inch equals one foot)
- 1" = 1'-0" (one inch equals one foot)

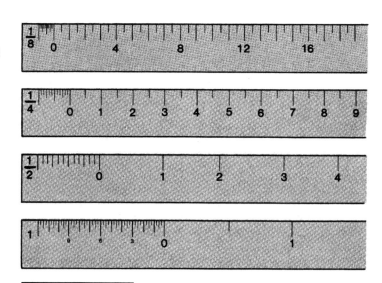

Figure 11-1. These are portions of four common scales used in architectural drafting. *What scale does each of these units represent?*

Notice how the use of numbers and symbols shortens the descriptions of measurement. Learn to use these numerals and symbols. You will need to use them when you prepare building plans.

Uses for these standard scales in drafting are listed in **Figure 11-2.** The scale 1/8" = 1'-0" is used for typical city-sized lots. Floor plans are generally drawn at 1/4" = 1'-0". Construction plans use larger scales to show greater detail. On construction details either 1/2" or 1" = 1'-0" is used.

SCALE SIZE	TYPE OF DRAWING
1/8" = 1'-0"	PLOT PLANS
1/4" = 1'-0"	FLOOR PLANS
1/2" = 1'-0" 1" = 1'-0"	CONSTRUCTION PLANS

Figure 11-2. This table shows the most common uses for the scales illustrated in Figure 11-1. *Why are the larger scales used for construction plans?*

METRIC SCALES

Most of the drafting you do will involve customary U.S. measurements in units of inches and feet. However, the use of metric measurements is standard in most of the world. The United States is committed to convert to metric measurements eventually.

The principles are similar. You have to get used to measurements expressed in meters (m) and millimeters (mm). One *meter* is slightly larger than one yard. A *millimeter* is 1/1000 of a meter.

Metric scales are usually based on ratios. A *ratio* is the relationship of one measurement to another. For example, metric plot plans are often drafted in ratios of 1:100. This scale is very close to the scale 1/8" = 1'-0" (1:96).

Metric floor plans are drawn in a ratio of 1:50. This is very close to a scale of 1/4" = 1'-0" (1:48).

Construction details may be drawn to metric scales of 1:20, 1:10, or 1:5. It should be noted that all dimensions in metric dimensions are in millimeters. Therefore, it is not necessary to use the symbol mm.

USING THE ARCHITECT SCALE

Most *architect's scales* are triangular in shape, as shown in **Figure 11-3**. Each surface of the triangle is marked with a different set of scales. Some scales are read from left to right. Others are read from right to left. Start the measurement at the zero point on the scale for feet, then read in the opposite direction from the zero point for the inches. A scale like the one in **Figure 11-3** has 11 different sets of measurements. Ten scales are in feet and inches. One scale is a ruler in inches only.

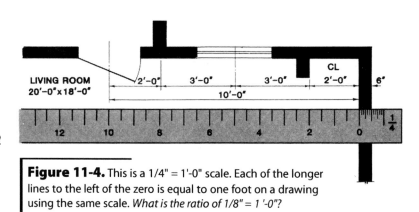

Figure 11-3. This is an architect's *triangular scale*. It has 11 different scales of measurement on its three sides. *In measuring a floor plan on the 1/4" scale of this unit, would you read to the right or left of the zero for feet?*

Figure 11-4 shows the use of a 1/4" = 1'-0" scale to measure a plan. To the right of the zero is a 1/4" unit that is divided into 12 parts (inches). Therefore, each quarter inch unit represents one foot.

Figure 11-4. This is a 1/4" = 1'-0" scale. Each of the longer lines to the left of the zero is equal to one foot on a drawing using the same scale. *What is the ratio of 1/8" = 1'-0"?*

Figure 11-5 illustrates the use of a 1/8" = 1'-0" scale. Because the scale is so small, each mark in the divided foot represents 2" (6 marks = 12").

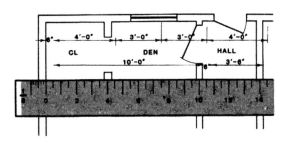

Figure 11-5. This is a 1/8" = 1'-0" scale. Each of the longer lines to the right of the zero is equal to one foot on a drawing using the same scale. *What is the ratio of 1/8" = 1'-0"?*

Figure 11-6 shows a 1/2" = 1'-0" scale. Because this is a larger scale, the inch divisions have an accuracy of 1/2".

Figure 11-7 shows a 1" = 1'-0" scale. With this scale, the inch divisions will have an accuracy of 1/4" (not shown in the illustration). Other measures available on an architect's scale are 3/32", 3/16", 3/8", 3/4", and full size. These scales are all read in the same manner: from right to left or left to right. For example the 3/8" and 3/4" markings are on the same blade (side or edge) of the scale. This is because 3/8 is half the size of 3/4. Thus, 3/8 reads from right to left and 3/4 from left to right. Inches are read from the opposite direction of the "0" mark. Each scale will have one foot divided into 12 equal parts (inches).

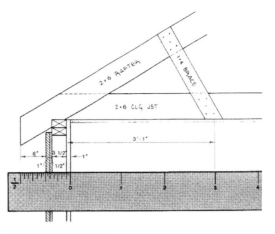

Figure 11-6. This is a 1/2" = 1'-0" scale. Notice that it is shown on a construction drawing. *What kinds of plans are commonly drawn in this scale?*

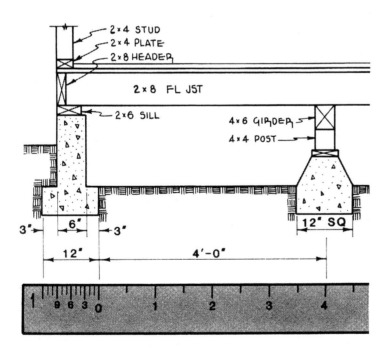

Figure 11-7. This is a 1" = 1'-0" scale. This scale is large enough so that it is used for specific construction details only. This scale means that drawings are actually one-twelfth as large as the structures they represent. *If a room measures 15' by 10', what size should the drawing paper be if the scale 1" = 1'-0" is used?*

UNIT 11 ACTIVITIES

VOCABULARY CHECKLIST

1. scale
2. ratio
3. architect's scale
4. meter (m)
5. millimeter (mm)
6. triangular scale

REVIEW QUESTIONS

1. How many measurement scales are on a triangular architect's scale?
2. What scale is most commonly used for plot plans?
3. What scale is most commonly used for floor plans?
4. What two scales are commonly used for construction plans?
5. On what units are metric scales based?
6. What are the criteria for the selection of a scale?

YOUR ARCHITECTURAL SCRAPBOOK

1. Find pictures and information on scales from a catalog of drafting supplies. Cut out pictures of scales and add them to your scrapbook. Label each scale.
2. Write in information about costs for different types of scales.
3. With a CAD system, dimension a floor plan with the ft./in. system and then with the metric system. Make hard copies and place them in your scrapbook.

CAD ACTIVITIES

After reading Unit 11, refer to Chapter 11 in the *Chief Architect Tutorials* and practice:

• Adding new tool buttons into a toolbar.
• Placing a hip roof on one of your floor plans.
• Placing a gable roof on one of your floor plans.

UNIT 12
ARCHITECTURAL LETTERING

IMPORTANCE OF LETTERING

The main function of architectural drawings is to communicate information. One of the important elements of communication in drawings is accurate, clear, and precise lettering.

Lettering provides the dimensions and descriptions of a structure. There is no place for carelessness or poor quality in the lettering of a drawing. If lettering is not clear, information can be misunderstood. Wasted time and costly errors can result.

LETTERING STYLES

To assure clarity, standard techniques must be used for the lettering of architectural drawings. Acceptable lettering styles are illustrated in **Figure 12-1**.

The clearest type of lettering is the *vertical single-stroke gothic style*. This is a clear, readable, style that provides a professional look to a drawing. It is the most commonly used lettering style for architectural and engineering drawings.

Architectural styles like those shown in Figure 12-1 can be developed. Each drafter will develop his or her own style to help speed up drawing and add character to lettering. Do not get too fancy, because correct communication is essential.

Use the alphabets and numbers in Figure 12-1 as guides for your own lettering. Each drafter eventually develops personal styles and preferences. Whatever style is used, the quality and the readability must be excellent.

VERTICAL SINGLE STROKE GOTHIC
ABCDEFGHIJKLMNOPQRSTUVWXYZ 1234567890

SLANT (68 DEGREES) SINGLE STROKE GOTHIC
ABCDEFGHIJKLMNOPQRSTUVWXYZ 1234567890

ARCHITECTURAL STYLE
ABCDEFGHIJKLMNOPQRSTUVWXYZ 1234567890

Figure 12-1 The vertical single-stroke gothic style (top line) is the most commonly used type of lettering in architectural drawings. The other two styles show acceptable alternatives used occasionally. *What is the purpose of lettering on architectural drawings?*

LETTERING SIZES AND POSITIONS

One of the marks of professional lettering is that all letters and numbers are drawn the same height. To assure uniform height, *guidelines* are used. **Figure 12-2** illustrates the drawing of guidelines.

ALWAYS USE TWO GUIDE LINES FOR LETTERING

1/8" GUIDE LINES

Figure 12-2. In preparation for lettering, start with lightly drawn guidelines. This assures that all letters and numbers will be of consistent height. On most drawings, lettering should be 1/8" in height. *What kind of pencil should be used to draw the guidelines?*

Guidelines should always have a very light line weight. Use a 4H pencil to keep the lines fine. In this way, the guidelines will not interfere with the readability of the letters. If the guidelines are light, they will fade away when making prints of your drawings.

Lettering on most architectural drawings is 1/8" tall. On large drawings, it is a good idea to use larger lettering. Heights can be increased to 3/16". This keeps the lettering proportional to the elements of the floor plan. Remember also that the height of lettering gives an indication of its importance. Key elements and major headings may be described in larger letters.

Fractions require greater height than ordinary letters and numbers. Fractions should be 3/16" or 1/4" in height. Use either of two techniques to letter fractions, as shown in **Figure 12-3**. One method is to draw a *horizontal fraction bar*. The other is to use a *diagonal fraction bar*. Follow your own preference in choice of methods; however, be consistent. Whichever method you choose, draw all fractions on a plan in the same style. With either method, individual numbers within fractions will be smaller than 1/8" in height.

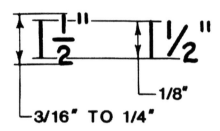

Figure 12-3. Two alternate styles may be used in lettering fractions. One has a horizontal fraction bar. The other uses a diagonal fraction bar. *How high are the numbers within fractions as compared with normal lettering?*

LETTERING TECHNIQUES

What follows are some hints for proper lettering technique.

- Use a soft pencil, but be careful not to choose a lead so soft that your lettering will smudge.
- Keep a sharp point on your pencil at all times.
- Rest your hand on a piece of paper to avoid smudging a drawing.
- Draw the pencil along the surface of the paper; do not push.

- Keep guidelines for descriptions and dimensions the same size throughout the drawing. The guidelines should be extremely light.
- Letter with a straight, quick, and positive motion. Don't hesitate or let your pencil linger when you letter.
- Whatever style you choose, be consistent. Be sure that spacing between letters and words is uniform. **Figure 12-4** provides an example of good lettering. This is compared with displays of some typical spacing problems.
- The drawing surface under the paper should be firm, but not hard.
- Sit comfortably when you letter; relax.
- Lean slightly toward the drawing board, but do not block your light.

DRAFTING CORRECT SPACING

EVENLY SPACED LETTERS – AREAS BETWEEN ALL LETTERS
ARE APPROXIMATELY THE SAME

DRAFTING

LETTERS SPACED TOO FAR – AREAS
BETWEEN LETTERS ARE TOO LARGE

DRAFTING

**INCORRECT
SPACING**

LETTERS SPACED TOO CLOSE – AREAS
BETWEEN LETTERS ARE TOO SMALL

DRAFTING

LETTERS UNEVENLY SPACED – AREAS   unevenly
BETWEEN LETTERS WILL VARY
FROM TOO SMALL TO TOO LARGE

Figure 12-4. *Consistent spacing* is important to quality lettering. For better judgment in spacing your lettering, don't bend too close to the drawing board. *What problem can occur if you bend too low over the drawing board?*

- If you are doing vertical lettering, practice the strokes shown in Figure **12-5**.
- If you are doing slanted lettering, practice the strokes in Figure **12-6**.
- For any letter or number, always draw the vertical strokes first; then add the horizontal strokes.
- Rotate your pencil so the point will not flatten out on one side.

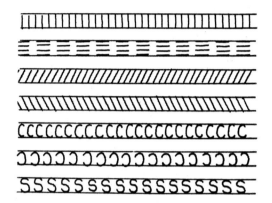

Figure 12-5. This set of practice strokes will help build your skills in vertical lettering. Practice will help improve the quality of your work. *Why is it important to the quality of your work to avoid using a pencil that is too soft?*

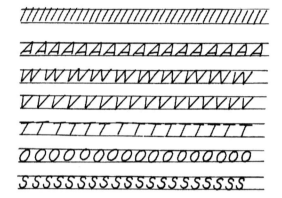

Figure 12-6. This set of practice strokes will help build your skills in slant lettering. *What is the value of resting your hand on a piece of paper, rather than on the drawing itself?*

USING A GUIDELINE TEMPLATE

A tool is available that can make lettering work easier and faster. This tool, shown in **Figure 12-7**, is a template for drawing guidelines. This guide is called an *Ames guideline template*.

The lettering guide has a series of holes into which you insert the point of a pencil with a hard, sharp lead. Select the holes that will provide the proper guidelines for your lettering. The lettering guide is then moved across the top of the T-square blade to form guidelines for the lettering.

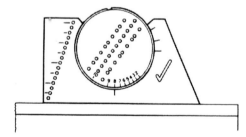

Figure 12-7. To make lettering work easier and faster, you can use a lettering guide. Place a pencil point in a hole and move the guide along the top edge of your T-square. *How can a lettering guide save you time?*

UNIT 12 ACTIVITIES

VOCABULARY CHECKLIST

1. vertical single-stroke gothic
2. guidelines
3. consistent spacing
4. fraction bar
5. Ames guideline template

REVIEW QUESTIONS

1. What is the height of most architectural lettering?
2. What is the basic style of most architectural lettering?
3. What method is used to assure that all letters are of consistent height?
4. Is actual lettering done with soft or hard pencils?

YOUR ARCHITECTURAL SCRAPBOOK

1. Letter a sample entry in each of the following styles: vertical single-stroke gothic, slant single-stroke gothic, and architectural.
2. Make hard copies of the various lettering fonts in your CAD system and place them in your scrapbook.

CAD ACTIVITIES

After reading Unit 12, refer to Chapter 12 in the *Chief Architect Tutorials* and practice generating the following drawings from one of your floor plans:

- Exterior perspectives.
- Interior perspectives.
- Exterior elevations.
- Interior elevations.
- Cross sectional views.
- Overview with a roof.
- Overview without a roof.

UNIT 13
ARCHITECTURAL SYMBOLS

FLOOR PLAN AND ELEVATION SYMBOLS

It is important that all details affecting the building of the home are shown on the floor plans and elevation drawings. There is not room or time to draw the exact appearance of every feature. Therefore, to indicate the actual features of an item on floor plans or elevations, small, simplified *symbols* are used. Often, the symbols on plans do not look like the items they represent. However, their meaning is clear because they are easily coded for reference by people using the plans. The builders who work with plans understand these symbols.

When drawing architectural symbols, it is important not to draw the symbol too small because they would be difficult to read on the plans. Conversely, do not draw the symbols too large or they will fill up too much space in the drawing of a room.

Architects prepare drawings other than floor plans. Construction drawings and their details are also required. Often pictorial drawings are included in a plan set. Pictorial drawings of buildings and rooms rarely use symbols. This is because pictorial drawings are not used in actual construction.

SYMBOL INFORMATION

- On floor plans, symbols rarely resemble the items they represent. This is largely because of space available. An example of how a symbol may represent may represent a telephone is shown in **Figure 13-1**.

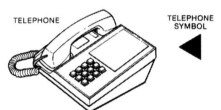

Figure 13-1. A triangle represents a telephone on a floor plan. This demonstrates that there may be no resemblance between items and their symbols on floor plans. *Why do symbols on floor plans rarely resemble the items they represent?*

- Another type of drawing is the elevation drawing. An *elevation drawing* shows vertical drawings of exterior and interior walls. On elevation drawings, the symbols usually look more like the actual items than they do on floor plans. This is because an elevation plan is closer to what people actually see in a building than a floor plan. To illustrate, **Figure 13-2** shows the kinds of symbols used to represent windows on elevation drawings.

Figure 13-2. Elevation symbols for glass and windows do resemble the actual items. *Why is it possible for symbols to resemble the items they represent on elevation drawings?*

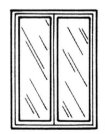

- It is not necessary to cover an entire surface with a material symbol. Covering only a small area will be adequate to alert the builders to the type of surface material to be installed.

- *Pictorial drawings* (perspectives) of buildings do not use symbols. They are drawn to look like a photograph and are not use for construction. The purpose of pictorial drawings are to give the clients a idea of how their home will look. They are also used by interior designers and for advertisements.

IDENTIFYING SYMBOLS

Figures 13-3 through 13-10 present sets of symbols for both floor plans and elevation drawings. They provide examples that you will follow as you begin to prepare architectural drawings. Study these illustrations carefully. Make sure you understand which symbols are used on floor plans and which belong on elevation drawings.

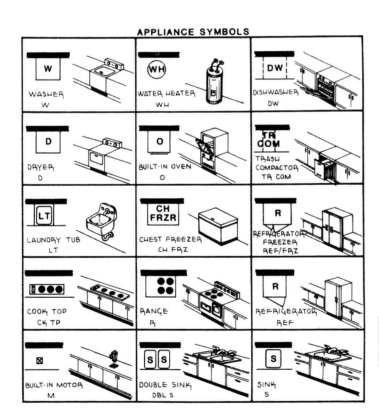

Figure 13-3. These are appliance symbols for the floor plan. Also shown are their pictorials and abbreviations.

BUILT-IN SYMBOLS

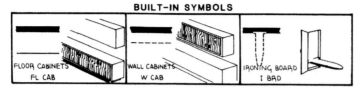

FLOOR CABINETS
FL CAB

WALL CABINETS
W CAB

IRONING BOARD
I BRD

Figure 13-4. These are symbols for built-in features often included in homes. The floor plan symbols, pictorials, and abbreviations are shown. *In which room or rooms would these symbols be used?*

PLUMBING SYMBOLS

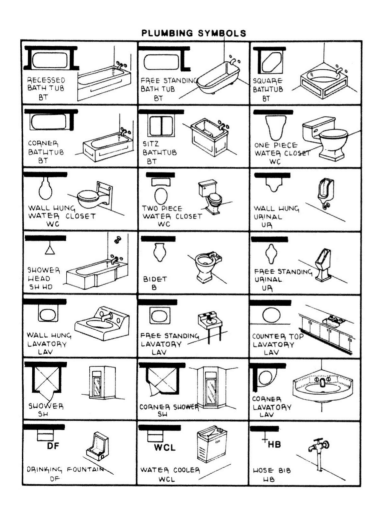

RECESSED BATH TUB
BT

FREE STANDING BATH TUB
BT

SQUARE BATHTUB
BT

CORNER BATHTUB
BT

SITZ BATHTUB
BT

ONE PIECE WATER CLOSET
WC

WALL HUNG WATER CLOSET
WC

TWO PIECE WATER CLOSET
WC

WALL HUNG URINAL
UR

SHOWER HEAD
SH HD

BIDET
B

FREE STANDING URINAL
UR

WALL HUNG LAVATORY
LAV

FREE STANDING LAVATORY
LAV

COUNTER TOP LAVATORY
LAV

SHOWER
SH

CORNER SHOWER
SH

CORNER LAVATORY
LAV

DF

WCL

HB

DRINKING FOUNTAIN
DF

WATER COOLER
WCL

HOSE BIB
HB

Figure 13-5. These are symbols for plumbing fixtures used in homes and commercial buildings. Floor plan symbols, pictorials, and their abbreviations are shown. *Which symbols would be used in home plans and which in commercial buildings?*

WINDOW SYMBOLS

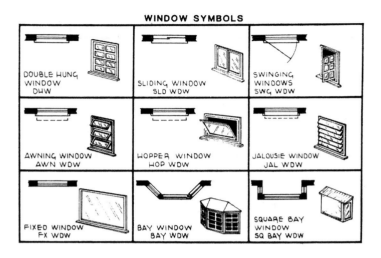

Figure 13-6. These are the floor plan symbols, abbreviations, and pictorials for different types of windows. Note that the floor plan symbols show how the windows operate. *How can you tell where the window's hinges are located?*

DOOR SYMBOLS

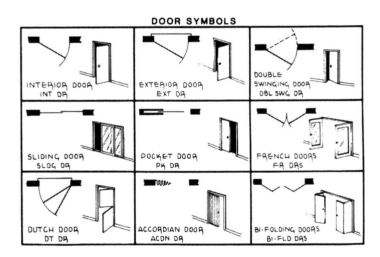

Figure 13-7. These are symbols used to represent doors on floor plans. Abbreviations and pictorials are also given. *Why is it important that a floor plan indicate the direction in which doors open and the amount of space taken up with the door's swing?*

Figure 13-8. These are symbols for electrical outlets. Floor plan and elevation symbols and their abbreviations are shown. *What should be the approximate diameter in the symbol for an electrical convenience outlet?*

HEATING/COOLING SYMBOLS

GAS OUTLET G	HEAT OUTLET HT OUT	THERMOMETER T	THERMOSTAT T
HEAT REGISTER R	RADIATOR RAD	ROOM AIR CONDITIONER RAC	DUCT DCT

Figure 13-9. These are the floor plan symbols used to show heating, ventilating, and cooling (HVAC) equipment. Abbreviations are also given. *Why are these symbols not required for elevation drawings?*

BUILDING MATERIAL SYMBOLS

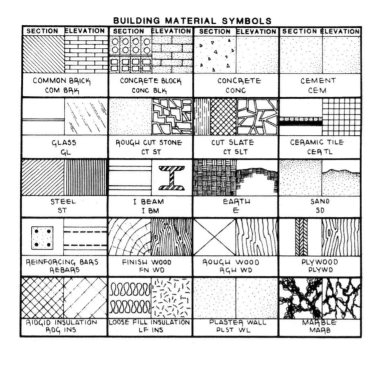

Figure 13-10. These are *sectional and elevation symbols* that indicate which building materials are being used. Abbreviations are included. *Why is it especially important that elevation symbols for building materials resemble the actual items?*

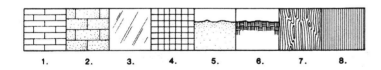

Figure 13-11. Use this illustration to answer Review Question 1.

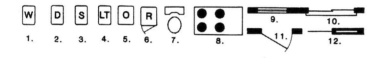

Figure 13-12. Use this illustration to answer Review Question 2.

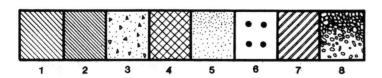

Figure 13-13. Use this illustration to answer Review Question 3.

UNIT 13 ACTIVITIES

VOCABULARY CHECKLIST

1. symbol
2. elevation drawing
3. pictorial drawing
4. sectional symbol
5. elevation symbol

REVIEW QUESTIONS

1. Name the architectural item represented by each of the twelve floor plan symbols in **Figure 13-11**.
2. Name the architectural item represented by each of the eight elevation symbols in **Figure 13-12**.
3. Name the architectural items represented by each of the eight symbols for building materials in **Figure 13-13**.

YOUR ARCHITECTURAL SCRAPBOOK

1. Draw at least ten examples of floor plan symbols in your scrapbook.
2. Draw at least ten examples of elevation symbols in your scrapbook.
3. On your scrapbook symbols, print their abbreviations.
4. If you do not have an architectural symbol library in your CAD system, create a series of symbols and save them to a file. Print a hard copy and place it in your scrapbook.

CAD ACTIVITIES

After reading Unit 13, refer to Chapter 13 in the *Chief Architect Tutorials* and complete the following:

• Create a plot plan for one of your floor plans.
• Add text to your floor plan (drawing title, scale, designer's name, address, etc).

UNIT 14
ARCHITECTURAL LINE WORK

TYPES OF LINES

All architectural drawings are based on a series of lines. These lines follow standards set by the American Society of Mechanical Engineers (ASME). Known as "Line Conventions," these standards give meaning to the lines in a drawing. Because there are standards, people who use drawings understand what the lines mean.

Different types of lines are used for different meanings. Lines differ in width, or thickness. They also differ in character. *Character* refers to the type of line. It may be made up of one unbroken line, or it may be composed of short or long dashes of different lengths. Each type of line has meaning and can be told apart from other lines.

You should be familiar with and be able to draw lines of three thicknesses. The thickness of a line on a drawing is called its *weight*. The three line weights found on architectural drawings are illustrated in **Figure 14-1**. These weights are thin, wide, and very wide lines. All lines should be dark black. This darkness is called *line density*. Density is necessary so lines will not disappear or fade when copies are made of drawings.

Figure 14-1. Examples of the three line weights used on architectural drawings: thin, wide, and very wide. *Why is it important that people reading your drawings be able to tell the width of your lines?*

The various architectural lines and their purposes are listed in **Figure 14-2**.

Thin Lines
- Hidden lines
- Extension lines
- Center lines
- Leaders
- Section lines
- Long break lines
- Dimension lines
- Construction lines

Wide Lines
- Visible lines
- Short break lines

Very Wide Lines
- Border lines
- Cutting plane lines

Each of these lines has a special meaning, and a special role, in architectural drafting. From this list, you can see that it is important to learn how to draw lines of three separate weights.

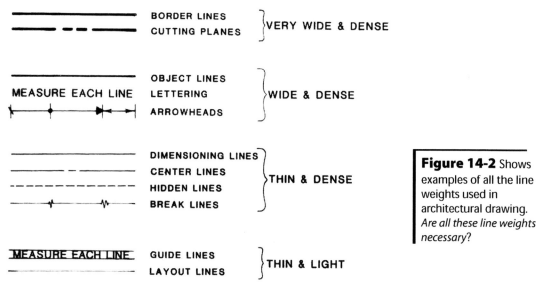

BORDER LINES	}	VERY WIDE & DENSE
CUTTING PLANES		
OBJECT LINES	}	WIDE & DENSE
LETTERING		
MEASURE EACH LINE	ARROWHEADS	
DIMENSIONING LINES	}	THIN & DENSE
CENTER LINES		
HIDDEN LINES		
BREAK LINES		
MEASURE EACH LINE	GUIDE LINES	}	THIN & LIGHT
	LAYOUT LINES		

Figure 14-2 Shows examples of all the line weights used in architectural drawing. *Are all these line weights necessary?*

NEED FOR CONSISTENCY

Regardless of their weight, all lines on architectural drawings must be dark black, or dense. Density is important because drawings are reproduced to provide copies to contractors and other workers. Reproductions from drawings and plans are called *prints*. It is vital that you draw dense and sharp lines if your drawings are to reproduce as good, clear prints. **Figure 14-3** shows the difference in readability between a dense line and a line that is too gray.

GOOD WEIGHT

TOO GREY

Figure 14-3. Examples of correctly-drawn and incorrectly-drawn lines. *What happens to prints made from your drawings if your lines are not sufficiently dark and dense?*

Each line weight must be drawn consistently. *Consistent* means that the quality of the work must be equal throughout each drawing. The thin lines must all be of the same weight. The same is true for the wide and very wide lines. A person reading a drawing should be able to tell the weight of lines just by glancing at a plan or print.

One way to keep lines consistent is to rotate your pencil as you work. If you do this, the lead will wear evenly all around. For an illustration of the importance of consistent lines, see **Figure 14-4**. There are two drawings in this figure. Drawing A is correct and consistent. Drawing B has lines that are inconsistent and represents sloppy, unacceptable work.

It is important to use the proper grade of drafting pencil and to prepare the point for the type of line to be drawn. See **Figure 14-5**.

ACCEPTABLE　　　　　**UNACCCEPTABLE**

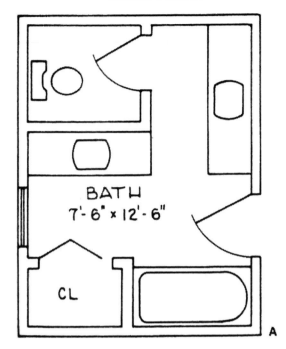
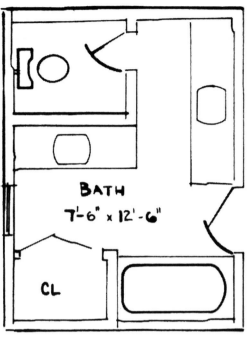

BATH
7'-6" x 12'-6"

CL

A　B

BATH
7'-6" x 12'-6"

CL

Figure 14-4. Examples of the three line weights used on architectural drawings: thin, wide, and very wide. *Why is it important that people reading your drawings be able to tell the width of your lines?*

THICK DARK LINES
OBJECT LINES
BORDER LINES
LETTERING

ROUNDED-OFF POINT, SOFT LEAD, H or F
THIN LEAD MECHANICAL PENCILS
0.7 mm or 0.9 mm

THIN DARK LINES
DOOR SWING
HIDDEN LINES
CENTER LINES
EXTENSION LINES
DIMENSION LINES

SHARP POINTED, SOFT LEAD, 2H, H or F
THIN LEAD MECHANICAL PENCILS
0.5 mm

THIN LIGHT LINES
LAYOUT LINES
GUIDE LINES

SHARP POINTED HARD LEAD, 2H, 3H or 4H
THIN LEAD MECHANICAL PENCILS
0.3 mm or 0.5 mm

Figure 14-5.
Preparing the pencil point is critical for drawing the correct line conventions. *Why is it necessary to have more than one drafting pencil when drawing a floor plan?*

Figure 14-6 is a drawing that illustrates use of all three line densities. Some of the uses for these lines are also identified. The uses for all of these lines are described below.

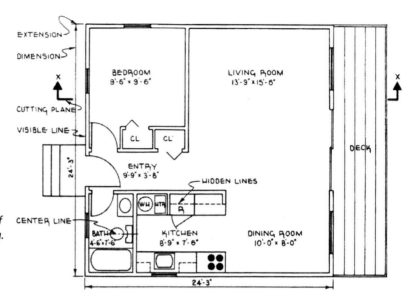

Figure 14-6.
This drawing demonstrates how the weight and consistency of lines in floor plans help to communicate information. *Identify the lines of different weights in this drawing.*

Thin Lines

- **Hidden lines** are shown by a dashed line. They represent an edge that cannot be seen because of something blocking the view of the edge.
- **Center lines** are long and short dash showing the center of an item.
- **Section lines** are usually drawn at a 45° angle and are sometimes called "cross-hatching." They represent surfaces exposed by being cut through.
- **Dimension lines** provide the length of the dimension.
- **Extension lines** are used to extend to the end of the dimension line.
- **Leaders** are lines drawn to notes or identification symbols.
- **Break lines** are used to show that part of the object has been removed or broken away. Long break lines are long, thin, ruled lines that are joined by freehand "zigzags."

Wide Lines

- **Visible lines** are used to show the edges that are seen when looking at an object.
- **Short break lines** are wide lines that are drawn freehand.

Very Wide Lines

- **Border lines** are used to frame drawings and should be the heaviest of all lines.
- **Cutting plane lines** are used to show where a section has been taken away. Arrows on end show the direction in which the section was taken.

UNIT 14 ACTIVITIES

VOCABULARY CHECKLIST

1. line weight
2. line density
3. prints
4. extension line
5. dimension line
6. cutting plane line
7. visible line

8. center line
9. hidden line
10. section line
11. leaders
12. break line
13. border line

REVIEW QUESTIONS

1. What weight of line is used for extension lines?
2. What weight of line is used for cutting plane lines?
3. What weight of line is used for a visible line?
4. What weight of line is used for a center line?

YOUR ARCHITECTURAL SCRAPBOOK

1. Cut out or copy at least one floor plan. Mark the width of the different lines used.
2. Draw the various types of lines used in architectural drawing. Label each line type.
3. With a CAD system, print out as many different line types that the software program has. Place the hard copy in your scrapbook for reference.

CAD ACTIVITIES

After reading Unit 14, refer to Chapter 14 in the *Chief Architect Tutorials* and practice with the following CAD tool buttons:

• Lines
• Arcs
• Splines
• Boxes
• Circles

• Point inserts
• Dimensioning
• Text
• Draw some irregular shaped furniture for one of your plans.

UNIT 15
ARCHITECTURAL DIMENSIONING

NEED FOR DIMENSIONS

Architectural drawings have three important parts. These are line work, dimensions, and notations.

Line work (line conventions) is covered in Unit 14.

Dimensions are numbers indicating the sizes of objects. Dimensions cover the overall building, the individual rooms, and all structural elements. Dimensions are used with lines and symbols that identify the parts of buildings they cover. Without a full set of dimensions, a home cannot be built.

Notations are notes and descriptions about specific parts of the structure. Examples of notations are the identifications of individual rooms, specific items, and construction notes.

Figure 15-1 is a drawing that has no dimensions and only minimal notations. A home could not be built from this limited information.

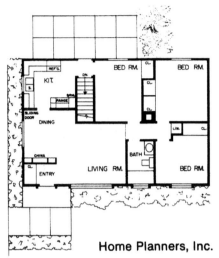

Home Planners, Inc.

Figure 15-1. This floor plan has no dimensions and very few notations. It would be impossible to build a house from this kind of floor plan. *What do dimensions show on a floor plan?*

Figure 15-2 is a drawing with only minimal dimensions provided. This is a type of drawing used in sales literature for homes. There is just enough information to give shoppers an idea of the general size of the building and its rooms. However, the dimensions are not detailed enough to be used in building the home.

For an example of a floor plan with enough dimensions for construction, see **Figure 15-3**. The dimensions are provided in feet and inches. Dimensions are indicated for all parts of the floor plan. It is important that the strings of dimensions add-up correctly to the overall dimensions.

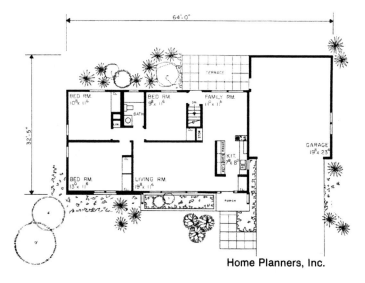

Figure 15-2. This floor plan has some dimensions. However, the dimensions are not sufficient for use in building a house. *What use could be made of a floor plan of this type?*

Home Planners, Inc.

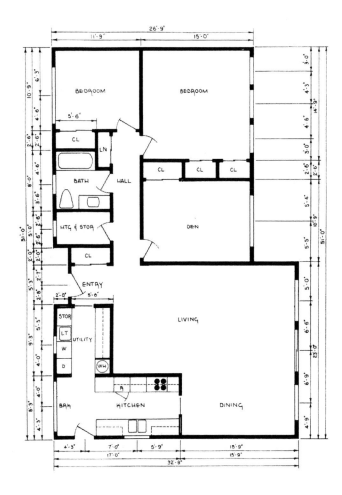

Figure 15-3. This floor plan has the types of dimensions needed for a construction drawing. Notice that there are as many as three sets of dimensions along individual exterior walls. *How would you make sure such strings of dimensions are accurate?*

PARTS OF ARCHITECTURAL DIMENSIONS

A dimension on a plan or drawing has several important parts. These parts are shown in **Figure 15-4**.

Dimension. The numbered description of the size of a structure and all of its parts.

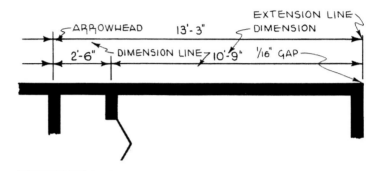

Dimension line. An unbroken line that runs the full length of the structure part to which the dimension applies. The dimension line is thin and dark.

Figure 15-4. This drawing illustrates the parts of an architectural dimension. *Which of the markings on this drawing is known as the dimension?*

Extension line. Lines that identify the end-points for which a measurement is given. The extension line is thin and dark.

Gap. A space, approximately 1/16" (2 mm), that is open between the extension line and the object drawn.

Arrowheads. Markings that indicate the ends of dimension lines.

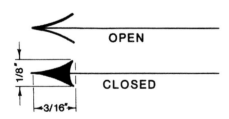

Figure 15-5. This drawing shows alternate styles that can be used in drawing arrowheads. *How are arrowheads used on architectural drawings?*

Two styles may be used for drawing arrowheads as shown in **Figure 15-5**. In one style, the arrowhead may be filled in and shown as solid. In the other, the arrowhead is open. With either style, the size of the arrowhead should be the same. The arrowhead is approximately 1/8" (3 mm) wide and approximately 3/16" (5 mm) long. Several optional styles for arrowheads are shown in **Figure 15-6**.

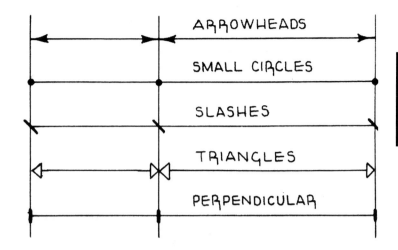

ARROWHEADS

SMALL CIRCLES

SLASHES

TRIANGLES

PERPENDICULAR

Figure 15-5. This drawing shows several optional markings that can be used to mark the ends of dimension lines. *Where are these markings placed when used on drawings?*

DIMENSIONING

Various applications apply for dimensioning floor plans and elevation drawings. *Floor plan dimensions* provide the length and width of a structure. *Elevation dimensions* provide the height of a structure.

Floor Plans

Dimensions should be lettered close but not touching the dimension lines. The dimensions should be positioned so that they can be read from either of two drawing positions. Horizontal dimensions are read straight up. The vertical dimensions are read from the right side as shown in the floor plan example in Figure 15-3.

Dimensions should be drawn and lettered in a certain order. Overall building dimensions should be on the outside of other dimensions. Smaller dimensions, for locating the center of interior walls, are then placed inside of the overall dimensions. The third row of dimensions, closest to the floor plan, starts with the outside of the exterior wall, and dimensions the centers of all windows, doors, and interior walls.

As previously stated, the *strings of dimensions* must always add up to the totals of the larger dimensions.

Room sizes may be shown in two ways. Dimension lines may be used, as in Figure 15-3. It is also acceptable to indicate room sizes as a general notation, shown in Figure 15-2. However, for construction purposes, the style in Figure 15-3 should be followed.

A different rule applies when an interior wall does not touch an outside wall. In this situation, the dimensions for location of the interior wall must be placed on the floor plan. For an example, see the dimensions in the entry of Figure 15-3.

Remember: Dimensions must represent the actual size of the building and its structural parts. Dimension sizes refer to the actual size of the building, regardless of the scale of the drawing. Dimensions for windows and doors are indicated from the center points of these openings. The dimensions and pertinent data is presented with window and door schedules. It is also acceptable to note the widths and heights of windows and doors on the floor plan.

Elevation Drawings

The major dimensions shown on elevation drawings are vertical measurements. The floor plan dimensions show only the length and width.

Figure 15-7 shows dimensions and notations that are placed on an elevation drawing. All vertical elevation dimensions are read from the right. Elevation dimensions should include:

- The distance from the foundation footing to the ground line. The *foundation footing* is the bottom of the structure. The *foundation* is the solid base, usually concrete, on which the house is built. The *footing* is the underground portion of the foundation. In cold areas, the footings must be deep enough to go beneath the level at which the ground freezes. The *ground line* is the level of the earth around the home.

- The distance from the ground line to the *floor line* (the level of the structures floor).

- The distance from the floor line to the top of the doors or windows.

- The distance from the floor line to the *ceiling line* (the level of the structures ceiling).

- The distance from the ceiling line to the ridge line. The *ridge line* marks the highest point on the roof.

- The distance from the ridge line to the top of the chimney.

- The pitch of the roof.

Figure 15-7.
This is an elevation drawing showing dimension markings. *What is the lowest point that should be indicated with dimension markings on an elevation drawing?*

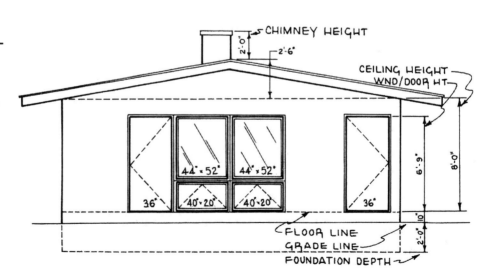

METRIC DIMENSIONS

All of the discussions and illustrations so far in this chapter deal with U.S. standard measurements. These are measurements with which you are familiar: inches, feet, yards, and miles. These standards of measurement were adopted in the United States on the basis of the British measuring system.

The rest of the world uses a different set of measurement standards, known as the *metric system*. Metric measures are followed in countries that use the standards set by the International Standards Organization (ISO). The ISO standards are being accepted and applied throughout the world as quickly as possible. This makes sense! People now travel and do business in many countries. Many countries do business with each other. Having uniform measurements would simplify things. Eventually, the metric system will be used throughout the United States. Some day soon, you will deal with metrics as part of your everyday life.

The commonly used metric system units of measure and their symbols are shown in **Figure 15-8.**

Commonly used metric system units and symbols:

Type of Measurement	Unit Name	Symbol
length, width, distance, thickness, girth, etc.	meter, centimeter, millimeter	m, cm, mm
mass (often called weight)	gram, kilogram*	g, kg
mass (larger)	metric ton	t
time	second	s
temperature	degree Celsius**	°C
area	square meter	m^2
area (land)	hectare	ha
volume (liquid or other)	liter, milliliter	L, mL***
volume (larger)	cubic meter, cubic centimeter	m^3, cm^3
density	kilogram per cubic meter	kg/m^3
velocity	meter per second	m/s
velocity (autos)	kilometer per hour	km/h
force	newton	N
pressure, stress	kilopascal	kPa
energy	kilojoule	kJ

Figure 15-8.
This chart lists most of the measurements used with the metric system. *Which units are used for measurements of distance?*

Metric Prefixes

These basic units of measure are used with a *prefix*. The prefix makes it possible to describe multiples of the basic units. The commonly used metric prefixes are shown in **Figure 15-9**. In architectural and industrial drawings, all dimensions are given in millimeters (mm). Because all the dimensions will be of the same prefix, no symbol is required for the dimensions. **Figure 15-10** is a floor plan with metric dimensions.

The meter is equal to 1.1 yards. The millimeter is one-thousandth of a meter.

Commonly used metric prefixes:

Prefix Name	Prefix Symbol	Prefix Value	
micro	μ	1/1 000 000 or 0.000 001	10^{-6}
milli	m	1/1000 or 0.001	10^{-3}
centi	c	1/100 or 0.01	10^{-2}
kilo	k	1 thousand or 1000	10^{3}
mega	M	1 million or 1 000 000	10^{6}
giga	G	1 000 000 000	10^{9}

Figure 15-9. This chart lists the commonly used prefixes. *Which prefix's value is one-thousandth?*

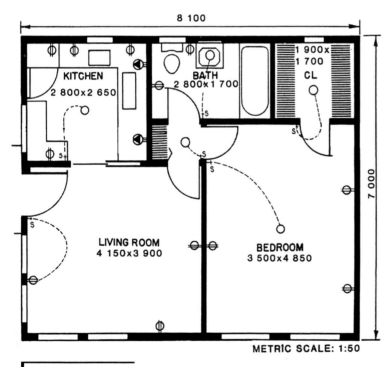

METRIC SCALE: 1:50

Figure 15-10. All dimensions of this floor plan are in millimeters. *How would you convert these dimensions to meters?*

UNIT 15 ACTIVITIES

VOCABULARY CHECKLIST

1. dimension
2. notation
3. gap
4. arrowheads
5. strings of dimensions
6. foundation
7. footing
8. ground line
9. floor line
10. ceiling line
11. ridge line
12. metric system
13. prefix

REVIEW QUESTIONS

1. Which architectural drawing contains the most horizontal dimensions?
2. Which architectural drawing contains the most vertical dimensions?
3. What symbol is used to show the limits (ends) of a dimension line?
4. What is the main purpose for providing detailed dimensions on an architectural drawing?
5. Why is the United States converting to the metric system?
6. What makes it possible to describe multiples of metric units?

YOUR ARCHITECTURAL SCRAPBOOK

1. Cut out or copy a dimensioned drawing. If the dimensions are not complete, indicate places where dimensions should be added.
2. Sketch a floor plan similar to the one in Figure 15-3. Indicate all of the dimensions needed for construction.
3. Make a chart, or table, of metric prefixes using one meter as the base unit
4. Use a CAD system to draw a floor plan and dimension it in millimeters.

CAD ACTIVITIES

After reading Unit 15, refer to Chapter 15 in the *Chief Architect Tutorials* and complete:

- Dimension a floor plan using the metric system (all dimensions are in millimeters - mm).
- Create a sunken living area (split level).
- Add steps at the split level.

UNIT 16
SHEET LAYOUTS

DRAWING MATERIALS AND SIZES

Architectural drawings can be prepared on three types of materials. These are drawing paper, tracing paper (vellum), and plastic film.

All of these materials are available in both sheets and rolls. The smallest sheet-drawing size is 8 1/2" by 11". This is known as a *size A* format. The largest sheet size, *E*, is 34" by 44". These and other standard *sheet formats* are listed in **Figure 16-1**. Standard metric sheet sizes are also shown. For drawings of larger sizes, materials may be purchased in rolls.

American Standards Association Paper Sizes

A	9" x 12" or 8 1/2" x 11"
B	12" x 18" or 11" x 17"
C	18" x 24" or 17" x 22"
D	24" x 36" or 22" x 34"
E	36" x 48" or 34" x 44"

International Standards Association Metric Paper Sizes

A 0	841 mm x 1189 mm
A 1	594 mm x 841 mm
A 2	420 mm x 594 mm
A 3	297 mm x 420 mm
A 4	210 mm x 297 mm
A 5	148 mm x 210 mm
A 6	105 mm x 148 mm
A 7	74 mm x 105 mm
A 8	52 mm x 74 mm
A 9	37 mm x 52 mm
A10	26 mm x 37 mm

Figure 16-1. This table shows U.S. standard and metric sizes for architectural drawing sheets. *Should you use different size sheets for the drawings in a set?*

A set of architectural working drawings requires many drawing sheets. These drawings are usually kept and used together as a set. Therefore, it is best to make all of the drawings in a set on sheets of the same size. Do this even if some drawings could fit onto smaller sheets. A set of drawings is easier to bind and handle if all sheets are the same size. See **Figure 16-2**.

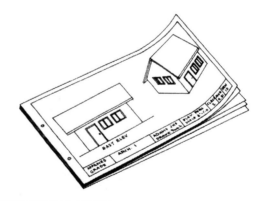

Figure 16-2. This drawing shows how architectural drawings or prints are usually bound in sets. *Why is it important that the title block be in the same position and be the same size on each drawing in a set?*

BORDERS AND TITLE BLOCKS

Before you begin your drawing, you should prepare each sheet's drawing *layout*. This preparation includes completing the borders and the title blocks.

A *border* is a heavy, solid line around the edge of a sheet of drafting material. It delineates the outside of the area that can be used by the drafter. On small drawings, borders are usually 1/2" (15 mm) from the edges of the sheet. On larger sheets, borders may be 1" (25 mm from the edges).

A *title block* is a compilation of information appearing on the bottom portion of a drawing's format. All drawings in the set of working drawings must have a title block. All title blocks should be the same size and in the same position on all drawings in a set. All title block information should be complete on every drawing.

Figure 16-3 shows a typical title block. Each title block should include the following information:

- Title of the drawing
- Scale
- Sheet number and total number of sheets in the set
- Job location
- Architect
- Designer
- Checker
- Date

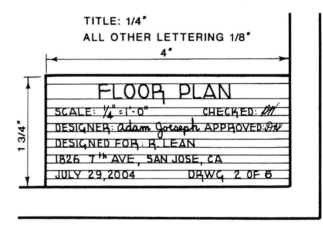

Figure 16-3. This is a typical title block for an architectural drawing. Note the page number notation. This is the second drawing in a set of six. *Why is it important to indicate the total number of drawings in a set?*

In addition, spaces are often provided for *notations* on changes or revisions. The date should always be changed when a drawing is revised. In reviewing prints, always work from the drawings with the latest revision dates.

Note that the entry for page (or drawing) number should include the total number of pages in the set. A typical notation might read: "4 of 8." This means page four of eight sheets in the set of drawings.

Drawing titles are normally lettered in 3/16" or 1/4" (6 mm or 8 mm) heights. For the remaining information, 1/8" (3 mm) lettering is normally used.

UNIT 16 ACTIVITIES

VOCABULARY CHECKLIST

1. sheet format
2. standard metric sheet
3. layout

4. border
5. title block
6. notation

REVIEW QUESTIONS

1. What is the value of a border on the sheet layout of an architectural drawing?
2. Why is it important that all drawings in a set be of the same size?
3. In what position should the title block be placed on drawings within a set after the first one?

YOUR ARCHITECTURAL SCRAPBOOK

1. Cut out or copy title blocks for at least two drawings. See if you can find title blocks with different information items. Note any differences.
2. Enter a list of title block information items in your scrapbook.
3. With a CAD system, prepare an A size sheet layout and save it for future use. Make a hard copy and place it in your scrapbook.
4. Prepare files of B and C formats with your CAD system. Make a hard copy and place it in your scrapbook.

CAD ACTIVITIES

After reading Unit 16, refer to Chapter 15 in the *Chief Architect Tutorials* and complete:

- Add a flight of stairs to one of your floor plans.
- Create a second floor.
- Create a stairwell opening.
- Complete the second floor (walls, windows, doors, fixtures, etc.).

PART V
Architectural Design & Drafting

Drawing Floor Plans

Drawing the Plot Plan

Drawing Elevations

Drawing Slab Foundations

Drawing T-Foundations

Drawing Roof Plans

Drawing Floor-Framing Plans

Drawing Wall-Framing Plans

Drawing Roof-Framing Plans

Drawing Electrical Plans

Drawing Plumbing Plans

PART V

ARCHITECTURAL DESIGN AND DRAFTING

SKILLS OF THE DRAFTER

You learned about the practices and procedures of the drafter in Parts II through IV. Now, a complete set of working drawings must be developed to obtain a building permit. The set of working drawings are then used for the construction of the building.

In Units 17 through 27, you will learn about standard drawing procedures and construction methods that are necessary to complete a set of residential working drawings. However, you should be aware that there are many alternative construction methods and procedures. Construction techniques will vary in different parts of the country. These variations are in response to a number of factors. The factors include climate, availability of material, site conditions, and personal preferences of homeowners.

YOUR LEARNING JOB

There are eleven units in Part V. These units, as listed below, cover all the areas for a residential set of working drawings that are required to obtain a building permit and have the contractors build the structure.

- Drawing floor plans
- Drawing plot plans
- Drawing elevations
- Drawing slab foundations
- Drawing T-foundations
- Drawing roof plans
- Drawing floor-framing plans
- Drawing wall-framing plans
- Drawing roof-framing plans
- Drawing electrical plans
- Drawing plumbing plans

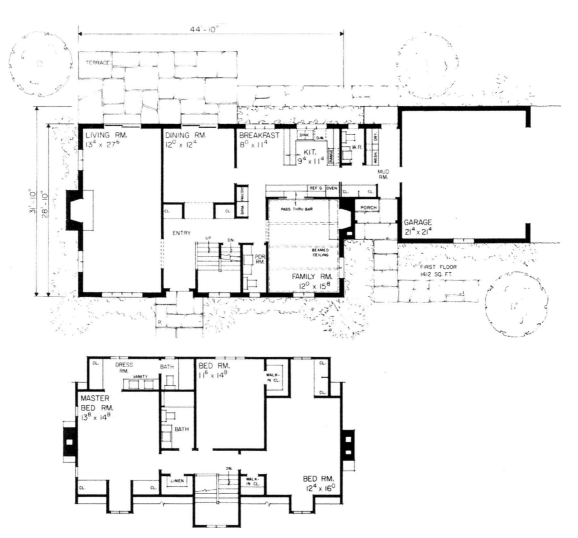

With the completion of these eleven units, you should be able to draw a full set of working drawings.

UNIT 17
DRAWING FLOOR PLANS

DRAWING FLOOR PLANS WITH MANUAL DRAFTING

A finished floor plan drawing is usually based on a design sketch developed by an architect or designer. The procedures for producing design sketches of floor plans are covered in Unit 7.

Before drawing a floor plan with manual drafting instruments, the appropriate scale must be selected. The scale used for most residential floor plans is 1/4" = 1 '-0". Using this scale, read and complete the following the steps.

Step A. Start by outlining the outside walls of the house. Draw the lines lightly with a 4H pencil. This provides a light line as a guide for the work that follows. These light lines are called *layout lines* and can be easily erased and changed. This beginning step is illustrated in **Figure 17-1**.

Step B. Draw the lines for inside surfaces of exterior walls. Typically, exterior walls of wood-framed homes are 6" wide. However, masonry walls may be 9" or 12" wide. In **Figure 17-2**, walls of 6" thickness are represented.

Step C. Measure and draw all interior partitions (walls) using *partition lines*. This delineates all the rooms and work areas within the home. Typical interior walls are 4 1/2" wide. (The wall studs are 3 1/2" wide with 1/2" sheetrock on each side.) However, plumbing walls and fire walls may be 6" to 9" wide. On the other hand, a non-supporting wall may be only 2 1/2" wide (The 3 1/2" x 1 1/2" studs are placed sideways with 1/2" sheetrock on two sides.) The appearance of the drawing at this point is shown in **Figure 17-3**. For convenience and speed, most drafters draw exterior and interior walls at a 6" width.

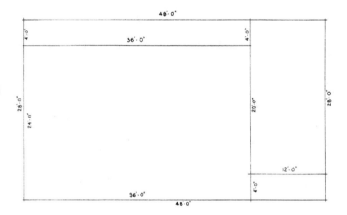

Figure 17-1. As the first step in developing a floor plan, use a 4H pencil to draw the outline of the building. The lines drawn at this point are called layout lines. *Why is a 4H pencil used for layout lines?*

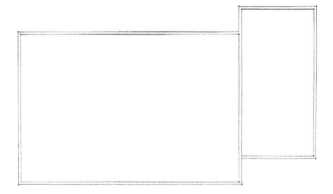

Figure 17-2. For the second step in floor-plan development, add layout lines for the interior walls of the structure. *What wall thickness is commonly used for the building of homes?*

Step D. Draw the locations of all openings in interior and exterior partitions, including all doors and windows. This step has been completed in **Figure 17-4**.

Step E. Add closets, cabinets, appliances, fixtures, and any built-in items. These additions are drawn to scale of 1/4" =1'-0", as shown in **Figure 17 -5**.

Step F. Complete the plan by drawing over the layout lines with an H or F pencil. Add all dimensions and notations. Erase any remaining layout lines. The completed floor plan should be similar to **Figure 17-6**.

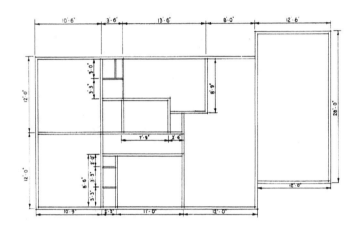

Figure 17-3. The third step in the development of a floor plan is the drawing of all interior walls and partitions. This sets up the room plan for the home. *What thickness is used for interior walls?*

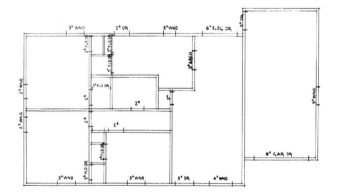

Figure 17-4. During the fourth step in drawing working floor plans, indicate the positions of all doors and windows. *What scale is used in positioning doors and windows?*

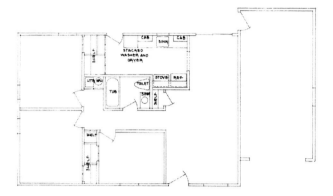

Figure 17-5. During the fifth step in floor plan development, closets and built-in components are added to the floor plan. *What tool can be used in drawing such built-in components as sinks and tubs?*

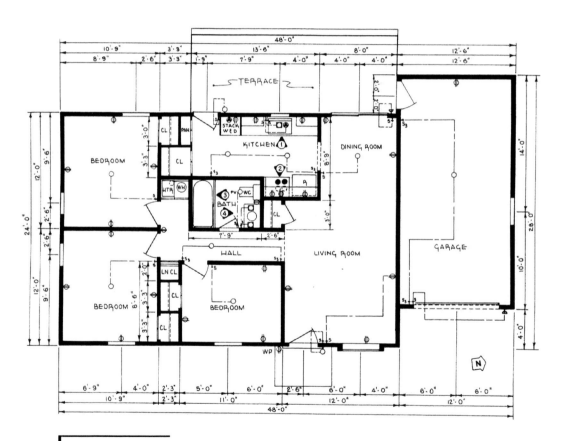

Figure 17-6. Final dimensions and descriptions are added. The layout lines are covered with the lines drawn with an H or F pencil. Unneeded layout lines are erased. *What is the purpose of drawing final lines with an H or F pencil?*

DRAWING FLOOR PLANS WITH A CAD SYSTEM

The CAD (computer-aided drafting) steps in **Figures 17-7** through **17-13** provide a general introduction on how to draw a small garage with an architectural drawing program. To learn the detailed procedures to activate and use the drawing commands of your specific architectural software program, you must use the *help menu* provided with the software program or an instructional CAD book.

Figure 17-7. Use a line drawing command to outline the garage. The overall dimensions are 10'-0" x 20'-0".

Figure 17-8. Using a line widen drawing command, widen the walls to six inches. Be certain to widen to the inside of the plan or you will increase the overall dimensions.

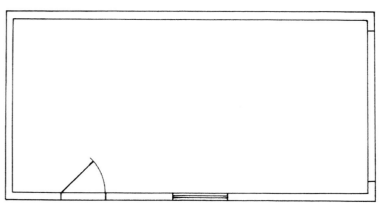

Figure 17-9. Using a line drawing command, outline the garage door. From an architectural symbol library, call up and position a 2'-6" door and a 3'-0" x 4'-0" window. If a symbol library is not available, you must draw the symbols. If you have to draw symbols, be sure to save them to a file so you can use them later.

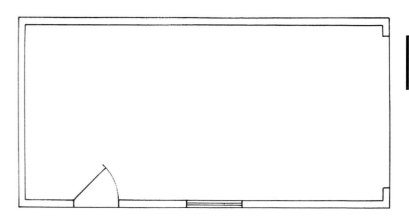

Figure 17-10. Use an edit command to remove the excessive lines from the doors.

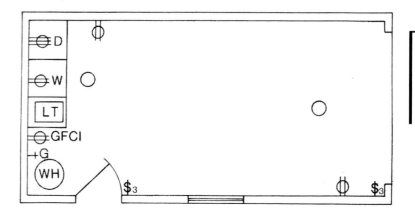

Figure 17-11. Either draw or call up from the symbol library all the electrical items, washer, dryer, laundry sink, water heater, and gas outlet. Place them in position as shown.

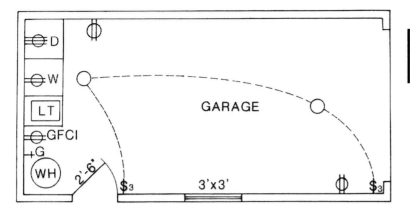

Figure 17-12. Use a text command to place the text. Use the spline command to connect a curved dotted line from the three-way switches to the light sources.

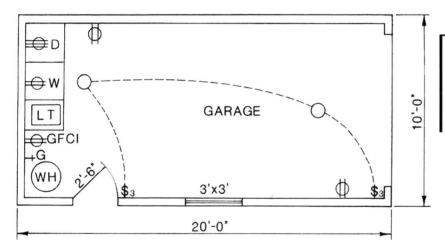

Figure 17-13. Use an architectural dimension command to dimension the garage to complete the floor plan of the garage.

UNIT 17 ACTIVITIES

VOCABULARY CHECKLIST

1. layout lines
2. partition lines
3. built-in components
4. help menu
5. CAD

REVIEW QUESTIONS

1. What scale is used for most residential floor plans?
2. Which hardness of pencil lead is used to draw layout lines?
3. What is the thickness of the exterior walls in the floor plans shown in this unit?
4. Which hardness of pencil lead is used to draw final structural lines on floor plans?

YOUR ARCHITECTURAL SCRAPBOOK

1. Write the steps required for developing a construction floor plan.
2. Copy the drawings in this unit showing each stage of floor plan development. These drawings can be sketched roughly. They should provide notes you can follow in developing floor plans of your own.
3. With a CAD system, draw the garage in **Figure 17-13**. Make a hard copy and place it your scrapbook.
4. Draw a small floor plan with a CAD system. Make a hard copy and place it in your scrapbook.

CAD ACTIVITIES

After reading Unit 17, refer to Chapter 17 in the *Chief Architect Tutorials* and complete:

- Drawing the garage in Figure 17-13.
- Drawing the floor plan in Figure 17-6.
- Design a large four-bedroom plan.

UNIT 18
DRAWING THE PLOT PLAN

PLOT PLAN INFORMATION

The drawing of the plot plan can begin after the zoning regulations are checked (see Unit 5). Specific information is required on a *plot plan* that is needed to obtain a building permit. This information includes:

- Property line and dimensions.
- An arrow indicating the direction of north.
- An outline of the building showing its location dimensions from property lines.
- Outlines of a garage or any other auxiliary buildings, including two location dimensions from property line.
- Driveway outline and dimensions.
- Walkway outline and dimensions.
- Street location indication.

Additional information that is not required, but is often added to plot plans includes:

- Positions of patios
- Lawns
- Gardens
- Roof outlines
- Landscaping features
- Contour lines

Contour lines show the elevation of the land. These lines indicate the rise and fall of land elevations.

PLOT PLAN DEVELOPMENT

The procedure for drawing a plot plan has four steps. These are described below and illustrated in Figures 18-1 through 18-4.

Step A. Using a 4H pencil, draw the outline of the *property line* (see **Figure 18-1**). A typical city building site is usually drawn to a scale of 1/8" = 1' - 0". *Broken lines* are used to show the property line. The dimensions of the property are noted during this step.

Step B. Measure and draw the lines for the zoning *setback*. This will identify the *buildable area*. These lines are drawn with *light dotted lines*. After building positions are indicated, these lines can be erased (see **Figure 18-2**). The setback distances are not shown on the drawing.

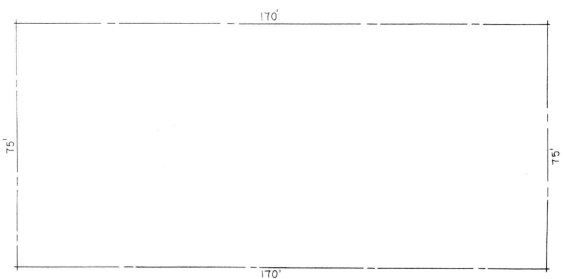

170'

75'

75'

170'

Figure 18-1. The first step in developing a plot plan is to draw a set of broken lines to indicate the property line. *What is the meaning of the dimension notations in this drawing?*

Step C. Measure and draw outlines for all structures and roof lines within the building area. Note, in **Figure 18-3**, how structure lines are broken and roof lines are solid. Dimensions for the distances from the property line to the building are given on all sides.

Step D. Draw in driveways, walkways, and patios. Add all dimensions and notes. Be sure to show all distances from the property lines to the structure. Add a north arrow to show the compass orientation of the lot. Indicate the scale used (see **Figure 18-4**).

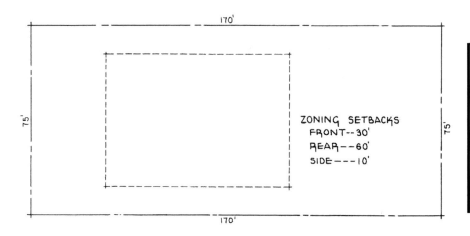

170'

75'

ZONING SETBACKS
FRONT--30'
REAR--60'
SIDE---10'

75'

170'

Figure 18-2. Step two in the development of a plot plan is to draw dotted layout lines indicating the *building area*. The building area is the space within the lot on which structures can be placed. *What are the distances between lot lines and building area lines called?*

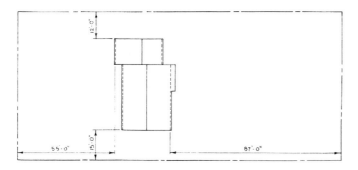

Figure 18-3. In the third step of plot plan development, indicate the *setback* locations of all structures. Indicate the dimensions for distances from the property line to the structure. *What do the broken lines in the drawing of the building show?*

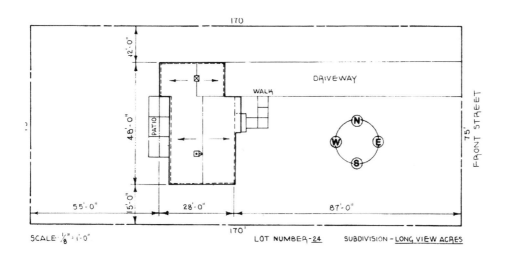

Figure 18-4. During the fourth step, the driveway, walkway, and patio are added. All lines are darkened. Dimensions and notes are added. Geographic orientation of the lot and the drawing scale are indicated. The plot plan is finished when the property is labeled. *What dimensions should you be sure to include during this step?*

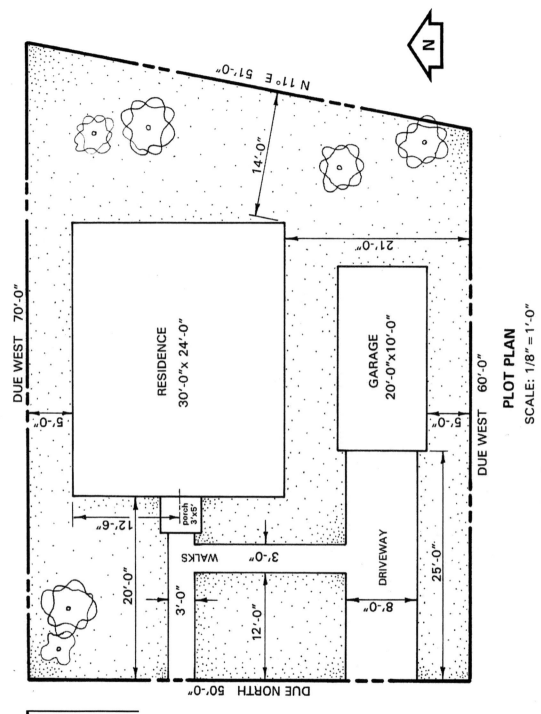

PLOT PLAN

SCALE: 1/8" = 1'-0"

N 11° E 51'-0"

14'-0"

DUE WEST 70'-0"

21'-0"

RESIDENCE
30'-0" x 24'-0"

GARAGE
20'-0" x 10'-0"

5'-0"

5'-0"

DUE WEST 60'-0"

12'-6"

porch
3'x5'

WALKS

3'-0"

DRIVEWAY

25'-0"

20'-0"

3'-0"

12'-0"

8'-0"

DUE NORTH 50'-0"

Figure 18-5. This is an example of a plot plan of a small home on a typical city lot. *Why is it important to give the compass orientation?*

UNIT 18 ACTIVITIES

VOCABULARY CHECKLIST

1. plot plan
2. contour lines
3. property line
4. broken lines
5. setback
6. building area

REVIEW QUESTIONS

1. What is the function of the property line?
2. What is a setback dimension?
3. What is a contour line?
4. Which division in the building department will check the plot plan?

YOUR ARCHITECTURAL SCRAPBOOK

1. List the items that must be shown on a plot plan.
2. List the optional items that are often shown on a plot plan.
3. Sketch a copy of the plot plan in **Figure 18-4**. This will be a guide in drawing future plot plans.
4. With a CAD system, draw a plot plan. Make a hard copy and place it in your scrapbook.

CAD ACTIVITIES

After reading Unit 18, refer to Chapter 18 in the *Chief Architect Tutorials* and complete:

- Copy the plot plan in Figure 18-5.
- Design and draw the plot plans for all the floor plans you have saved.

UNIT 19
DRAWING ELEVATIONS

THE NEED FOR ELEVATION DRAWINGS

The elevation drawings are drawn after the floor plan is finalized. They are necessary to show the dimensions and information that cannot be shown on the floor plans. The elevation drawings show the exterior finish materials and the architectural styling. Many different architectural styles may be designed from the same floor plan as shown in **Figure 19-1**. Appearances of a structure can be changed by the use of different exterior finish materials, windows, doors, and roof styles.

Figure 19-1.
It is possible to design many different architectural styles from the same floor plan. *What exterior building features effects the architectural style?*

Figure 19-2.
Examples of a minimal exterior elevations drawings. *What additional information should be given to the builders to change these elevation drawings into working drawings?*

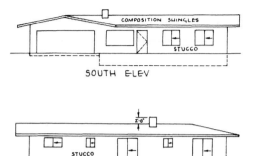

COMPOSITION SHINGLES

STUCCO

SOUTH ELEV

WEST ELEV

STUCCO

2'-0"

STUCCO

NORTH ELEV

STUCCO

EAST ELEV

The placement of exterior elevation drawings on a set of working drawings is shown in **Figure 19-2**. These elevation drawings are an example of minimum line technique. Each elevation should be labeled by *compass orientation* (**Figure 19-3**). Note that the elevation call outs are oriented to the compass and not to the property lines.

Only the length and width dimensions are shown on the floor plan. The height dimensions can only be shown on the elevation drawings as shown in **Figure 19-4**.

Finished details of the exterior building materials may be shown to make the elevation attractive for the client. Some exterior finish materials are shown in **Figure 19-5**. Shading and landscaping may also be applied to the elevation for a realistic appearance (**Figure 19-6**). These types of elevation drawings are referred to as *presentation drawings* and are not useful for construction purposes.

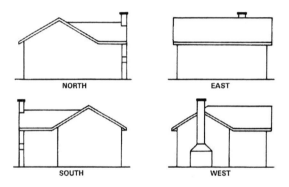

NORTH

EAST

SOUTH

WEST

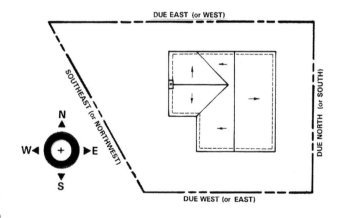

DUE EAST (or WEST)

SOUTHEAST (or NORTHWEST)

DUE NORTH (or SOUTH)

DUE WEST (or EAST)

N
W + E
S

Figure 19-3. Exterior elevations must always be oriented with a compass direction. *What is the relationship of the compass headings between the elevation callouts and the property line directions?*

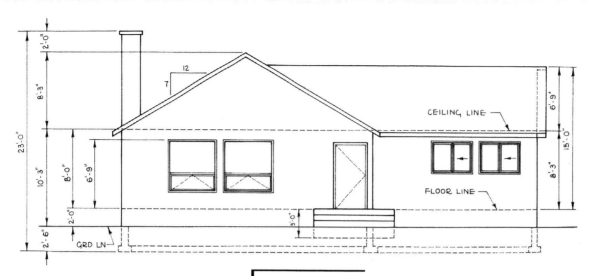

Figure 19-4. Example of a dimensioned exterior elevation drawing. *What additional information must the builders have to complete the construction?*

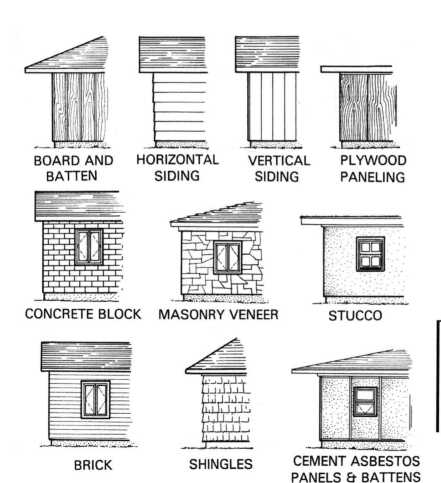

BOARD AND BATTEN

HORIZONTAL SIDING

VERTICAL SIDING

PLYWOOD PANELING

CONCRETE BLOCK

MASONRY VENEER

STUCCO

Figure 19-5. Examples of various types of exterior finish materials. *What are some other exterior finish materials and combinations of materials for the exterior finishes.*

BRICK

SHINGLES

CEMENT ASBESTOS PANELS & BATTENS

Figure 19-6. Examples of rendered and landscaped exterior elevations. *What is the use for rendered exterior elevations?*

DRAWING EXTERIOR ELEVATIONS

Elevation drawings are usually drawn to the same scale as the floor plan. The process of drawing exterior elevations is carried out in four steps.

Step 1. Draw the major horizontal height lines for the south side of the structure (**Figure 19-7A**). These lines include the *foundation footing line*, the finished *grade line*, the floor line, the height of the windows and doors, the ceiling line, and the chimney's height.

Step 2. Tape the floor plan to the top of your drawing area. Using a T-square and triangle, project down the corners of walls, windows, doors, fireplace, etc. as shown in **Figure 19-7B**.

Step 3. Complete the outline of all the structural features. Design a roof and add the slope diagram (**Figure 19-7C**). Determining the slope of a roof is covered later in this unit. The elevation details may now be added with the following features (**Figure 19-7D**).

- vertical dimensions
- siding materials
- window and door styles
- shutters
- trim
- gutters and down spouts
- fireplace and chimney

The remaining elevations may now be drawn using the same procedures (**Figures 19-8A, B, and C**).

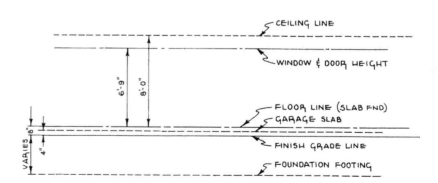

Figure 19-7A.
When preparing an exterior elevation, start by indicating the basic horizontal lines of the structure. *Why are these elevation heights critical for the drawing of an exterior elevation?*

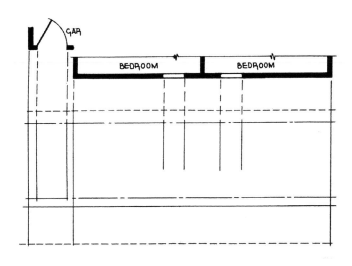

Figure 19-7B.
The next step is to project down from the floor plan wall corners, windows, doors, and other key structural items. *What drafting tools are used to project the vertical lines for the elevation's drawing?*

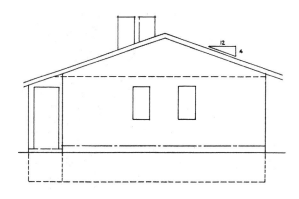

Figure 19-7C. Design and outline the roof, windows, doors, and other key structural items. *Why is it important to know the location and size of the built-in items when designing the size of the windows?*

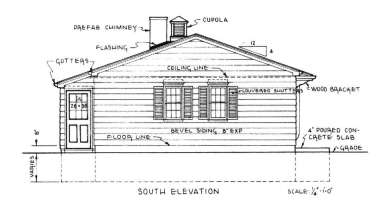

Figure 19-7D. The last steps for the completion of the exterior elevations are to add all the elevation's details, darken the line work, add the dimensions, and notes. *What is the advantage of completing all the details for an elevation as compared to a minimal outline of the elevation?*

Figure 19-8A.
The finished west exterior elevation. *How many exit doors are shown in this elevation?*

Figure 19-8B.
The finished east exterior elevation. *What type of windows are to be installed?*

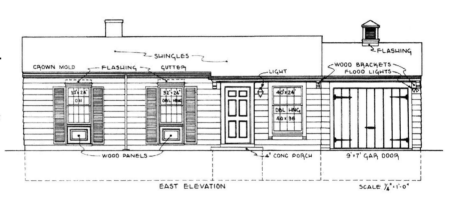

Figure 19-8C.
The finished north exterior elevation. *What is the pitch of the roof?*

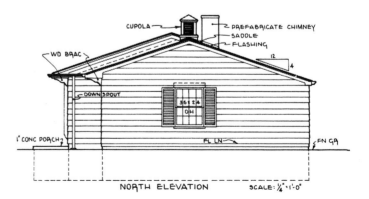

ROOF DESIGN

The various types of roof slopes are shown in **Figure 19-9**. Determining the slope of the roof is the responsibility of the architect or designer. Items to consider are the architectural style of the design and the runoff for water and snow. After drawing the roof on the elevations, a slope diagram must be added. The procedure to draw a slope diagram is shown in **Figure 19-10**. The horizontal line is the *run* and it is always in units of 12. The vertical line is the *rise* and will change with the different roof slopes.

Builders calculate the roof's pitch from the slope diagram's information. To obtain the *pitch*, you must double the run to 24 (span). This becomes the denominator, and the rise becomes the numerator. An example of a slope diagram with a run of 12 and a rise of 6 is: 6/24 = 1/4 pitch. **Figure 19-11** shows several calculations for the roof pitch.

Figure 19-12 shows several styles of roofs. Most residential roofs are of the gable and hip architectural style.

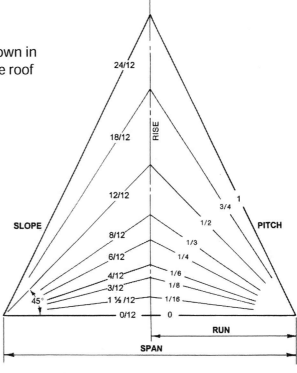

Figure 19-9. The selection for your roof's pitch may taken from this drawing. *What is the difference between a slope diagram and the roof's pitch? What is the roof pitch of a roof with a 12/12 slope?*

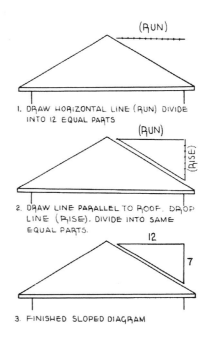

Figure 19-10. This illustration shows the steps to draw the roof slope diagram. The run will always be in units of 12. The rise will change with angle of the roof. *How would the roof pitch for this roof be written?*

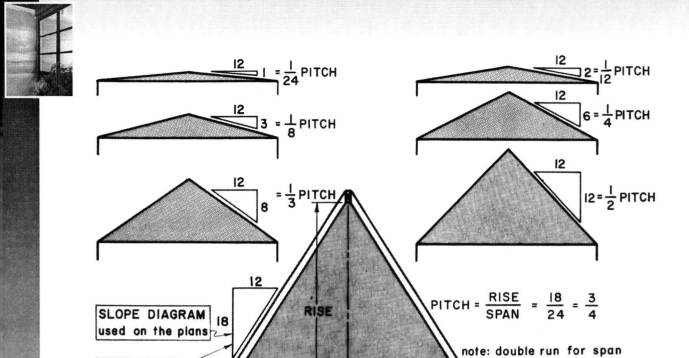

Figure 19-11. Examples of calculations for various roof slopes. *Why is the roof pitch critical information for the builders?*

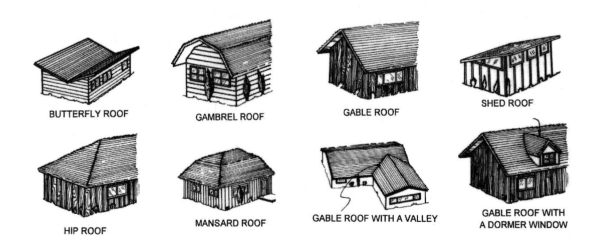

Figure 19-12. Examples of residential roofs. *Which roof style would you use with your design?*

INTERIOR ELEVATION DRAWINGS

Interior elevation drawings are needed for the builders to finish the interior construction details. *Interior elevations* have the instructions to construct and install the built-in features of the home. Some of these features are cabinets, fireplaces, fixtures, appliances, trim, mirrors, and surface covers.

The techniques for drawing an interior elevation are similar to the exterior elevation. All the dimensions of the interior elevation must match the floor plan and exterior elevation dimensions.

The interior elevations (**Figures 19A** through **19D**) are typical examples showing finishes, cabinets, built-ins, appliances, fixtures, etc. If any item is not shown, the builders have to become the designers on what items to purchase and install or build.

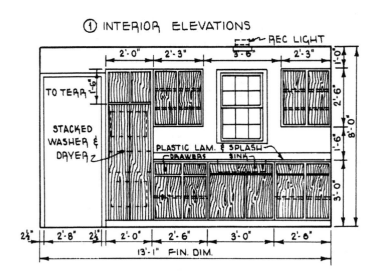

Figure 19-13A. An example of an interior elevation from the kitchen. *What additional information must be given to finish the construction of this kitchen?*

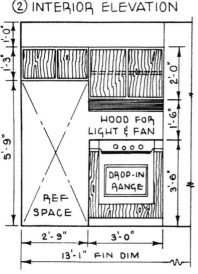

Figure 19-13B. An example of another wall in the kitchen. *What are the dimensions for the refrigerator's space?*

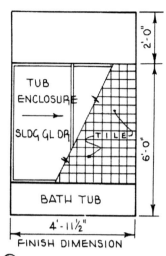

BATH TUB

4'-11½"

FINISH DIMENSION

③ INTERIOR ELEVATION

Figure 19-13C. An example of an interior elevation from the bathroom. *What additional information must be given to the builders to complete the construction of the bathroom?*

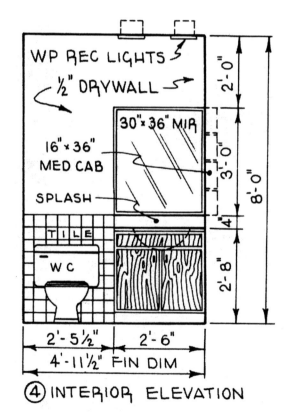

④ INTERIOR ELEVATION

Figure 19-13D. An example of another wall in the bathroom. *What is the FIN. DIM?*

UNIT 19 ACTIVITIES

VOCABULARY CHECKLIST

1. compass orientation
2. presentation drawings
3. exterior elevations
4. foundation footing line
5. grade line

6. run
7. rise
8. pitch
9. interior elevations

REVIEW QUESTIONS

1. What role do elevation drawings have with the construction of a home?
2. How are the dimensions of a floor plan related to those of an exterior elevation drawing?
3. What is the meaning of roof pitch?
4. What information do builders obtain with the roof pitch fraction?
5. What is the meaning of the roof slope diagram?
6. Why is it critical that the floor plan and elevation dimensions are identical?

YOUR ARCHITECTURAL SCRAPBOOK

1. Make a list of all the elements that should be included for an exterior elevation.
2. Make a list of all the elements that should be included for an interior elevation.
3. Cut out or copy several elevation drawings from publications that you find attractive and add them to your scrapbook.
4. With a CAD system, draw several different architectural style elevations from the same floor plan. Make hard copies and add them to your scrapbook.

CAD ACTIVITIES

After reading Unit 19, refer to Chapter 19 in the *Chief Architect Tutorials* and complete:

- Create the exterior elevations for all the floor plans you have saved.
- Create several interior elevations from each of your floor plans.

UNIT 20
DRAWING SLAB FOUNDATIONS

TYPES OF FOUNDATIONS

A *foundation* is the base upon which a structure is built. The framing of the structure is fastened to the foundation system, which is securely anchored into the earth.

There are various types of foundation systems used for residential construction. The selection depends on the soil condition, contours of land, and the homeowner's preference. The foundation systems are as follows (see **Figure 20-1**).

- T-foundation
- Slab foundation
- Column system
- Pier system
- Pile system

The commonly used foundations for residential construction are the T and slab. **Figure 20-2** shows examples of T and slab foundations. The T-foundation will be covered in Unit 21.

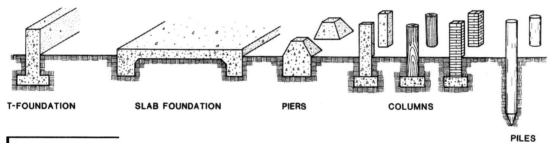

Figure 20-1. Examples of various types of residential foundations. *What type of foundation would the best for a steep hillside? What type of foundation should be selected to keep building costs down?*

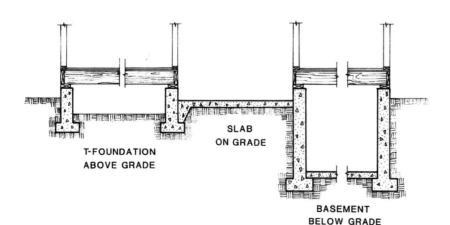

Figure 20-2.
The use of T and slab foundations. *When would the T and slab foundation be used together?*

THE SLAB FOUNDATION

The structural design of a slab foundation is shown in **Figure 20-3**. The major feature of a *slab foundation* is the concrete that is poured on the ground under the entire floor area of the home. The slab foundation must be situated on compact soil. The forms for the footings and the slab are prepared then concrete is poured. The following items must be positioned and installed before the pour.

- fill
- insulation
- water lines
- heating ducts
- vapor barrier
- plumbing lines
- gas lines
- steel reinforcements (**Figure 20-4**)

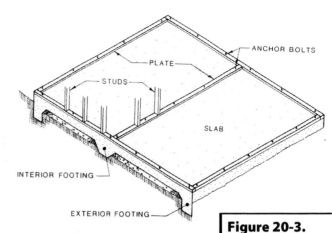

Figure 20-3.
The first wood member on the slab is the plate which is firmly attached. *What is used to attached the plate to the slab? Why is the plate treated?*

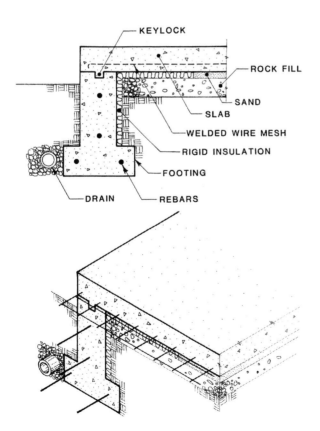

Figure 20-4.
Examples of reinforcing bars *(rebars)* and *welded wire mesh* (WWM) in a slab foundation. *What is the purpose of placing steel in a slab foundation?*

The thickness for a residential slab on firm soil is 3 1/2" to 4". The width and depth of the footings, under bearing walls are 12". Slab foundations built on land fill or poor soil conditions must have the foundation designed by an architect or soils engineer. Typical slab foundation details are shown in **Figure 20-5**. The construction of an adjacent slab foundation for a garage to a home's T-foundation is shown in **Figure 20-6**. Note the steel dowels (rebars) between the slab and T-foundations, used to secure the two foundations together.

There are many variations for the construction of a slab foundation. A typical type is a monolithic pour. The footings and the slab are poured at the same time. The first wood member is a *treated plate* that repels termites, dry rot, and fungus. The exterior wall plate is attached with *anchor bolts* at every four feet. The interior walls are usually attached with *concrete nails*.

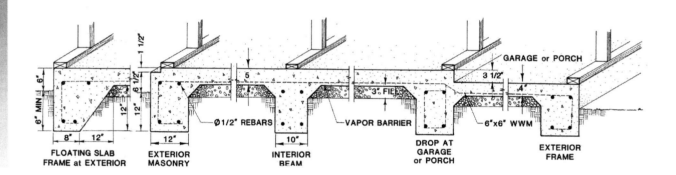

Figure 20-5. There are many variations of the slab construction. *What are some reasons for the design variations of the same construction detail?*

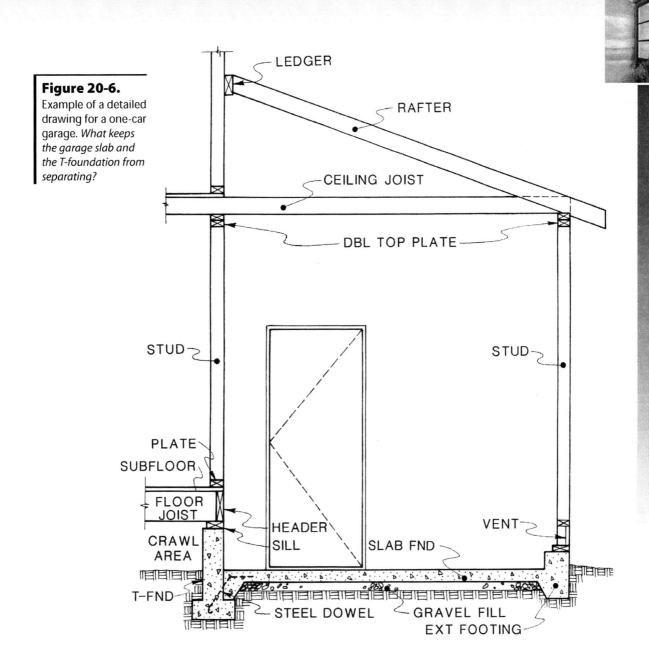

Figure 20-6.
Example of a detailed drawing for a one-car garage. *What keeps the garage slab and the T-foundation from separating?*

LEDGER

RAFTER

CEILING JOIST

DBL TOP PLATE

STUD

STUD

PLATE
SUBFLOOR

FLOOR
JOIST

CRAWL
AREA

HEADER
SILL

SLAB FND

VENT

T-FND

STEEL DOWEL

GRAVEL FILL
EXT FOOTING

Footings are poured deep enough in the earth to assure a solid base for the foundation. In cold climates, footings must reach below the frost line. The width of footings for most residential slabs is 12". A typical monolithic slab plan and construction details are shown in **Figure 20-7**.

Slab foundations have advantages and disadvantages. Advantages include lower cost, quieter walk areas, a lower profile for the home, and less construction costs. There are several disadvantages. One of these is the hard walking surface that can be tiring. Another is that slab floors tend to retain cold temperatures. Also, it can be expensive to repair pipes under a slab.

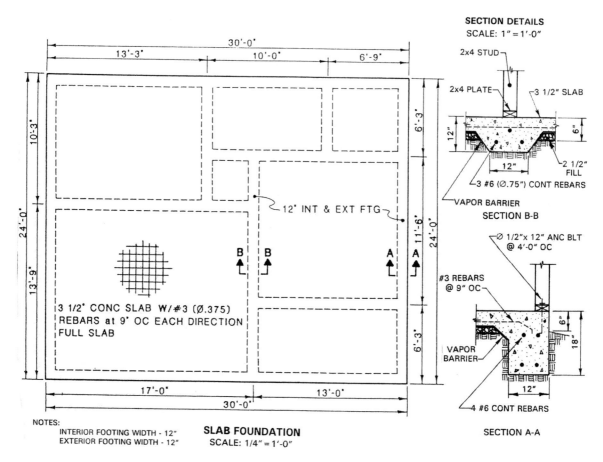

Figure 20-7. Example of a completed slab foundation plan and details for a small home. *What is the symbol for diameter? What is the spacing for the anchor bolts?*

THE DRAFTING PROCESS

A plan for a slab foundation is developed in three steps.

Step 1. Trace the outline of the house, garage, and other foundation areas from the floor plan. This means that you will use the same scale as you use for the floor plan. After you have traced the outside line, draw a line indicating the thickness of the 12" footing (**Figure 20-8**).

Step 2. Draw the 12" footing lines under the bearing interior partitions (walls). These footings should be centered under the partitions (**Figure 20-9**).

Step 3. Add dimensions and notations about structural details to complete the foundation plan (**Figure 20-10**).

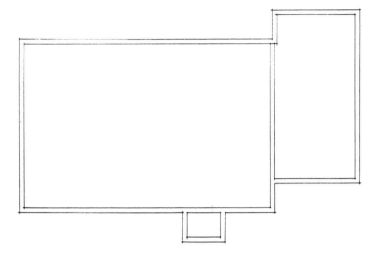

Figure 20-8.
Trace from the floor plan the outside of the structure, then draw the 12" footings. *What is the advantage of tracing the foundation outlines from the floor plan?*

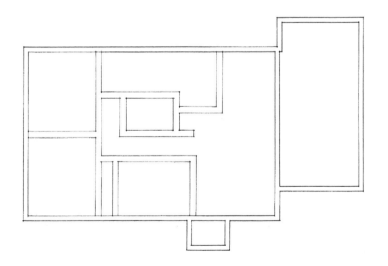

Figure 20-9.
Trace the 12" interior footings from the interior walls. The footings must be centered under the interior walls. *Why must the footings be centered under the interior walls?*

Figure 20-10.
Completed slab foundation plan with dimensions, notes, and symbols. *What do the X-X and Y-Y callouts represent?*

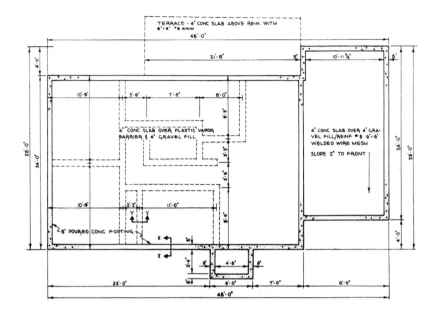

A vapor barrier of plastic sheeting or hop-mopped building paper must be placed between the slab and gravel fill to stop moisture from pentetrating into the house (**Figure 20-11**).

Figure 20-11.
Note the placement of the vapor barrier and the gravel fill. *What is the purpose of the vapor barrier and gravel fill?*

UNIT 20 ACTIVITIES

VOCABULARY CHECKLIST

1. slab foundation
2. welded wire mesh
3. rebar
4. treated plate
5. anchor bolt
6. concrete nail

REVIEW QUESTIONS

1. What are the advantages of slab foundations?
2. What are the disadvantages of slab foundations?
3. What is the thickness of most residential slabs?
4. What are the functions of footings under slab foundations?
5. Why is a bed of gravel fill placed under a slab foundation?
6. What is the purpose of the anchor bolts?
7. What is the purpose of a vapor barrier?
8. What is the purpose of the steel used in a foundation?

YOUR ARCHITECTURAL SCRAPBOOK

1. Find the building code information covering slab foundations in your area. Add this information to your scrapbook.
2. Find or sketch plans for slab foundations in your area. Include all dimensions.
3. With a CAD system, draw a slab foundation and details for the floor plan you designed. Make a hard copy and place it in your scrapbook.

CAD ACTIVITIES

After reading Unit 20, refer to Chapter 20 in the *Chief Architect Tutorials* and complete:

- Copy the slab foundation in Figure 20-10.
- Copy the slab foundation construction details in Figure 20-7.
- Design a slab foundation and construction details for one of your floor plans.

UNIT 21
DRAWING T-FOUNDATIONS

T-FOUNDATION CONSTRUCTION

If a home requires a basement or if the floor is to be raised above the ground, a T-foundation is required. This type of foundation gets its name from its appearance. The foundation is built in the shape of an inverted letter T. The floor system rests on the top of the T-foundation. The structural principle and key features of a T-foundation are illustrated in **Figure 21-1**.

The *T-foundation*, like a slab foundation, provides a base for the building of a home. Its purpose is to raise the home above the finished grade (ground) line. Specifications for the foundation's dimensions depend on the condition of the soil and the weight of the structure.

The T-foundation is constructed of solid concrete. There are also interior concrete *piers* to support the center of the floor system. **Figure 21-2** shows the parts of a T-foundation system. Included are the girders and joists that support the floor system. Also shown are the *mud sill* and *anchor bolt* that join the floor system to the foundation. Building codes, architects, or structural engineers determine the size and amount of the structural building materials that can be used in each area for foundations and structural supports.

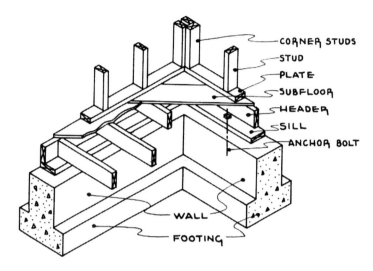

Figure 21-1. This is a detail showing the key features of a T-foundation. The footing is the base of the T-foundation. It distributes the weight of the structure into the ground. A wood frame floor system is built across this type of foundation. *What feature of this construction gives the T-foundation its name?*

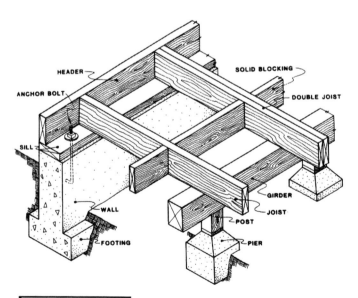

Figure 21-2. This drawing shows the structural principles and elements for the floor framing system within a T-foundation. *What is the major difference between a slab foundation and a T-foundation?*

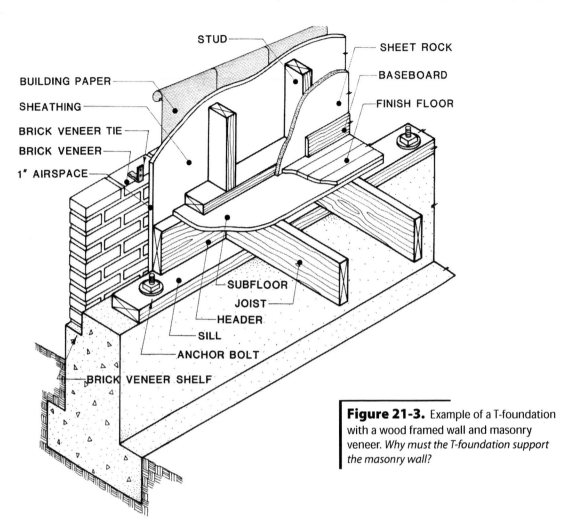

STUD

SHEET ROCK

BUILDING PAPER

BASEBOARD

SHEATHING

FINISH FLOOR

BRICK VENEER TIE

BRICK VENEER

1" AIRSPACE

SUBFLOOR

JOIST

HEADER

SILL

ANCHOR BOLT

BRICK VENEER SHELF

Figure 21-3. Example of a T-foundation with a wood framed wall and masonry veneer. *Why must the T-foundation support the masonry wall?*

If the structure is to have a wood frame wall with a masonry veneer wall, a wider T-foundation with a shelf to support the weight of the masonry wall is required (**Figure 21-3**).

There are specific engineering standards for foundation construction. An example of building code requirements for T-foundations on firm soil for one- and two-story homes is shown **Figure 21-4**.

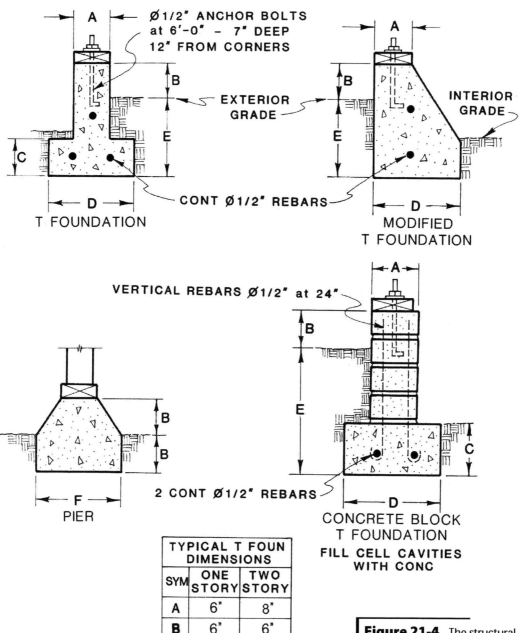

Ø1/2" ANCHOR BOLTS
at 6'-0" – 7" DEEP
12" FROM CORNERS

EXTERIOR
GRADE

INTERIOR
GRADE

CONT Ø1/2" REBARS

T FOUNDATION

**MODIFIED
T FOUNDATION**

VERTICAL REBARS Ø1/2" at 24"

PIER

2 CONT Ø1/2" REBARS

**CONCRETE BLOCK
T FOUNDATION**
FILL CELL CAVITIES
WITH CONC

TYPICAL T FOUN DIMENSIONS		
SYM	ONE STORY	TWO STORY
A	6"	8"
B	6"	6"
C	6"	8"
D	12"	16"
E	12"	18"
F	12"	16"

Figure 21-4. The structural sizes of foundation elements will vary according to the supported weight and the soil conditions. *What is the purpose of the rebars inside the concrete?*

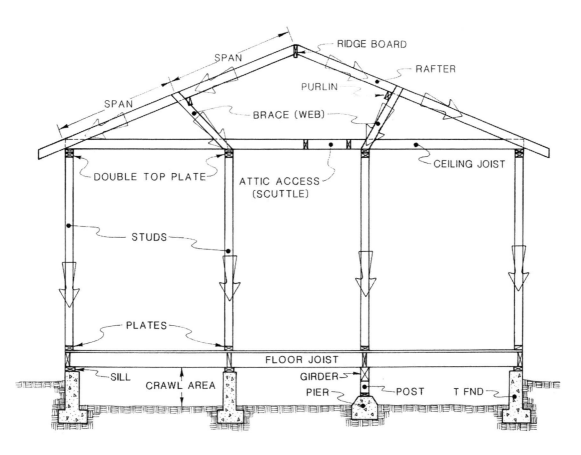

Figure 21-5. The dead load is transmitted from the roof, walls, floor, and foundation into the ground. *What makes up the total load?*

A critical part of foundation design is the area of the *footings* that distributes the weight of the structure into the ground. **Figure 21-5** shows how the weight from the roof, ceiling, walls, and floor system is distributed into the ground. The weight from all the permanent structural parts is called the *dead load*. The weight from free-standing furniture, snow, people, and wind pressure, makes up the *live load*. Added together, the dead load and the live load, makes up the *total load* used to calculate the size of the foundation.

BASEMENTS

In very cold climates, it is critical to have the foundation footings below the frost line. If the ground freezes below the footing, the foundation will be lifted and seriously damaged. If the frost line is deep, it would be a simple operation to excavate the extra soil to accommodate a basement (**Figure 21-6**). A standard concrete slab will form the floor for the basement.

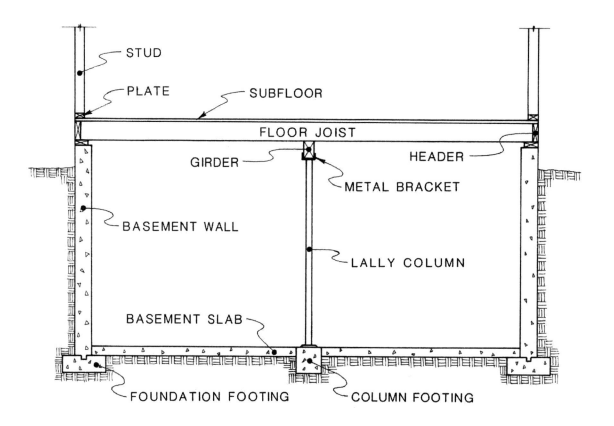

Figure 21-6. An example of a basement foundation system. *What is the purpose of a lally column?*

DEVELOPING T-FOUNDATION PLANS

To draw a T-foundation plan, follow the five-step process.

Step 1. Trace the outside lines of the structure from the floor plan, then draw the line representing the inside of the exterior foundation. Indicate a wall thickness of 6". Add dotted lines indicating a 3" space on either side of the exterior wall. These dotted lines indicate the position of the T-foundation footing. The result of this step is shown in **Figure 21-7A**.

Step 2. Add lines for any additional concrete foundations to be poured. These may be for a garage, porches, patio, walk, etc. Footings for these slab or T-foundations should be indicated. See **Figure 21-7B**.

Step 3. Indicate the positions of girders and piers. **Figure 21-7C** shows a 4" by 6" girder supported by piers. A *girder* can be made of steel or wood. It is the main horizontal support beam for the floor system. *Piers* are support bases of concrete. Treated plates and posts are placed above the piers to support the girder. In Figure 21-7C, piers are placed every four feet along the length of the girder. Placement of piers and use of girders depends on the location of near-by walls and the weight of the structure.

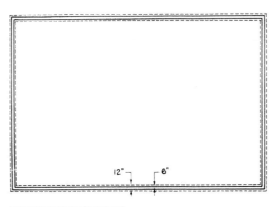

Figure 21-7A. The first step to draw the plan for a T-foundation is to trace the T-foundation's wall and footing from the floor plan. The wall is 6" wide and the footing (hidden lines) is 12" wide. *Why is it easier to trace the walls?*

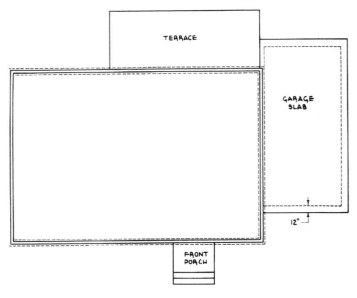

Figure 21-7B. The second step is to indicate supplementary concrete such as terraces, patios, garage slab, porches, and stairs. *What is used to stop the separation of separate concrete pours?*

Step 4. Indicate positions of the floor joists. *Joists* are wooden beams that support the floor of a building. In **Figure 21-7D**, the joists are 2" by 8"s. *Double joists* are used under parallel walls for support. This means that two 2" by 8"s are positioned together so that their center points are 16" OC (on center). Positioning of joists must be accurate. When the home is built, flooring material will be attached to the joists. Under the walls that are perpendicular to the floor joists, solid blocking is applied for added strength.

Step 5. The finished T-foundation plan will have dimensions, notes, and section detail callouts. See **Figure 21-7E**.

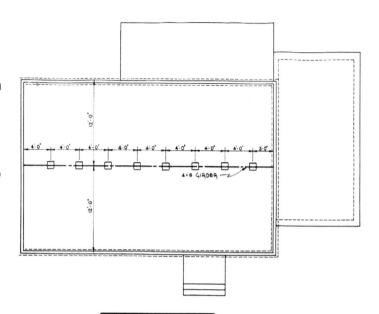

Figure 21-7C. The third step is to indicate the position of the girders and the piers. *What purpose does the girder have within the floor system?*

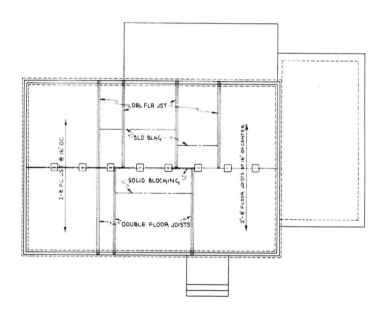

Figure 21-7D. The fourth step is to indicate the direction, size, and spacing of the floor joists. Also indicate the solid blocking and double floor joists under the interior walls. *Why should this part of the T-foundation plan be traced from the floor plan?*

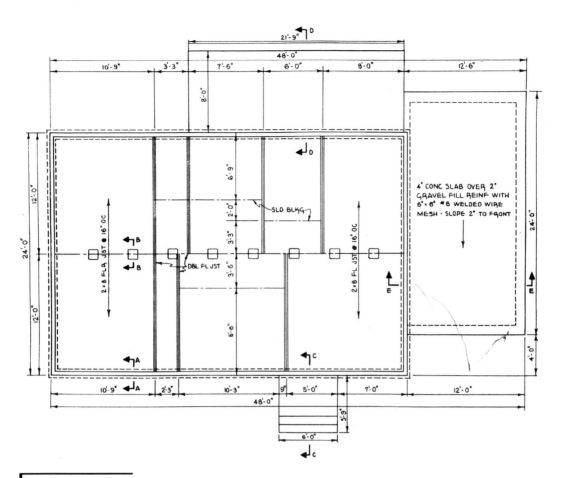

Figure 21-7E. To complete the T-foundation plan, add the dimensions, notations, and section callouts. *What is the purpose of the solid blocking and double floor joists?*

T-FOUNDATION DETAILS

Detail drawings are needed to show construction techniques for each major part of a T-foundation. A number of typical detail drawings are included in **Figures 21-8A through E**.

Figure 21-8A shows a section of the exterior of a T-foundation. This indicates the depth of the footing, the ground line, and the crawl space. The *crawl space* is the area between the ground and the bottom of the floor joists in a T-foundation's floor system. Also detailed is part of the floor system.

Figure 21-8B shows the detail construction of one of the piers and the positions of the girder and floor joists above the pier.

Figure 21-8C is a detail drawing showing how the front porch and the T-foundation are joined. The porch is anchored to the foundation walls with *steel dowels* (rebars).

Figure 21-8D is a detail showing the joining of the T-foundation and the slab for the terrace, if it is required.

Figure 21-8E is a detail showing the garage slab joining the T-foundation of the house.

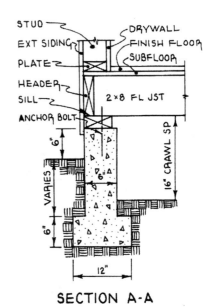

SECTION A-A

Figure 21-8A. An example of a sectional drawing of a T-foundation. *What is the purpose of the crawl space?*

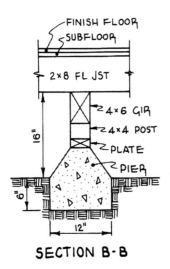

SECTION B-B

Figure 21-8B. An example of a sectional drawing of a pier and girder. *What is the purpose of the plate and post under the girder?*

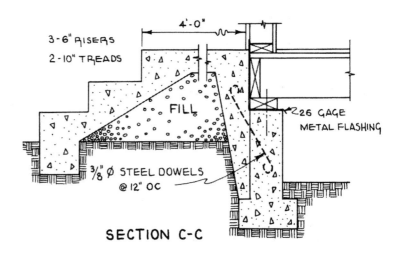

SECTION C-C

Figure 21-8C. An example of a sectional drawing of the front stairs and porch. *What is the function of the steel dowels (rebars)?*

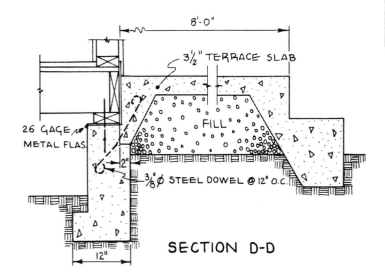

Figure 21-8D. An example of a sectional drawing of the terrace. *What is the purpose of the 26-gage metal flashing?*

SECTION D-D

8'-0"

3½" TERRACE SLAB

FILL

26 GAGE METAL FLAS.

2"

⅜" Ø STEEL DOWEL @ 12" O.C.

12"

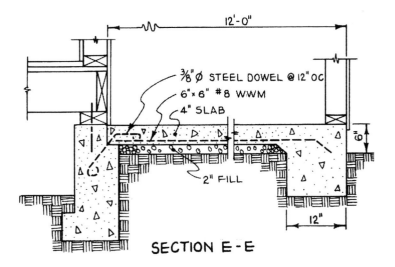

Figure 21-8E. An example of a sectional drawing of the garage slab. *How far above grade is the garage's plate? What must be done to this plate?*

SECTION E-E

12'-0"

⅜" Ø STEEL DOWEL @ 12" OC

6" × 6" #8 WWM

4" SLAB

2" FILL

6"

12"

Note that the drawings for the porch, terrace, and garage are broken in the middle. This is because the drawings show details only. They do not include the full width of the slab that has no new details. It also saves space on the drawing's format. The broken portion of the drawing indicates that the slab is continued through the full width. The dimension lines are drawn to indicate that a portion of the structure is deleted.

There is a third option of a foundation that uses piles. *Piles* are columns of wood, concrete, and/or steel (**Figure 21-9**). They are less than 24" in diameter and driven into the ground to carry a vertical load or to provide lateral support. **Figure 21-10** shows the use of the slab, T, and pile foundations.

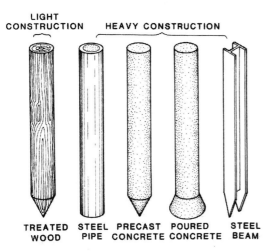

LIGHT CONSTRUCTION | HEAVY CONSTRUCTION

TREATED WOOD | STEEL PIPE | PRECAST CONCRETE | POURED CONCRETE | STEEL BEAM

Figure 21-9. A third option for a foundation system is with piles. *What type of pile would you use for a small vacation house build on a sandy beach?*

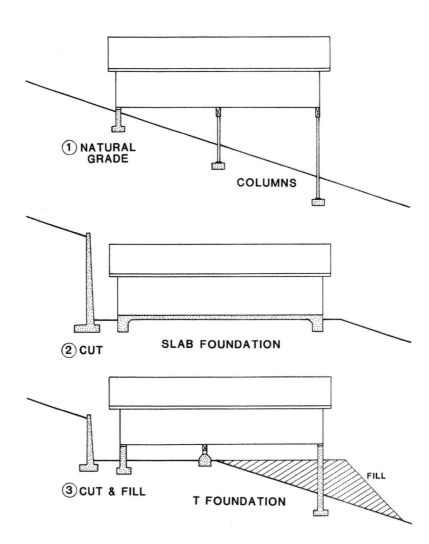

① NATURAL GRADE

COLUMNS

② CUT

SLAB FOUNDATION

③ CUT & FILL

T FOUNDATION

FILL

Figure 21-10. Examples of various site conditions using the three foundation systems. *What is the major advantage of the pile foundation system?*

UNIT 21 ACTIVITIES

VOCABULARY CHECKLIST

1. T-foundation
2. footing
3. dead load
4. live load

5. girder
6. pier
7. joist
8. double floor joists

9. crawl space
10. steel dowel
11. pile

REVIEW QUESTIONS

1. What part of a T-foundation distributes the total load of a structure into the ground?
2. Why are internal supports needed for floor system, and what are they called?
3. Why is a girder needed and what is its function?
4. What are floor joists and where are they located?
5. What is a crawl space and where is it located?
6. What type of structure requires a T and a slab foundation?

YOUR ARCHITECTURAL SCRAPBOOK

1. List the specifications for T-foundations in your area. Get these from the copy of the local building code that you have been using.
2. Sketch a T-foundation and several of the details.
3. With a CAD system, draw a T-foundation with its details for your floor plan. Make a hard copy and place it in your scrapbook.
4. With your CAD system, design a pile foundation for your floor plan and add it to your scrapbook.

CAD ACTIVITIES

After reading Unit 21, refer to Chapter 21 in the *Chief Architect Tutorials* and complete:

- Copy the T-foundation in Figure 21-7E.
- Copy the T-foundation construction details in Figures 21-8A, 21-8B, 21-8C, 21-8D, and 21-8E.
- Design and draw a T-foundation and construction details for one of your floor plans using the building code tables in this unit.

UNIT 22
DRAWING ROOF PLANS

THE ROOF PLAN

The *roof plan* is usually incorporated into the plot plan as shown in **Figure 22-1**. In some situations, however, separate roof plans are necessary. This need occurs when the small scale of the plot plan does not show enough of the roof's details. An example of a completed roof plan that should be drawn to a larger scale for clarity is shown in **Figure 22-2**.

It must be noted that none of the roof's sloping surfaces will appear to be true size in a roof plan.

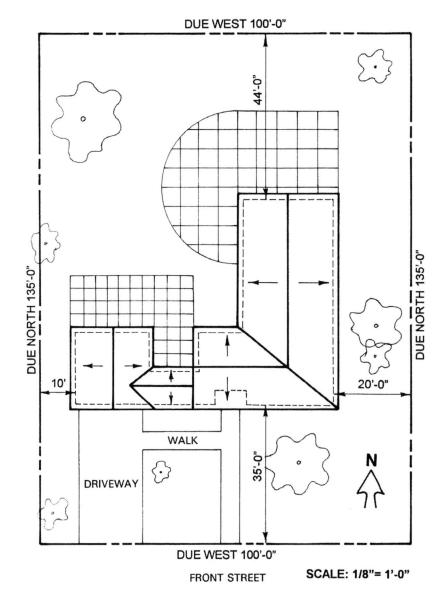

Figure 22-1.
The roof plan is often shown with the plot plan drawing. *Why is the roof plan shown with the plot plan?*

DUE WEST 100'-0"

44'-0"

DUE NORTH 135'-0"

DUE NORTH 135'-0"

10'

20'-0"

WALK

35'-0"

DRIVEWAY

N

DUE WEST 100'-0"

FRONT STREET

SCALE: 1/8"= 1'-0"

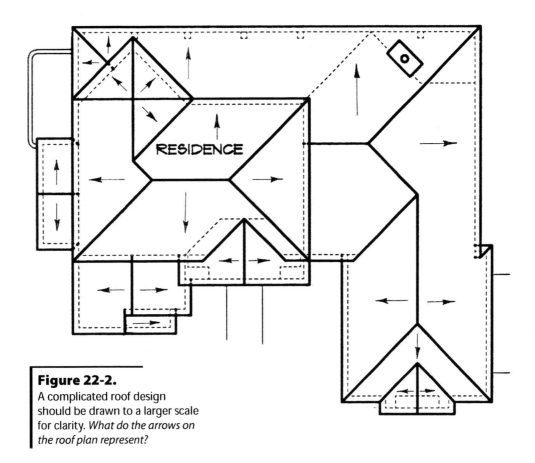

Figure 22-2.
A complicated roof design
should be drawn to a larger scale
for clarity. *What do the arrows on
the roof plan represent?*

DRAWING THE ROOF PLAN

The drawing of a roof plan is a three-step process.

Step 1. If you are drawing the roof plan to the same scale as the floor plan, you should trace the outline of the house from the floor plan. This is accomplished with hidden lines as shown in **Figure 22-3**.

Step 2. Measure the amount of roof overhang from the elevation design, then draw the outline of the roof's overhang. Use a solid line to show the outside edge of the roof. See **Figure 22-4**.

Step 3. Measure the size and location of the ridge boards from the elevation design. The *ridge board* establishes the *ridge line*, the highest point on the roof. Draw these ridge boards on your roof drawing with solid lines as shown in **Figure 22-5**.

Figure 22-3. The first step in drawing the roof plan is to draw the outline of the structure. If drawing the roof plan to the same scale as the structure it may be traced. *Why is important to draw the outline of the structure accurately?*

Figure 22-4. The second step in drawing the roof plan is to accurately draw the overhang with a solid line. *How is the amount of overhang determined?*

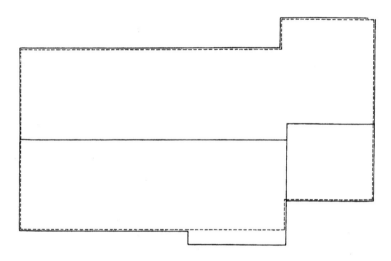

Figure 22-5. The third and final step in developing a roof plan is to draw in the ridge board, chimney, saddle, cupola, and slope lines. *What is a ridge board?*

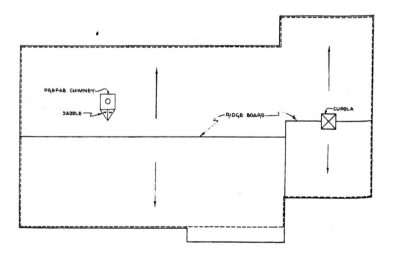

Add the arrows showing the direction of the slope on all roof surfaces. The arrows point in the direction of the downward slope.

Locate and draw the position of the chimney, cupola, or other structures such as dormer windows, and skylights that are above the roof line. A *cupola* is a small structure on a roof to help ventilation in the attic.

Figure 22-6 shows the relationship of the elevations to the roof's design. It is critical that the roof's dimensions on the roof plan are identical to the roof's dimensions on the elevation drawings.

Figure 22-6.
The dimensions of the roof's drawing must be identical on the roof plan and all the exterior elevation drawings. *Will a sloping surface on the roof plan appear true size?*

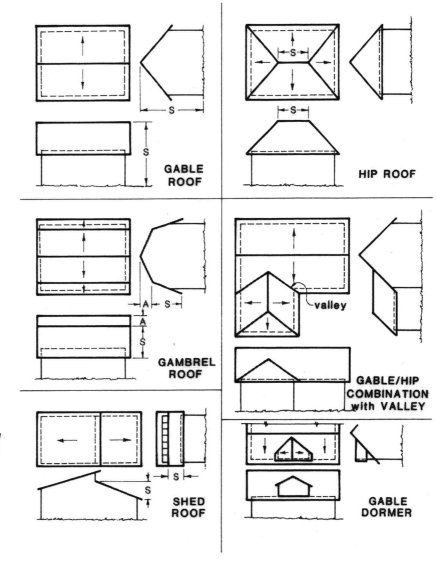

UNIT 22 ACTIVITIES

VOCABULARY CHECKLIST

1. roof plan
2. ridge board
3. ridge line
4. cupola

REVIEW QUESTIONS

1. Which types of drawings will show the roof plan?
2. What structural member is the highest point on the roof line?
3. How is the outline of the house shown on a roof plan?
4. How is the direction of roof slope shown on a roof plan?
5. Why is the elevation design important when drawing the roof plan?

YOUR ARCHITECTURAL SCRAPBOOK

1. Cut out or copy several various types roof plans. Add these to your scrapbook.
2. Sketch a roof plan of your house and place in your scrapbook.
3. With a CAD system, draw several different types of roof designs for your floor plan. Make hard copies and add them to your scrapbook.

CAD ACTIVITIES

After reading Unit 22, refer to Chapter 22 in the *Chief Architect Tutorial*s and complete:

• Bring up your floor plan and add the following roofs - hip, gable, shed, gambrel, and mansard roofs.

UNIT 23
DRAWING FLOOR-FRAMING PLANS

THE FLOOR-FRAMING PLAN

A *floor-framing* plan shows the position and sizes of all the structural members that make up the floor system. Typical floor-framing construction members on a T-foundation are shown in **Figure 23-1**. The structural members making up the floor system are:

Girder - The *girder* is a horizontal beam that supports the central part of the floor system (**Figure 23-2**).

Sill - The *mud sill* is the first member resting on the concrete of the T-foundation. The sill must be treated to repel termites, dry rot, and fungus.

Floor Joist - *Floor joists* are horizontal structural members that support the subfloor.

Header - The *header* or rim joist joins at the ends of the floor joists to enclose the floor system.

Subfloor - The *subfloor* usually consists of 4'x 8' plywood panels. The combined thickness of the subfloor and finish floor is between 1.5" and 2" depending on the building code.

Plate - The *plate* rests on the subfloor and is the base for the wood frame stud walls.

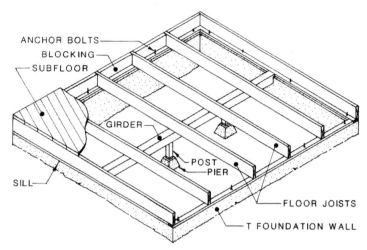

Figure 23-1. An overview of a standard floor system on a T-foundation. This system is called platform or Western framing. *Can this floor system be used with a slab foundation?*

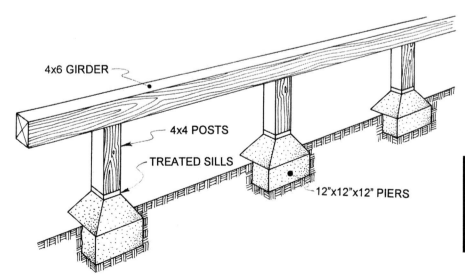

Figure 23-2
The girder or beam is used to reduce the span for the floor joists. *Why is the plate on the pier treated?*

FLOOR SYSTEM SUPPORT

The floor system is supported around its perimeter with a T-foundation. If the floor joists have a long span, a support (girder) or a T-foundation wall should be placed beneath as shown in **Figure 23-3**. *Piers* and *posts* are used to support the girder. Note the pocket support for the end of the girder in the T-foundation wall in **Figure 23-4**. For a two- or three-story structure not having a firm soil condition, a continuous T-foundation should be used to support the floor system. **Figure 23-5** shows the detail drawings.

Figure 23-3.
For the interior support for a floor system, a girder with piers or continuous T-foundation wall may be used. *What is the advantage of a T-foundation wall over a girder and piers?*

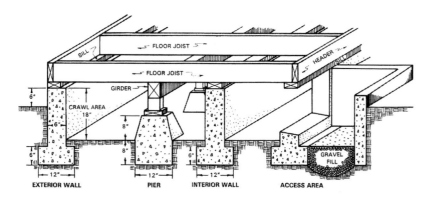

Figure 23-4.
This construction detail shows the girder pocket in the T-foundation wall. *Why must the top of the girder be level with the top of the mudsill?*

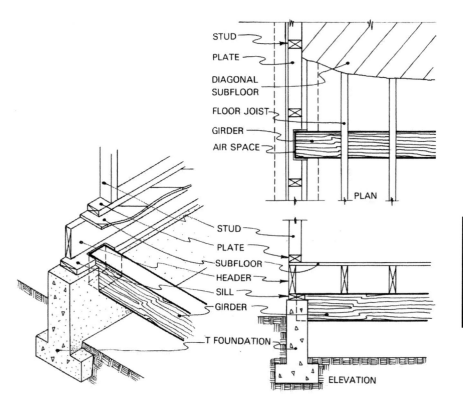

Figure 23-5.
An interior T-foundation provides better support for a floor system than a girder and piers. *Name two situations where a T-foundation internal floor support should be used.*

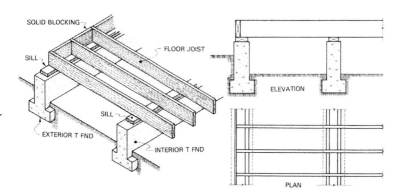

FLOOR JOISTS

Floor joists may rest on top of a girder or be hung off the sides of the girder using metal joist hangers. This will lower the profile of the structure. The floor joist may be in one continuous piece or shorter floor joists can be overlapped on a girder (**Figure 23-6**).

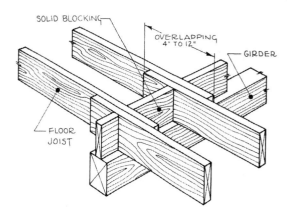

Figure 23-6. The joining of two continuous floor joists must be joined over a girder. *Why are floor joists joined over the girder?*

BEARING WALLS

Interior walls that help support the roof's load are classified as *bearing walls*. Bearing walls that are parallel to the floor joists must have a double floor joist placed directly under the wall (**Figure 23-7**). Bearing walls that are perpendicular to the floor joists must have solid blocking or bridging between the floor joists directly below the wall (**Figure 23-8**). Non-bearing walls do not require the additional framing support.

OPENINGS

Openings in the floor system for stairwells and fireplaces must be framed with double construction members on four sides as shown in **Figure 23-9**. This is also true for the ceiling and roof systems for chimneys, skylights, and dormer windows.

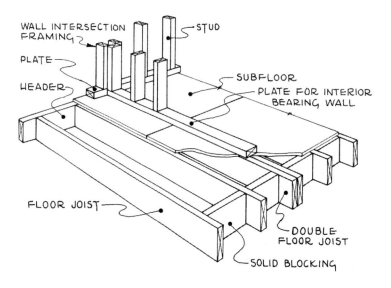

Figure 23-7. Double floor joists must be placed directly under bearing walls that are parallel to the floor joists. *Are double floor joists under a non-bearing wall required?*

WALL INTERSECTION FRAMING

STUD

PLATE

HEADER

SUBFLOOR

PLATE FOR INTERIOR BEARING WALL

FLOOR JOIST

DOUBLE FLOOR JOIST

SOLID BLOCKING

Figure 23-8. *Blocking* or bridging must be placed directly under bearing walls that are perpendicular to the floor joists. *What purpose does the blocking serve?*

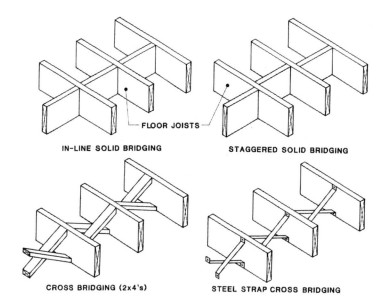

FLOOR JOISTS

IN-LINE SOLID BRIDGING

STAGGERED SOLID BRIDGING

CROSS BRIDGING (2x4's)

STEEL STRAP CROSS BRIDGING

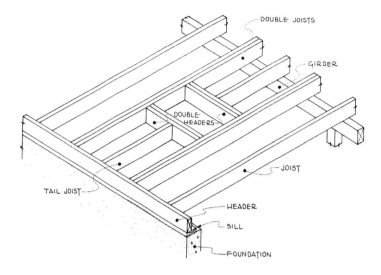

Figure 23-9. An opening in the floor system must be double-framed on all sides. *Is this true for openings in the ceiling and roof?*

STEEL REINFORCEMENTS

Steel *reinforcement bars (rebars)* greatly increase the strength of the T-foundation (**Figure 23-10**). Most building codes require placing rebars in the T-foundation.

FLOOR JOIST ENGINEERING

To calculate the size of floor joists from an engineering table, an understanding of span and spacing must be clear. *Span* is the supported distance of a single structural member. *Spacing* is the distance between similar structural members as shown in **Figure 23-11**. The engineering table used to calculate the joist size and spacing is shown in **Figure 23-12**. This table uses number 2 grade Douglas fir (DF) for construction grade building materials. Number 1 grade is high quality wood and used for interior finishes and trims. Number 3 and 4 grades are less expensive, but are of poor quality and requires more or larger materials for construction because of its lack of strength.

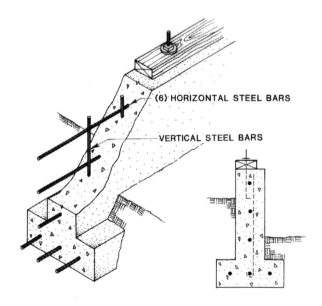

Figure 23-10. Placing steel inside the foundation's concrete greatly increases its strength. *What is the synonym for the steel bars?*

Figure 23-11.
Before reading engineering tables, you must have an understanding of span and spacing. *What is an advantage of having a short span?*

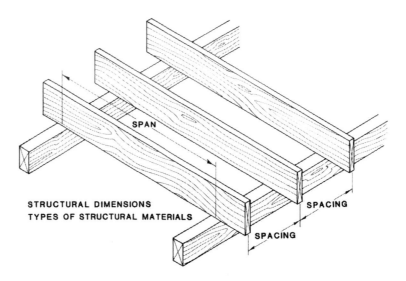

SPAN

STRUCTURAL DIMENSIONS
TYPES OF STRUCTURAL MATERIALS

SPACING

SPACING

FLOOR JOISTS SPANS

JOIST SIZE	JOIST SPACING	JOIST SPAN
2" x 4"	12"	10'-0"
	16"	9'-0"
	24"	7'-0"
2" x 6"	12"	13'-0"
	16"	12'-0"
	24"	10'-0"
2" x 8"	12"	14'-0"
	16"	13'-0"
	24"	11'-0"
2" x 10"	12"	16'-0"
	16"	15'-0"
	24"	12'-0"
2" x 12"	12"	20'-0"
	16"	18'-0"
	24"	15'-0"
2" x 14"	12"	23'-0"
	16"	21'-0"
	24"	17'-0"

Figure 23-12. An example of an engineering table for floor joists. *What size floor joist must be used for a 16'-0" span? What is the spacing?*

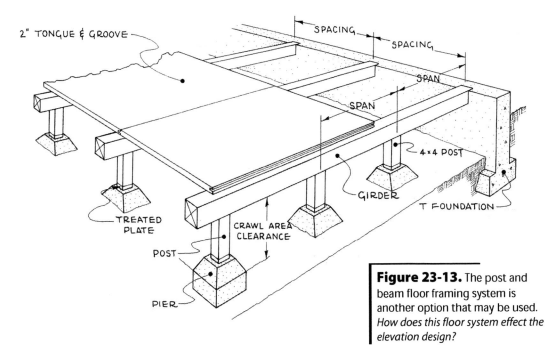

Figure 23-13. The post and beam floor framing system is another option that may be used. *How does this floor system effect the elevation design?*

POST AND BEAM FLOOR SYSTEM

Another type of floor system for a T-foundation is the post and beam floor system. Girders are placed on four foot centers and 4' x 8' x 1" *tongue and groove* (T&G) plywood and are fastened to the girders. (**Figure 23-13**). This floor system eliminates the floor joists, is faster to build, and gives the structure a lower profile.

STAIRS

When designing multilevel floors, it is important to understand the principles of stair design (**Figure 23-14**). Stairs may be designed to fit most conditions in multilevel structures. **Figure 23-15** shows the length of the run for various pitch and stair sizes for a standard eight-foot ceiling height. The floor system for the second floor is usually 12 inches thick making the total height 108".

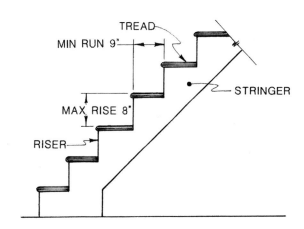

Figure 23-14. Parts of a stair system. *Why must the tread not be less than 9"?*

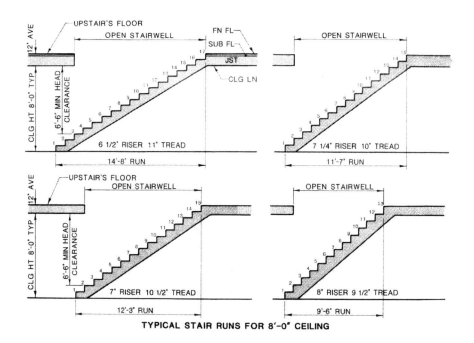

Figure 23-15.
Various stair designs.
What is the advantage of a flight of stairs with a low pitch? What is the disadvantage?

TYPICAL STAIR RUNS FOR 8'-0" CEILING

DRAWING THE FLOOR FRAMING PLAN

The procedure to drawing a floor-framing plan as shown in **Figure 23-16** is shown below.

1. Trace the outline of the T-foundation from the floor plan.
2. Draw the positions of the girders and label their size.
3. Draw the required piers under a 4" x 6" girder. A girder near a bearing should have spacing of 3'-6". If no bearing wall is nearby, the spacing should be 5'-0". The spacing will change with the soil conditions and the weight of the structure.
4. Measure the span for the floor joists and obtain the size and spacing from the engineering table in **Figure 23-12**. Draw a single line representation of the floor joists.
5. Add dimensions and the size and spacing of the floor joists.
6. Draw construction details that will help the builders with the construction (**Figures 23-17** and **18**).

Often it is necessary to draw the subfloor panel system to help the contractor calculate the number of 4' x 8'x 1" T & G plywood panels required and with the construction for the floor system (**Figure 23-19**).

Figure 23-16.
When drawing a floor-framing plan, trace the exterior T-foundation from the floor plan. *List three reasons why having the floor plan drawing under the vellum paper of the floor-framing drawing is advantageous?*

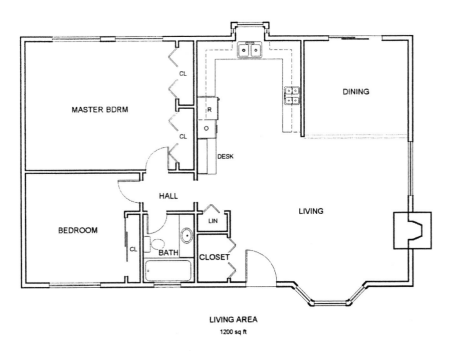

MASTER BDRM

CL

CL

DESK

R

DINING

HALL

BEDROOM

CL

BATH

LIN

CLOSET

LIVING

LIVING AREA
1200 sq ft

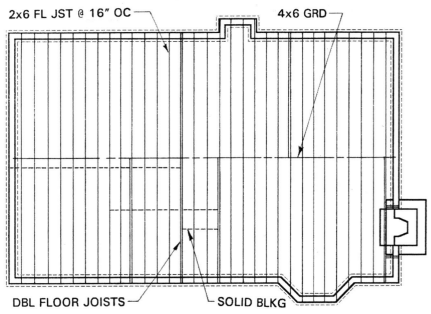

2x6 FL JST @ 16" OC

4x6 GRD

DBL FLOOR JOISTS

SOLID BLKG

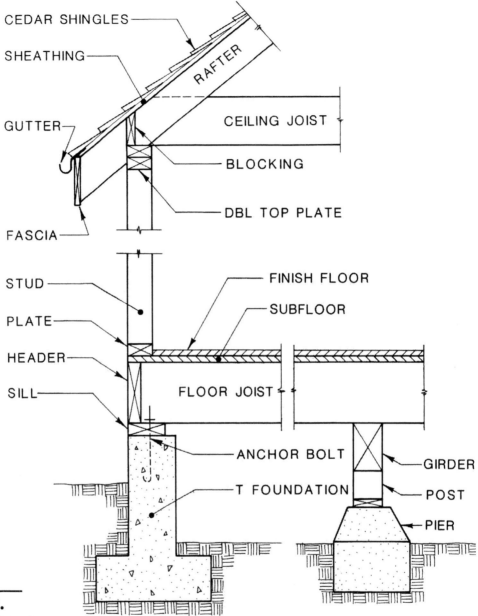

CEDAR SHINGLES

SHEATHING

RAFTER

GUTTER

CEILING JOIST

BLOCKING

DBL TOP PLATE

FASCIA

STUD

FINISH FLOOR

PLATE

SUBFLOOR

HEADER

SILL

FLOOR JOIST

ANCHOR BOLT

GIRDER

T FOUNDATION

POST

PIER

Figure 23-17.
A section detail through the foundation, wall, and roof. *What are the advantages of construction details?*

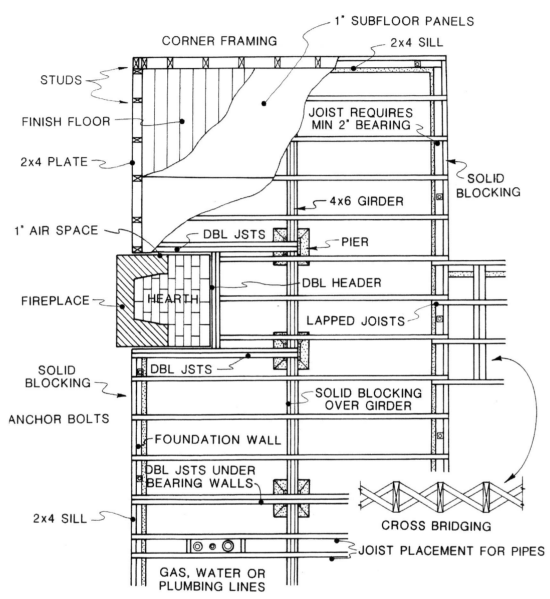

Figure 23-18. This is a double-line floor framing detail. *What are the advantages and disadvantages of a double-line detail drawing and a single-line detail drawing?*

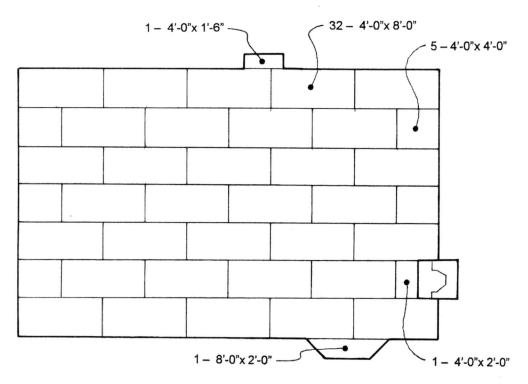

1 – 4'-0"x 1'-6"   32 – 4'-0"x 8'-0"   5 – 4'-0"x 4'-0"

1 – 8'-0"x 2'-0"   1 – 4'-0"x 2'-0"

SUBFLOOR PANEL SYSTEM

Figure 23-19. An example of a subfloor panel floor system. *What is the modular size of plywood construction panels?*

UNIT 23 ACTIVITIES

VOCABULARY CHECKLIST

1. girder
2. mud sill
3. floor joist
4. header

5. subfloor
6. pier
7. post
8. bearing wall

9. blocking
10. span
11. spacing

REVIEW QUESTIONS

1. What is the first structural wood member resting on the T-foundation?
2. Define the span of a structural member.
3. Define the spacing of structural members.
4. What does the girder support?
5. What supports the girder?
6. What is the purpose of treated wood?

YOUR ARCHITECTURAL SCRAPBOOK

1. Make a freehand sketch of a floor framing system for your floor plan and add it to your scrapbook.
2. With a CAD system, draw the floor-framing system and add it to your scrapbook.
3. With a CAD system, draw the subfloor plan for your floor plan and add it to your scrapbook.

CAD ACTIVITIES

After reading Unit 23, refer to Chapter 23 in the *Chief Architect Tutorials* and complete:

- Draw the floor framing plan for one of your plans using the building code table in Figure 23-12.
- Draw a subfloor panel system plan for your floor plan.
- Draw a sectional detail of your floor system (refer to Figure 23-17).

UNIT 24
DRAWING WALL-FRAMING PLANS

FRAMING MEMBERS

Wall-framing drawings show the elevation of exterior and interior walls. The structural wall members are shown with siding materials removed. Exterior wall-framing drawings are prepared and identified with a compass orientation. The interior wall-framing must be identified by room name and with a compass orientation. Before you begin drafting wall-framing drawings, you should be familiar with the names of the wall-framing members shown in **Figure 24-1**. A definition of the terms follows:

Studs are the vertical members framing the wall on 16" centers. A standard 2" x 4" stud for an 8'-0" ceiling height is 92 1/2" in length (**Figure 24-2**). The finished stud's dimensions after the surfacing operation are 1 1/2" x 3 1/2".

Corner framing and *wall intersection framing* consists of three studs and spacer blocks (**Figure 24-3**).

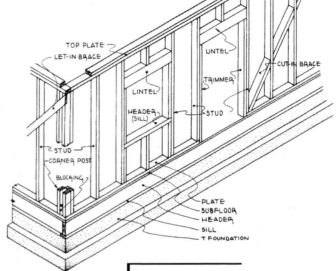

Figure 24-1. A general overview of the wall-framing members. *What is the top structural member for window and door openings?*

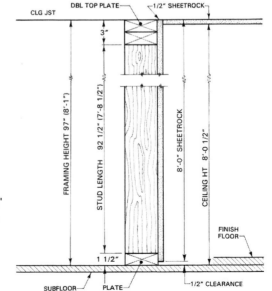

Figure 24-2. The stud length of 92 1/2" is used for a standard 8' - 0" ceiling height. *Why are wall studs less than eight feet?*

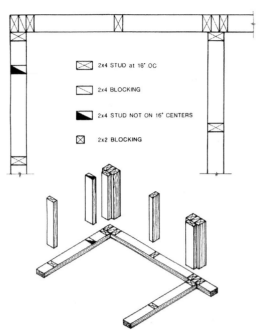

Figure 24-3. Wall-framing for corners and intersecting walls. *How many studs are required for the framing of intersecting walls? What is the purpose of the spacer blocking?*

2x4 STUD at 16" OC

2x4 BLOCKING

2x4 STUD NOT ON 16" CENTERS

2x2 BLOCKING

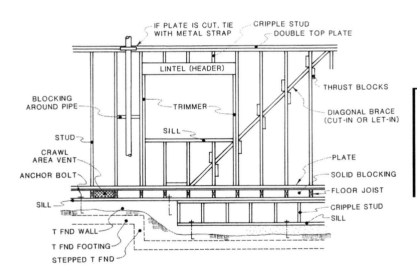

IF PLATE IS CUT, TIE WITH METAL STRAP

CRIPPLE STUD

DOUBLE TOP PLATE

LINTEL (HEADER)

THRUST BLOCKS

BLOCKING AROUND PIPE

TRIMMER

DIAGONAL BRACE (CUT-IN OR LET-IN)

SILL

STUD

CRAWL AREA VENT

PLATE

SOLID BLOCKING

ANCHOR BOLT

FLOOR JOIST

SILL

CRIPPLE STUD

SILL

T FND WALL

T FND FOOTING

STEPPED T FND

Figure 24-4. This is a partial wall-framing plan with a stepped T-foundation. Note the cripple wall to increase the height of the T-foundation's wall. Two trimmer studs support the window's lintel. *Why are cripple studs placed above the lintel?*

A *lintel* or *header* is a horizontal brace over a window or door opening (**Figure 24-4**). The larger the span of the opening, the larger the lintel must be. See the engineering table for lintel spans in **Figure 24-5**.

A *window sill* is a horizontal brace at the bottom of the window's framing opening. See **Figure 24-4**.

The *bottom plate* is the bottom part of the wall framing. It is placed directly over the subfloor. **Figure 24-6** shows the plate and the alignment and coding of the studs.

LINTEL SPANS

Supporting roof and ceiling only		Supporting floor, roof and ceiling only	
SIZE	SPAN	SIZE	SPAN
4x4	3'-6"	4x4	3'-0"
4x6	5'-0"	4x6	4'-0"
4x8	6'-0"	4x8	5'-0"
4x10	7'-0"	4x10	6'-6"
4x12	8'-6"	4x12	8'-0"
4x14	9'-6"	4x14	10'-0"
4X16	10'-0"	4x16	12'-0"

Figure 24-5. An engineering table for calculating lintels. *What size lintel should be used for an opening width of 6' - 0" for a one-story house? What size lintel should be used for an opening width of 4' -0" for the first floor of a two-story house?*

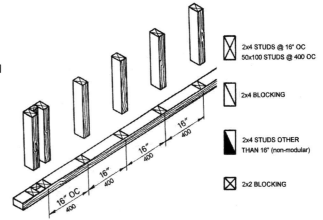

Figure 24-6. An example of a wall plate and the stud's coding. *What is the meaning of 400?*

Cut-in braces and *let-in braces* are diagonal braces that strengthen the wall from lateral forces from winds and earthquakes (**Figure 24-7**).

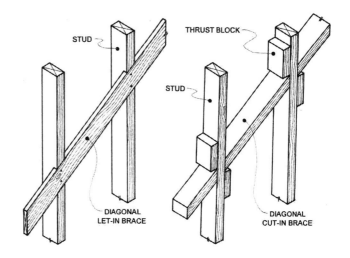

Figure 24-7. Diagonal let-in and cut-in bracing increase the lateral support. *What natural forces apply lateral pressures?*

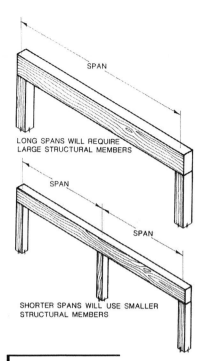

SPAN

LONG SPANS WILL REQUIRE
LARGE STRUCTURAL MEMBERS

SPAN

SPAN

SHORTER SPANS WILL USE SMALLER
STRUCTURAL MEMBERS

Figure 24-8. Reducing the span of a structural member. *What is the purpose of reducing the span?*

Trimmer studs are the structural studs that are placed at the inside of door and window openings. Trimmers support the lintel. See **Figure 24-1**.

A *top plate* consists of two 2 x 4s placed at the top of the studs. The roof rafters rest on the top plate. See **Figure 24-1**.

STRUCTURAL ENGINEERING

The sizes and spacing of structural members are engineered to safely span a specific distance. The greater the span (distance), the larger the structural members must be, and/or spaced closer together. If the size of the structural member is too large, it may be reduced by reducing the distance of the span with additional vertical supports (**Figure 24-8**).

Often in a set of working drawings, a full section of the structure, through the foundation, wall, and roof framing are prepared (**Figure 24-9**). These sectional drawings are very helpful for the construction crew.

Figure 24-9.
A full sectional drawing through the complete structure is a great help to the builders. *What is the purpose of the thrust blocks?*

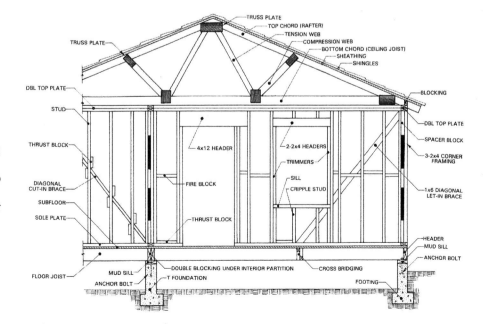

DEVELOPING WALL-FRAMING DRAWINGS

Wall-framing drawings are developed with a six-step process.

Step 1. Draw light horizontal lines representing the top and bottom plates and the standard height of 6' - 9" for the tops of windows and doors. Use the height of the ceiling height in your elevations as your guide for the distance between plates. This step is shown in **Figure 24-10**.

Figure 24-10. The first step to draw a wall-framing plan is to draw the horizontal line heights of the structural members. *Why is it a good idea to draw the wall-framing plan to the same scale as the exterior elevations and floor plan?*

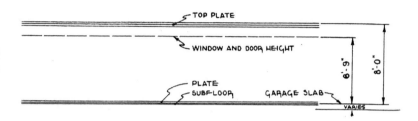

Step 2. Place the floor plan or the elevation drawing above the wall-framing drawing. Project down the major structural intersections of the floor plan. This procedure is illustrated in **Figure 24-11**.

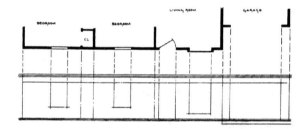

Figure 24-11. From the floor plan, project down walls and openings. *What is another option if you do not project from the floor plan?*

Step 3. Add trimmers and lintels to window and door openings. See **Figure 24-12**.

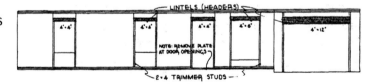

Figure 24-12. Add the trimmers and lintels. *What function does the trimmer perform?*

Step 4. Add studs (*king studs*) adjacent to the trimmers, then add the *window sills*. See **Figure 24-13.** The rough-framed opening for windows and doors should be slightly larger than the actual windows and doors.

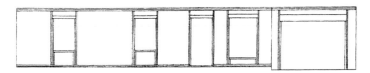

Figure 24-13. Add the king studs and window sills. *What is the standard height of windows and doors?*

Step 5. Draw in the corner posts and interior wall intersection posts, as shown in **Figure 24-14.**

Figure 24-14. Add the corner and wall intersection framing. *How many studs are used for a corner framing?*

Step 6. Add studs and braces, as shown in **Figure 24-15.**

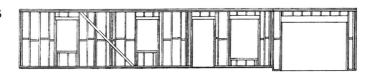

Figure 24-15. Add all the studs and cripple studs at 16" OC (on center). *Why is 16" a modular dimension?*

Complete the wall-framing elevation by darkening in all lines. An example of a wall-framing drawing projected from an exterior elevation is shown in **Figure 24-16**. Note that projecting from the exterior elevation or floor plan, the wall-framing plan and a stud-layout plan can be drawn.

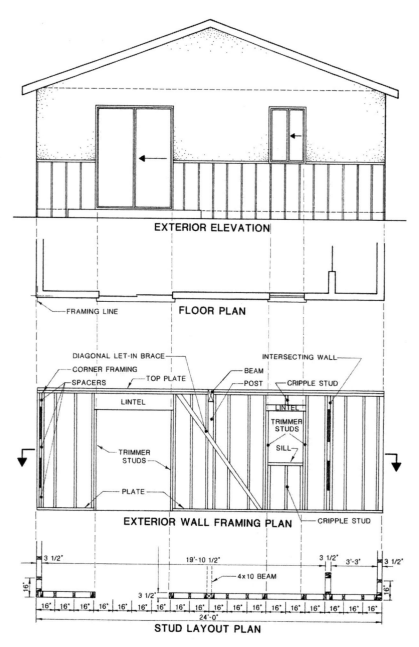

Figure 24-16. This is an example of a finished wall-framing plan and a stud-layout plan projected from an exterior elevation and a floor plan. *What is the relationship between the floor plan, exterior elevation, wall-framing plan, and the stud-layout plan?*

Detail drawings for stucco and brick exterior walls are shown in **Figure 24-17** and **Figure 24-18**.

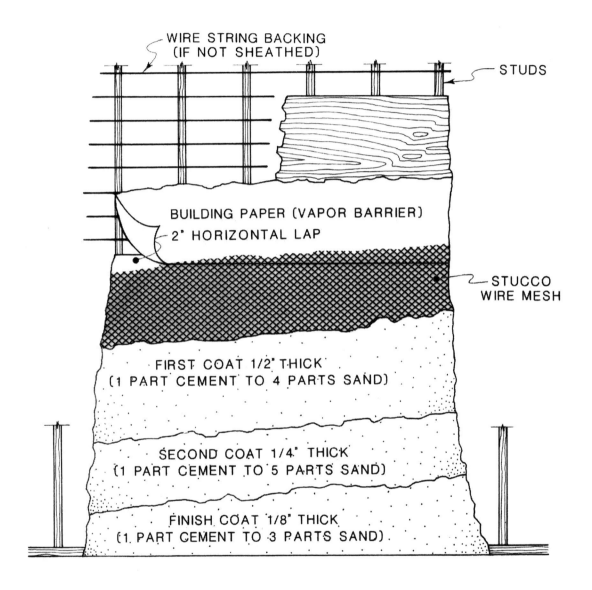

WIRE STRING BACKING
(IF NOT SHEATHED)

STUDS

BUILDING PAPER (VAPOR BARRIER)

2" HORIZONTAL LAP

STUCCO
WIRE MESH

FIRST COAT 1/2" THICK
(1 PART CEMENT TO 4 PARTS SAND)

SECOND COAT 1/4" THICK
(1 PART CEMENT TO 5 PARTS SAND)

FINISH COAT 1/8" THICK
(1 PART CEMENT TO 3 PARTS SAND)

Figure 24-17. A detail-drawing for a stucco wall. *Why should specific instructions be given in a detail-drawing?*

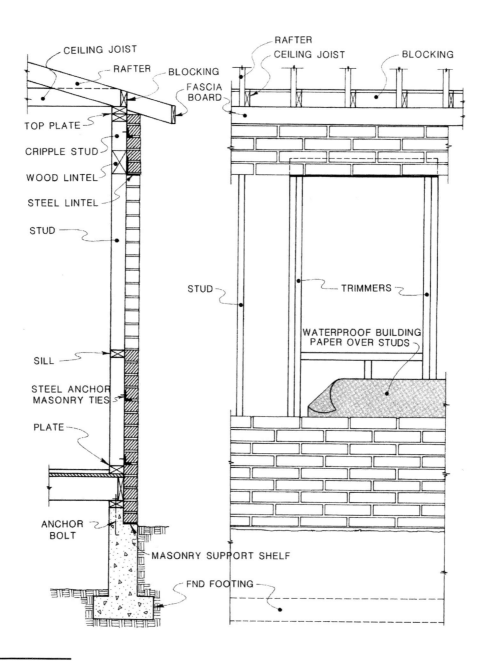

Figure 24-18. Sectional and elevation detail-drawings for a brick veneer wall. *How is the brick veneer wall supported?*

UNIT 24 ACTIVITIES

VOCABULARY CHECKLIST

1. wall-framing drawings
2. stud
3. lintel
4. header
5. window sill
6. bottom plate
7. let-in brace
8. cut-in brace
9. trimmer stud
10. top plate
11. king stud

REVIEW QUESTIONS

1. How does a wall-framing drawing differ from an elevation drawing?
2. What are the main vertical framing supports for a wall?
3. What construction member supports the lintel?
4. What is the normal spacing of studs?
5. What is the highest construction member for a framed wall?
6. What construction member frames in the tops of the windows and doors openings?

YOUR ARCHITECTURAL SCRAPBOOK

1. List the construction members in a framed wall for your scrapbook
2. Using a CAD system, draw a wall-framing elevation from your floor plan. Identify the members with notations. Make a hard copy and place in your scrapbook.

CAD ACTIVITIES

After reading Unit 24, refer to Chapter 24 in the *Chief Architect Tutorials* and complete:

- Copy the wall framing plan in Figure 24-16.
- Draw the front elevation wall framing plan from one of your floor plans (refer to Figure 24-5 for the building code table for the lintels).

UNIT 25
DRAWING ROOF-FRAMING PLANS

THE ROOF PLAN

The style of the roof is usually determined when designing the exterior elevations (see Unit 9 for the various architectural styles of roofs). The required information before drawing the roof- framing plan is: the roof style, the pitch, and the overhang. The roof-framing plan must ensure that the roof's design is structurally sound and safe from snow loads and lateral forces from winds and earthquakes.

The basic parts of a roof are shown in **Figure 25-1**. The two roof styles for most residential designs are the *gable roof* (**Figure 25-2**) and the *hip roof* (**Figure 25-3**). The roof-framing drawings in **Figures 25-2** and **25-3** are single-line representations of the structural members. It is much faster to draw structural members with a single line rather than double lines for the structural members as shown in **Figure 25-4**.

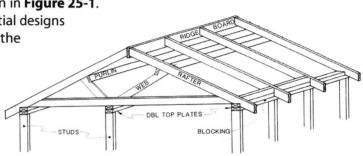

Figure 25-1. The basic parts of a roof.
What is the purpose of a purlin?

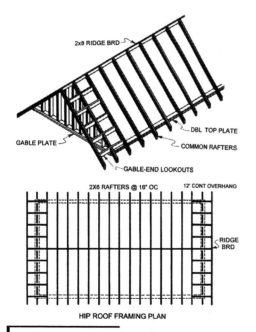

Figure 25-2. The gable roof for a rectangular plan will have two sloped surfaces. *What structural member is used to extend the overhang on the gable end?*

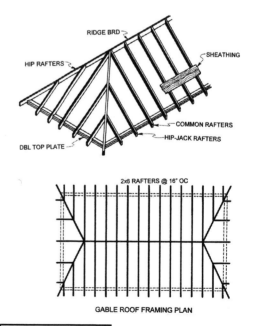

Figure 25-3. The hip roof for a rectangular plan will have four sloped surfaces. *What is the difference between a common rafter and a hip-jack rafter?*

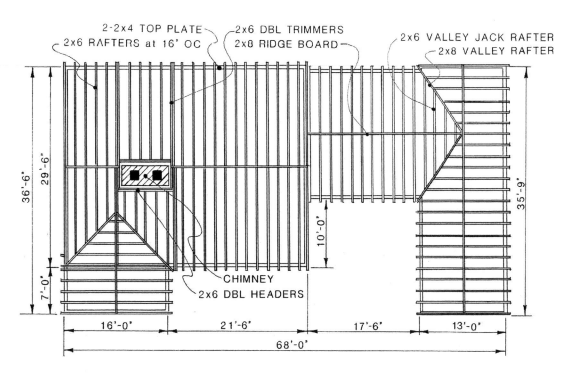

Figure 25-4. An example of a double line roof-framing plan for a gable house. *Why are the rafters doubled around the chimney?*

A roof design may incorporate more than one style for its design. The L-shaped roof in **Figure 25-5** uses the hip and gable roof for its design. Note the double framing around the opening for the chimney and the *collar beams* used to strengthen the rafter tie-in.

On a roof-framing plan, the sloping structural members are not shown as true size. Sometimes, for clarity, it is necessary to draw the roof-framing elevations as shown in **Figure 25-6**. The end-gable view is the only drawing to show the true size of the *rafters*. Note that each drawing is in-line with each other so the views can be projected.

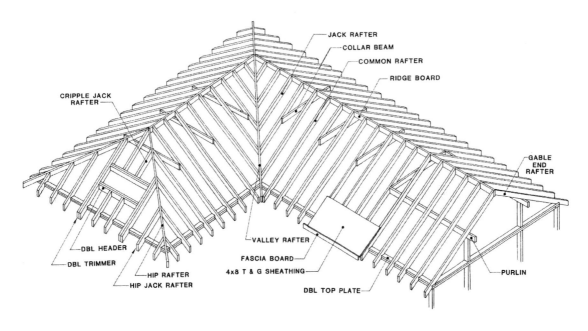

JACK RAFTER

COLLAR BEAM

COMMON RAFTER

RIDGE BOARD

CRIPPLE JACK
RAFTER

GABLE
END
RAFTER

DBL HEADER

DBL TRIMMER

HIP RAFTER

HIP JACK RAFTER

VALLEY RAFTER

FASCIA BOARD

4x8 T & G SHEATHING

DBL TOP PLATE

PURLIN

Figure 25-5.
Note the valley and the additional roof framing stiffeners in this L-shaped roof plan. *What two roof styles are incorporated into this roof design?*

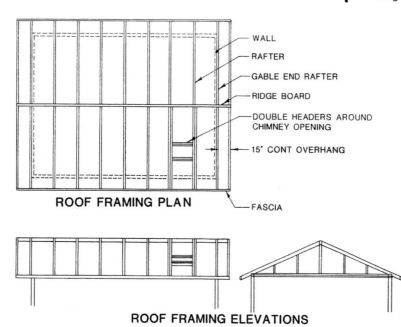

WALL

RAFTER

GABLE END RAFTER

RIDGE BOARD

DOUBLE HEADERS AROUND
CHIMNEY OPENING

15' CONT OVERHANG

ROOF FRAMING PLAN

FASCIA

ROOF FRAMING ELEVATIONS

Figure 25-6.
An example of a roof-framing plan and the elevation drawings of the roof framing. *In which view are the rafters shown as true size?*

ROOF CONSTRUCTION DETAILS

Because of the large size of the roof-framing plans, special construction details cannot be clearly shown. Therefore, sectional details drawn at a larger scale are provided. The scales usually selected are 1/2" to 1" = 1' - 0".

EAVE DETAILS

There are many different architectural designs for *eave details*. Two typical eave details are shown in **Figure 25-7**. A highly-detailed pictorial drawing, showing all the members that constitute an eave detail is shown in **Figure 25-8**.

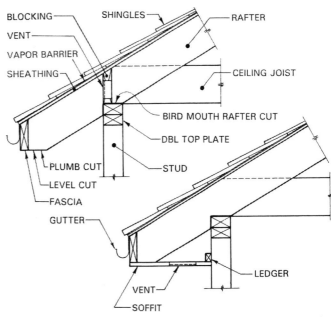

Figure 25-7. Enlarging the drawing scale for the eave detail makes it easier to add all the constructions required for the builders. *What special type of cut is made in the rafters so it can rest firmly on the double top plate?*

Figure 25-8. Sometimes a construction detail is drawn with a pictorial. *What is the advantage of a pictorial over a two-dimensional drawing?*

CHIMNEY ROOF FRAMING DETAIL

A chimney's framed opening through the roof is shown in **Figure 25-9.** To double frame the opening, the rafters are doubled on the sides and double headers are placed on the other sides. The same process is framed through the ceiling system with double ceiling joists, and through the floor system with double floor joists with *double headers.*

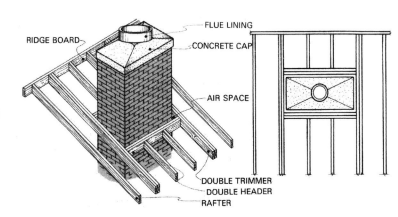

Figure 25-9. Framed openings through the roof, ceiling, and floor systems must be double framed. *What is the purpose of the air space between the chimney's bricks and the wood framing?*

DORMER WINDOW DETAIL

If an attic is converted into a livable space, *dormer windows* may be added to allow more floor space and head clearance. The opening in the roof for the dormer window is the same as for the chimney. This requires a double rafter on the sides, and double headers for the other sides (**Figure 25-10**).

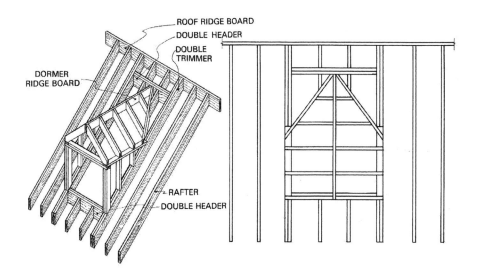

Figure 25-10. In order to gain more floor space and headroom in an attic room, dormer windows may be installed. The dormer window also adds a distinctive styling to the exterior design. *How is the opening in the roof framed for a dormer window?*

SKYLIGHT DETAILS

To allow more light into the home, *skylights* may be installed into the roof. **Figure 25-11** shows a basic fixed-skylight detail. The skylight in **Figure 25-12** is a more advanced model, therefore requiring more detailed information in the its detail drawing. By opening the width of the skylight's well, more sunlight will enter into the room.

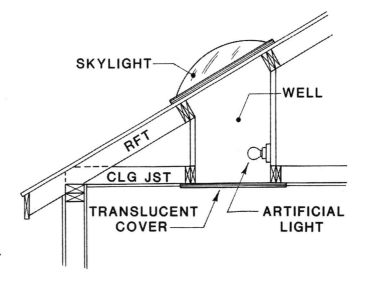

Figure 25-11. An example of a construction detail for a basic design of a fixed skylight. *What is the purpose of the light bulb in the skylight's well?*

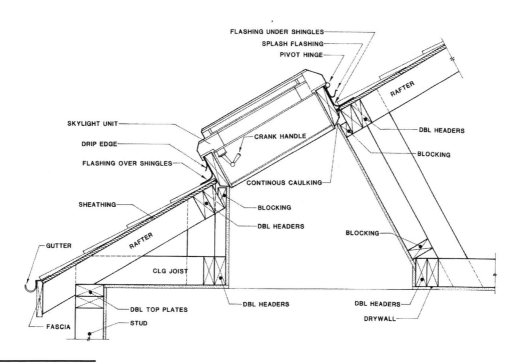

Figure 25-12. An example of a complex opening skylight construction detail. *What is the advantage of a wide opening in the skylight's well?*

ROOF SHEATHING PLAN

The *sheathing* cover on a roof is usually 4' x 8' x 1/2" plywood. A roof-sheathing plan will help to speed up the work and assist with the ordering of the panels (**Figure 25-13**).

The overall dimensions of the roof and the floor plan were designed with a four-foot module. This means that there will be no waste of 4 x 8 panels being applied to the roof's sheathing and subfloor.

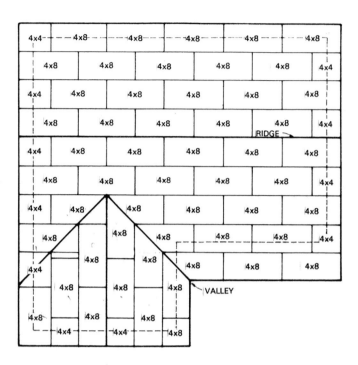

Figure 25-13. A roof panel detail drawing will help with the construction of the roof. *How does the roof sheathing help with the ordering of the 4' x 8' x 1/2" plywood panels?*

ENGINEERING TABLES

Most of the engineering data required for basic residential design may be acquired in engineering tables obtained from your local building department. The tables in **Figure 25-14** and **Figure 25-15** are calculated for #2 DF (Douglas fir). To read the tables, check the floor plan for the span of the structural member and select the size and spacing. If the span is greater than what the tables have, then an architect or structural engineer must calculate the sizes and spacing for the structural members.

CEILING JOIST SPANS

SIZE	JOIST SPACING	SPAN
2" x 4"	12"	10'-0"
	16"	9'-0"
	24"	8'-0"
2" x 6"	12"	16'-0"
	16"	14'-6"
	24"	12'-6"
2" x 8"	12"	21'-6"
	16"	19'-6'
	24"	17'-0"

Figure 25-14. The engineering table for the ceiling joists spans goes up to 21' - 6". *How is the size of a ceiling joist with a span of 21'-6" obtained? What is the spacing?*

RESIDENTIAL RAFTER SPANS

SIZE	RAFTER SPACING	LESS THAN 4:12 PITCH	MORE THAN 4:12 PITCH
2" x 4"	12"	9'-0"	10'-0"
	16"	8'-0"	8'-6"
	24"	6'-6"	7'-0"
	32"	5'-6"	6'-0"
2" x 6"	12"	14'-0"	16'-0"
	16"	12'-6"	13'-6"
	24"	10'-6"	11'-0"
	32"	9'-0"	9'-6"
2" x 8"	12"	19'-0"	21'-6"
	16"	17'-0"	18'-6"
	24"	13'-6"	15'-0"
	32"	11'-6"	13'-0"
2" x 10"	12"	23'-0"	25'-0"
	16"	21'-0"	22'-6"
	24"	17'-6"	19'-0"
	32"	15'-0"	16'-6"
2" x 12"	12"	27'-0"	29'-0"
	16"	25'-0"	27'-0"
	24"	21'-0"	23'-6"
	32"	19'-0"	21'-6"

Figure 25-15.
The engineering table for residential roof rafters spans goes up to 29' - 0". *Why is a low pitched roof designed structurally stronger than a high pitched roof?*

DRAWING THE ROOF-FRAMING PLAN

When you are ready to draw the roof-framing plan, trace the outline, ridges, valleys, and adjacent surface edges from the roof plan, then calculate and draw the rafter sizes and spacing. Draw the rafters with a single or double line and add the dimensions and notations. **Figure 25-16** shows a finished roof-framing plan after it was traced from the roof plan.

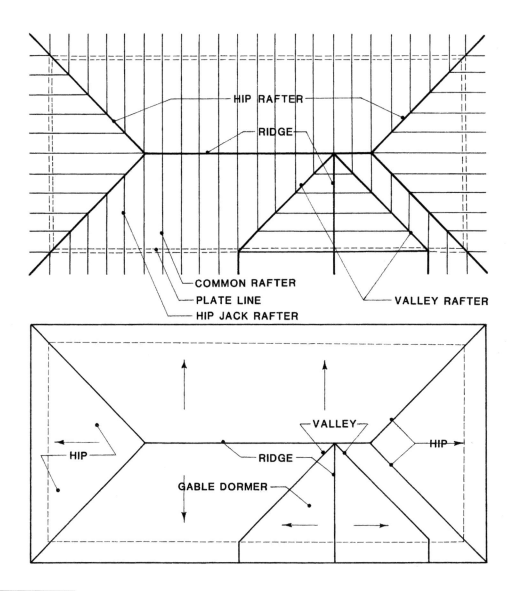

Figure 25-16. A roof-framing plan may be quickly drawn if the details of the roof plan are first traced. *What is the intersection of the hip roof and the gable roof called?*

UNIT 25 ACTIVITIES

VOCABULARY CHECKLIST

1. gable roof
2. hip roof
3. collar beams

4. rafters
5 eave details
6. double headers

7. dormer window
8. skylight
9. sheathing cover

REVIEW QUESTIONS

1. What is the difference between a roof plan and a roof-framing plan?
2. What do the dotted lines on a roof-framing plan represent?
3. How is the spacing of rafters shown on a roof-framing plan?
4. What type of framing member permits a large overhang on the gable side?
5. Are the rafters in roof-framing plans drawn to actual size?

YOUR ARCHITECTURAL SCRAPBOOK

1. Make a list for all the structural members in a roof-framing plan and add it to your scrapbook.
2. Using a CAD system, draw the roof-framing plans for your floor plan of a gable, hip, and shed roof. Make hard copies and add them to your scrapbook.

CAD ACTIVITIES

After reading Unit 25, refer to Chapter 25 in the *Chief Architect Tutorials* and complete:

• Copy the eave details in Figure 25-7.
• Draw a roof sheathing plan for the roof of one of your plans (refer to Figure 25-13).
• Draw a roof framing plan for one of your floor plans (refer to Figure 25-15 for the building code table for the spans and spacing of the rafters).

UNIT 26
DRAWING ELECTRICAL PLANS

THE RESIDENTIAL ELECTRICAL PLAN

The electrical plan for a home consists of the placement of electrical symbols drawn on the floor plan. Several of the most common symbols are shown in **Figure 26-1**. The electrical circuits have switches that control the flow of electricity (**Figure 26-2**). These symbols guide the installation of all the electrical items. Additional electrical symbols are described in Unit 13.

When drawing the electrical symbols, care must be taken not to draw them too large or too small. **Figure 26-3** shows examples for 1/4" and 1/8" scale floor plans with the proportional sizes for electrical symbols.

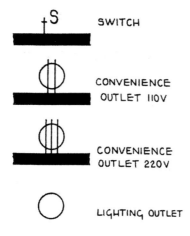

Figure 26-1. Commonly-used electrical symbols on a floor plan drawing. *Must the electric symbol look like the actual electrical item?*

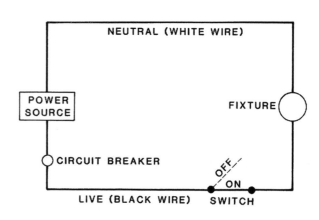

Figure 26-2. An electric circuit must be composed of a: power source, wired circuit, fixture, switch, and circuit breaker. *How does the switching mechanism work?*

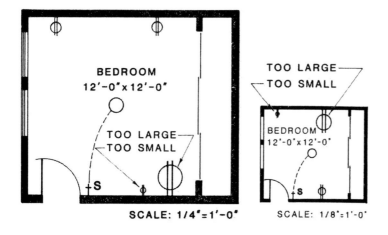

Figure 26-3. It is important to draw the electrical symbols to the correct size. If they are too small, they will be difficult to read. If they are too large, they will take up too much room in the drawing. *Will the electrician install the wires from the switches to the light fixtures exactly as shown on the drawing?*

THE RESIDENTIAL ELECTRICAL PLAN

When planning the electrical layout for a residential plan, the following items should be incorporated.

1. Electric outlets (110 v & 220 v)
2. Lighting fixtures
3. Floor outlets
4. Phone systems
5. Computer systems
6. Music and home theater systems/speakers
7. Alarm systems
8. TV cable or satellite systems
9. Intercom system
10. Thermostats
11. Types of circuits:
    General purpose circuits (110 v)
    Small appliance circuits (110 v)
    Dedicated circuits (110 v and 220 v)
    Lighting circuits (110 v)

ELECTRICAL PLANNING FEATURES

1. Plan light switches so one does not have to enter or leave a dark room.
2. Light switches must be on the handle side of the door (**Figure 26-4**).

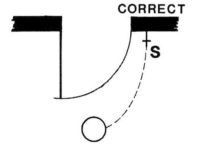
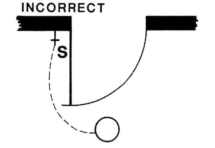

Figure 26-4. The light switch must be placed on the door handle side of the door. *Why is it incorrect to place the switch on the hinge side of the door?*

3. Plan for *GFCI* (ground fault circuit interupter) outlets near all water sources.
4. Note the height of the following outlets above the floor:
   • over kitchen cabinets 40"
   • wheelchair accessible 24"
   • clock outlets about 6 '- 6"
5. Dimension all ceiling and walls light fixtures that are critical to furniture location, art, etc.
6. Do not place outlets or switches behind bathroom wall mirrors.
7. Each room should have a minimum of two light sources; each on a different circuit.
8. Plan music centers, home theaters, TV's, and computers on the same circuits.
9. Plan all equipment using an electric motor on circuits other than the entertainment circuits.
10. Do not overload circuits.

ELECTRICAL PLANNING FEATURES continued

11. Place thermostats on interior walls.
12. All major appliances in the kitchen and service will require a dedicated circuit.
13. Plan TV cable, satellite, and/or telephone outlets near your computer for easy internet access.
14. Regular phone lines use 24-gauge, 6 pair category #3 wiring (maximum of 3 phone lines).
15. Phone lines using 6 pair category of #5 wiring will allow more phone lines and networking with computers.
16. For the best quality reception for TVs, computers, and telephones install 100% shielded coaxial cable to eliminate signal leakage.
17. *Electrical and magnetic fields* (EMF) are present wherever electricity flows. Studies are mixed on their harmful effects on the body. To reduce exposure:
    • Do not stay any closer than necessary to electrical appliances.
    • Keep use of personal appliances such as hair dryers to a minimum.
    • Turn off the electric blanket when going to sleep.
    • Do not keep clocks, radios, etc. near your head when asleep.
18. Use extension cords with the proper rating for the electrical appliance. Common *wire gauges* are 18, 16, 14, 12, and 10, with 10 being the heaviest gauge wire. A 16 gauge wire will carry 5 to 8 amps and 960 watts safely. A 10-gauge wire will carry 15 to 20 amps and 2,400 watts safely.

ELECTRICAL LAYOUTS

Typical room-by-room electrical layouts provide you with a general idea of good electrical planning.

   • Entry (**Figure 26-5**)
   • Kitchen (**Figure 26-6**)
   • Dining room (**Figure 26-7**)
   • Service room (**Figure 26-8**)
   • Stairs and halls (**Figure 26-9**)
   • Bedroom (**Figure 26-10**)
   • Closets (**Figure 26-11**)
   • Bathroom (**Figure 26-12**)
   • Basement/mechanical room (**Figure 26-13**)

A completed electrical plan is shown in **Figure 26-14**. This electric plan has taken in accord the needs of the occupants with the placements of the electrical items.

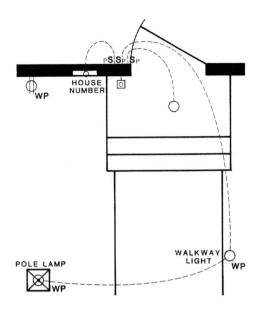

Figure 26-5. A typical electrical layout for a residential entry. *Why do the entry switches have pilot lights?*

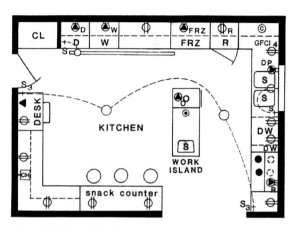

Figure 26-6. An electrical plan for an island kitchen. *Why are S₃ switches installed?*

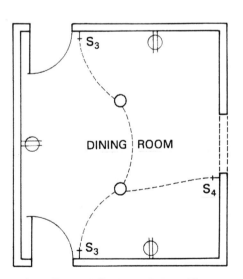

S₃ = THREE-WAY SWITCH (3 WIRES)
S₄ = FOUR-WAY SWITCH (4 WIRES)

Figure 26-7. A typical electrical layout for a dining room. *What is the purpose of a 4-way switch?*

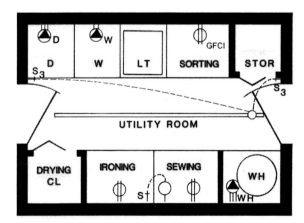

Figure 26-8. A typical electrical plan for a utility/laundry room. *What do the black triangles in the electrical symbols mean?*

Figure 26-9. An example of the switching systems for stairs and hallways. *Why are so many switches used in this example?*

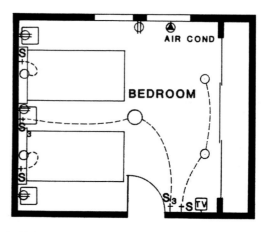

Figure 26-10. An example of the electrical layout for a bedroom. *What is the reason for having three light switches at the head of the beds?*

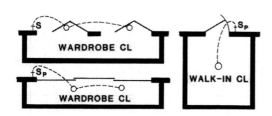

Figure 26-11. Examples of lighting layouts for wardrobe and walk-in closets. *When are switches with a pilot light used for closets?*

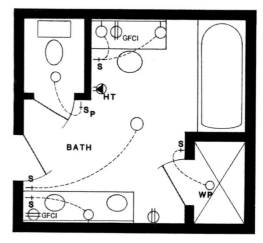

Figure 26-12. An electrical layout for a large bathroom. *What type of light fixture is installed in the shower?*

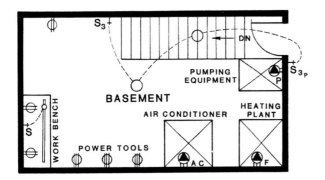

Figure 26-13. The room housing the mechanical system must have several 220v dedicated outlets for the equipment. *Why are 3-way switches installed at stairs?*

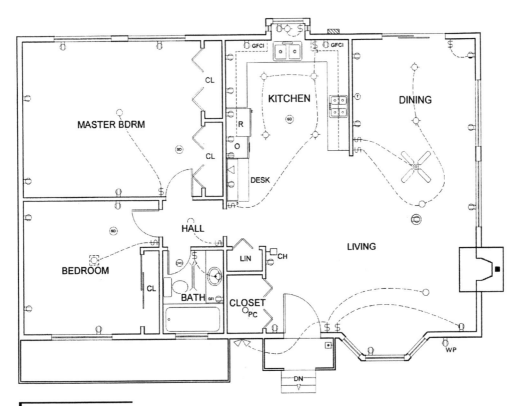

Figure 26-14. A completed electrical layout for a residential plan. *What is the symbol SD in a circle? Why is it required in all homes?*

UNIT 26 ACTIVITIES

VOCABULARY CHECKLIST

1. GFCI
2. EMF
3. wire guages

REVIEW QUESTIONS

1. Why is the placement of light switches important?
2. What is the difference between the following symbols: S, S3, S4?
3. What is a GFCI outlet?
4. What are 220V circuits used for?
5. Is the path of the connecting electric wires from the switch to the light source on the floor plan the true wiring path?

YOUR ARCHITECTURAL SCRAPBOOK

1. Sketch an electrical plan for your floor plan.
2. Add pictures of various lighting fixtures.

CAD ACTIVITIES

After reading Unit 26, refer to Chapter 26 in the *Chief Architect Tutorials* and complete:

- Draw the floor plan in Figure 26-14 and all the electrical symbols.
- Add all the electrical symbols necessary to your floor plans.

UNIT 27
DRAWING PLUMBING PLANS

THE PLUMBING SYSTEM

The plumbing system is basically simple. It consists of a gravity waste system with outgoing drainage pipes and an incoming water pressure system. Plumbing working drawings show the piping systems that carry the waste materials to the sewer disposal system and the pipes that supply the hot and cold water to the fixtures. With the exception of the water fixtures, the piping systems are mainly concealed within the structure.

THE GRAVITY WASTE SYSTEM

The *gravity waste system* works on the principle of gravity. Liquid and solid waste products flow down a horizontal pipe that has a slope of 1/4" per foot to a sewage system (**Figure 27-1**). The ends and the turns of directions in this pipe must have a *cleanout* so blockages may be removed. Because the system is a gravity flow, the pressure must be equal in the line. A *vent* equalizes the pressure in the pipe and also routes sewer gases in the line outside.

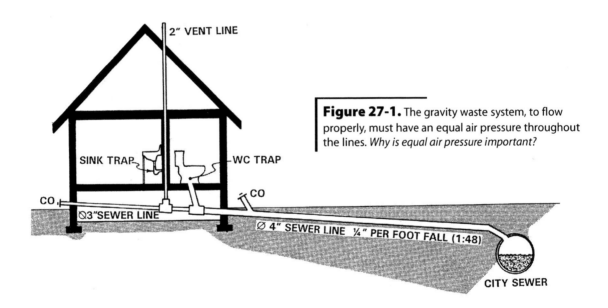

Figure 27-1. The gravity waste system, to flow properly, must have an equal air pressure throughout the lines. *Why is equal air pressure important?*

Figure 27-2 shows the waste system for a two-story house with a basement. The waste system line from the toilet to the city sewer system or septic tank must have a 4" diameter. The lines before the toilet may have a 3" diameter that leads into the 4" line.

Figure 27-3A is a floor plan of a bathroom showing the plumbing symbols for the waste system. **Figure 27-3B** is a pictorial for the same bathroom. **Figure 27-3C** and **Figure 27-3D** are elevation details and elevation schematics for the lavatory (bathroom sink) and bathtub.

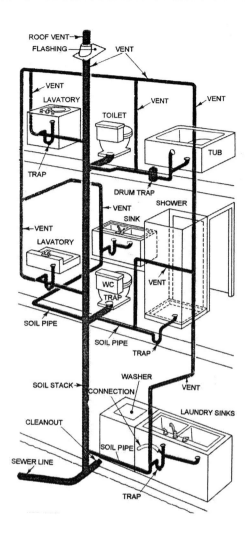

Figure 27-2. All sewer gases are vented to the outside air. *What is the purpose of the traps at each fixture?*

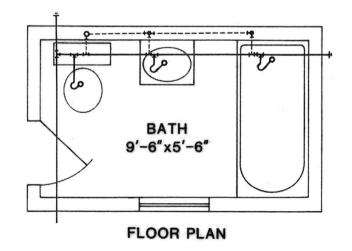

Figure 27-3A. A waste system floor plan for a bathroom. *What does the dotted line represent?*

FLOOR PLAN

BATH
9'-6"x5'-6"

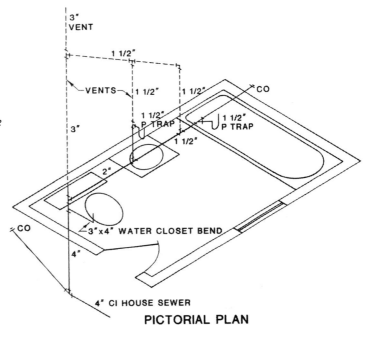

Figure 27-3B. A pictorial drawing of the bathroom's waste system. *Where is the trap for the water closet?*

3"
VENT

1 1/2"

VENTS

1 1/2"

1 1/2"

CO

3"

1 1/2"
P TRAP

1 1/2"
P TRAP

1 1/2"

2"

CO

3"x4" WATER CLOSET BEND

4"

4" CI HOUSE SEWER

PICTORIAL PLAN

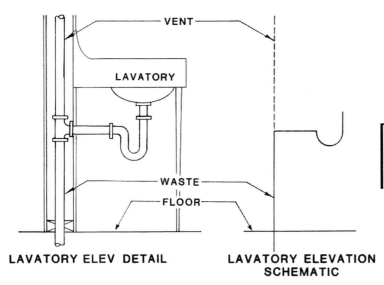

VENT

LAVATORY

WASTE

FLOOR

LAVATORY ELEV DETAIL

LAVATORY ELEVATION SCHEMATIC

Figure 27-3C. An elevation detail and elevation schematic of the bathroom's lavatory. *Why are plumbing schematics preferred over the detail drawings?*

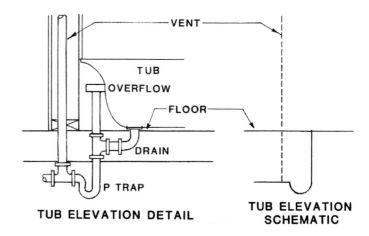

Figure 27-3D. The elevation detail and elevation schematic of the bathroom's bathtub. *What is the purpose of the overflow in the bathtub?*

VENT

TUB OVERFLOW

FLOOR

DRAIN

P TRAP

TUB ELEVATION DETAIL

TUB ELEVATION SCHEMATIC

THE PRESSURE WATER SYSTEM

The water line enters the house under pressure from local pumping stations or elevated water tanks. Be certain to have the water line entering the house buried below the *frost line*. The water is routed to the hot water heater where hot and cold water is routed to the fixtures. It is a good idea to insulate the hot water lines to stop heat loss. Each fixture should have a *cutoff (shut off) valve* to allow work on the faucets (**Figure 27-4**). The diameter of water pipes depends on the available water pressure available and the building codes. Typical sizes are shown in **Figure 27-5**.

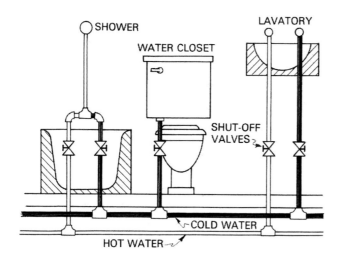

SHOWER

WATER CLOSET

LAVATORY

SHUT-OFF VALVES

COLD WATER

HOT WATER

Figure 27-4. Cutoff (shut off) valves are provided for all the water fixtures. *What is the purpose of the cutoff valves?*

MINIMUM PLUMBING PIPE DIAMETERS

Figure 27-5. Typical pipe diameters for the pressure water system and gravity waste system. *Which fixture requires the largest waste line? Which fixture requires the largest vent line?*

FIXTURE	COLD WATER	HOT WATER	SOIL, WASTE	VENTS
SINKS	½"	½"	1 ½" to 2"	1 ¼" to 1 ½"
LAVATORY	½" to 3/8"	1 ¼" to 3/8"	1 ¼" to 2"	1 ¼" to 1 ½"
TOILET	½" to 3/8"	None	4"	2"
BATHTUB	½"	½"	1 ½" to 2"	1 ¼" to 1 ½"
SHOWER	½"	½"	2"	1 ¼"
WATER HTR	¾"	¾"	None	4"
WASHER	½"	½"	2"	1 ½"

An overview of the *pressure water system* is shown in **Figure 27-6**. Because of water pollution, it is advisable to install *filter systems* as shown in **Figure 27-7**.

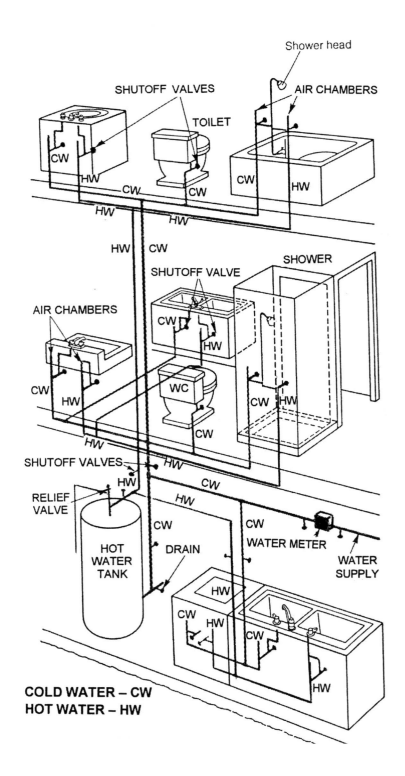

Figure 27-6.

A pressure water supply system for a two-story house with a basement. *What is the purpose of the air chambers at the water fixtures?*

COLD WATER – CW
HOT WATER – HW

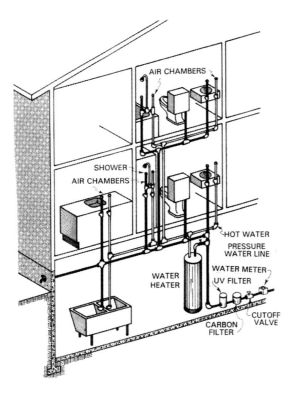

AIR CHAMBERS

SHOWER
AIR CHAMBERS

HOT WATER
PRESSURE
WATER LINE

WATER
HEATER

WATER METER
UV FILTER

CARBON
FILTER

CUTOFF
VALVE

Figure 27-7. A water supply system should be provided with a filter system. *What is the purpose of a filter system?*

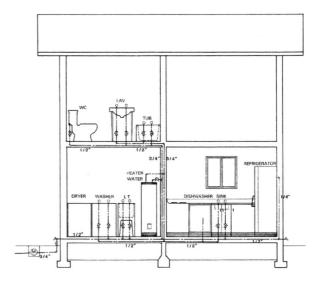

Figure 27-8. An elevation of a two-story home's pressure water supply system. *Why is there a 1/4" water line at the refrigerator?*

Figure **27-8** is an example of a two-story elevation drawing for the pressure water system. Plumbers prefer three-dimmensional (3D) pictorial drawings for piping layouts because they are easier to interperet Figure **27-9.**

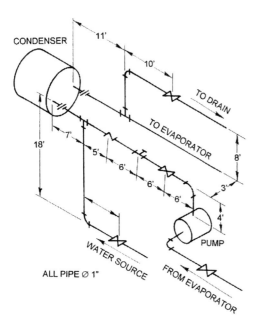

CONDENSER

TO DRAIN

TO EVAPORATOR

PUMP

WATER SOURCE

FROM EVAPORATOR

ALL PIPE ∅ 1"

11'
10'
18'
7'
5'
6'
6'
6'
8'
3'
4'

Figure 27-9. An example of a 3D piping layout. *Why is a 3D drawing often easier to read than a 2D drawing?*

COMPLETED PLUMBING SCHEMATICS

To simplify the plumbing system, earlier illustrations separated the waste system and the water system. The finished working drawing for plumbing systems must show the entire system. **Figure 27-10** shows the finished plumbing elevation for a bathroom. **Figure 27-11** shows the finished plan for the bathroom's plumbing plan. **Figure 27-12** is a plumbing plan for a utility room, and **Figure 27-13** shows the completed plumbing floor plan and elevation for a small house.

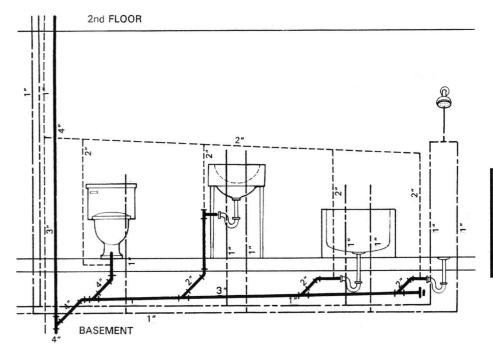

Figure 27-10.
The bathroom's elevation showing the waste and water systems together. *Why do some water lines vary in diameter?*

Figure 27-11. A bathroom floor plan showing the waste and water systems together. *Why is the water closet the only water fixture with no hot water?*

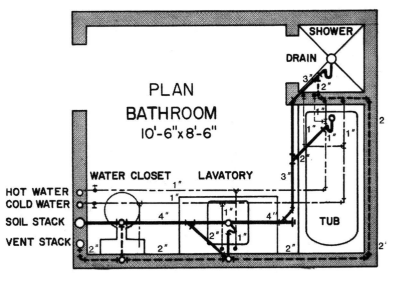

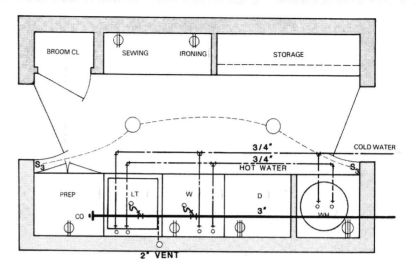

Figure 27-12. A typical plumbing layout for a laundry room. *What is the diameter of the waste line?*

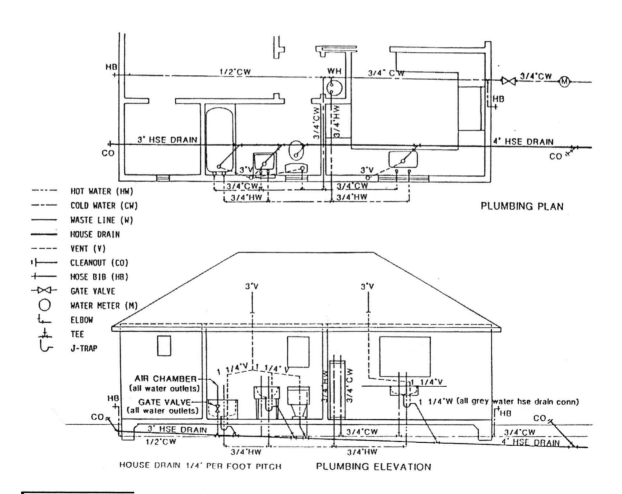

HOT WATER (HW)
COLD WATER (CW)
WASTE LINE (W)
HOUSE DRAIN
VENT (V)
CLEANOUT (CO)
HOSE BIB (HB)
GATE VALVE
WATER METER (M)
ELBOW
TEE
J-TRAP

PLUMBING PLAN

AIR CHAMBER
(all water outlets)
GATE VALVE
(all water outlets)

1 1/4"W (all grey water hse drain conn)

HOUSE DRAIN 1/4" PER FOOT PITCH

PLUMBING ELEVATION

Figure 27-13. An example of a finished plumbing working drawing with a legend of all the plumbing parts. *What is the purpose of the J-traps? What are the symbols for hot and cold water lines?*

HOT WATER

If the hot water heater is a great distance from the fixtures, a lot of cold and hot water is wasted. To eliminate some of this waste, a continual *hot water circulating system* may be installed (**Figure 27-14**). A small pump keeps hot water circulating so instant hot water is always available. There will be some loss of heat and a small cost to keep the pump running.

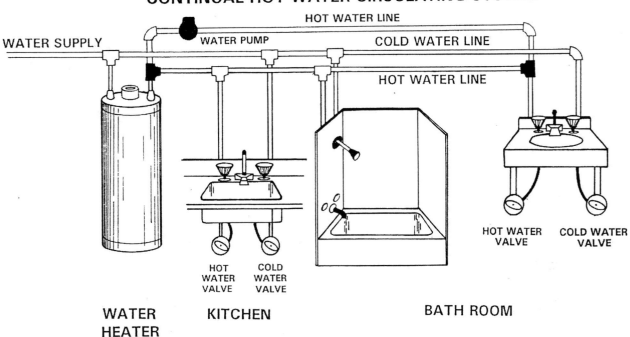

CONTINUAL HOT WATER CIRCULATING SYSTEM

Figure 27-14. A diagram of the workings for a continual hot water circulating system. *What keeps the hot water circulating?*

Another hot water system is the tankless water heater (**Figure 27-15**). The *tankless water heater* produces hot water only when a hot-water valve is opened. This ignites the heat source, which may be natural gas, propane, or electricity. Cold water enters a coil of copper pipe in a heat exchange. Hot water is produced and is quickly delivered to the fixture; no more running out of hot water during long showers. The system is economical because there is no heat loss in the hot water lines and no periodic reheating of water in a hot water heater's tank.

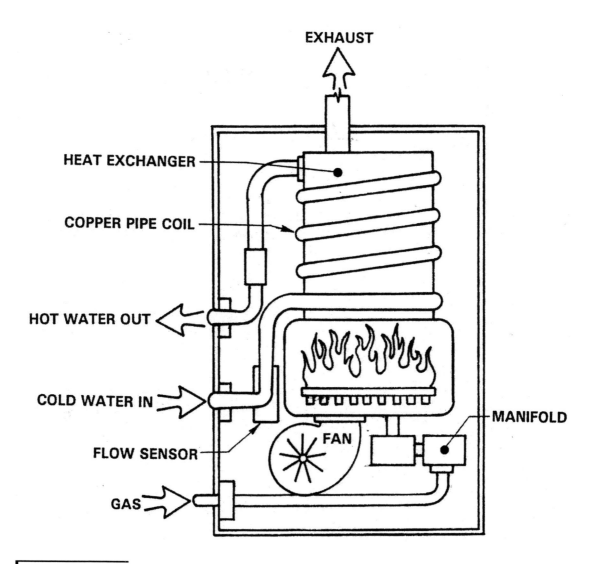

Figure 27-15. A diagram of a tankless water heater. *What are some of the advantages for a tankless water heater system?*

UNIT 27 ACTIVITIES

VOCABULARY CHECKLIST

1. gravity waste system
2. cleanout
3. vent
4. water system pressure
5. frost line
6. cutoff valve
7. filter system
8. hot water circulating system
9. tankless water heater

REVIEW QUESTIONS

1. Why must the pressure in the gravity waste system be equal throughout?
2. What is used to equalize the pressure in the gravity waste system?
3. Name two sources from where the water supply's pressure is produced.
4. What is the purpose of a cutoff valve?
5. Why is it advisable to have a filtering system in the pressure water line?
6. Name several ways that water and heat is wasted in a plumbing system.

YOUR ARCHITECTURAL SCRAPBOOK

1. Clip out or copy various water fixtures and appliances from magazines for your scrapbook.

CAD ACTIVITIES

After reading Unit 27, refer to Chapter 27 in the *Chief Architect Tutorials* and complete:

- Copy the plumbing plan in Figure 27-3A.
- Copy the lavatory elevation schematic in Figure 27-3C.
- Copy the tub elevation schematic in Figure 27-3D.
- Draw the plumbing plans for your floor plans.

PART VI
SETS OF WORKING DRAWINGS

Plan Set for a Cabin

Plan Set for Potting Shed

Advancements in Design & Construction

UNIT 28
PLAN SET FOR A CABIN

PLAN SET FOR A CABIN

Throughout this text, you have learned about the principles of residential design, construction, and drawing techniques. It is now possible for you put all this information together and complete a full set of architectural *working drawings* for a residence. With a set of working drawings, you will be able to obtain the *building permits* and have the builder construct the house. Whether you use manual drafting techniques, or a CAD system to produce the drawings, the finished set of working drawings will be almost identical.

ASSEMBLING THE WORKING DRAWINGS

The architect or designer that creates the set of working drawings is responsible for gathering all areas of information for the client's needs, site data, and the basic design. They must also complete all the drawings, and carefully check all of the drawings for errors and consistency.

All the drawings in a set of working drawings must be matched. If the length of the house is 40 feet, then the plot plan, elevations, foundation, and related construction details must be 40 feet. You can see the problem if the foundation is drawn at 38 feet. If a design change is made on one drawing, than all other drawings containing that feature of the design must be changed. Working with an architectural CAD system, you can make design changes very easily and quick as compared to manual drafting.

The following set of architectural working drawings for a small cabin may be copied or redesigned for a class project. Regardless of the size of the residence, the set of plans must have the following drawings.
1. Floor plan
2. Plot plan
3. Exterior elevations
4. Interior elevations
5. Foundation plan
6. Sectional construction details

Figure 28-1.
This floor plan is part of a full set of architectural working drawings for a small cabin. *What are the overall dimensions for this cabin?*

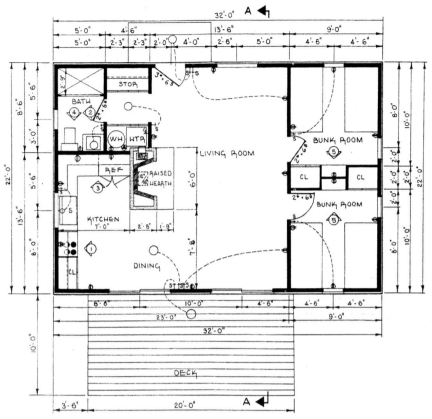

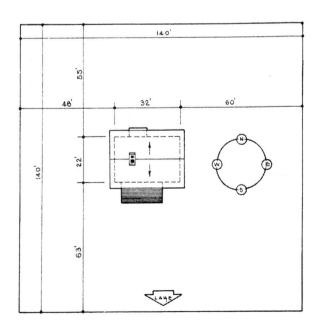

Figure 28-2. This is the plot plan for the cabin. *How is the cabin oriented to the sun?*

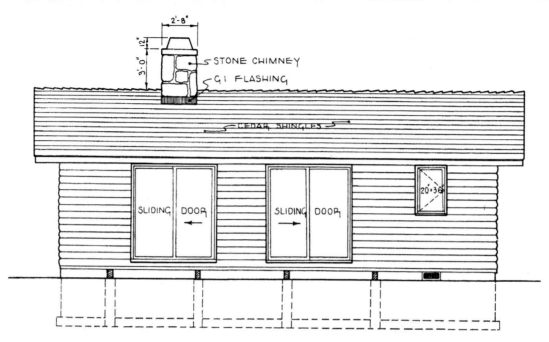

Figure 28-3. The south exterior elevation is shown in this drawing. *What is the rise of the chimney's structure above the roof? Why is it so high?*

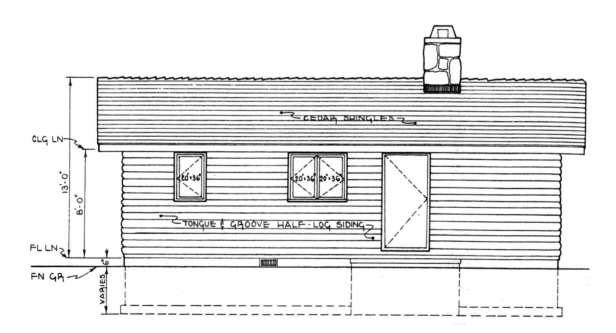

Figure 28-4. The north exterior elevation is shown in this drawing. *Why would this side of the cabin be the most likely to have dry rot and termites?*

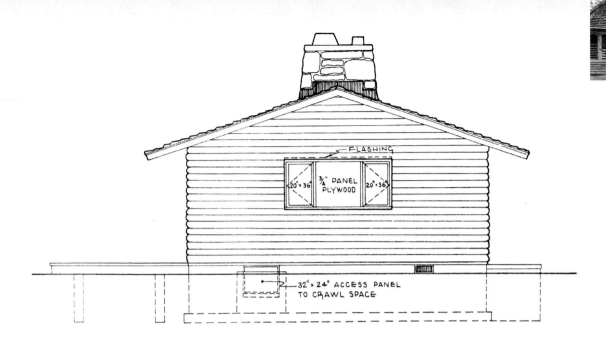

Figure 28-5. The east exterior elevation is shown in this drawing. *What is the purpose for the access panel in the T-foundation's wall?*

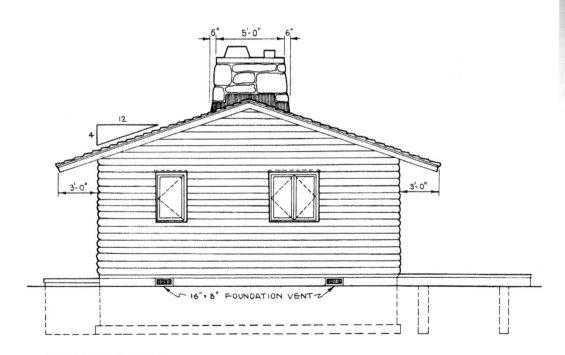

Figure 28-6. The west exterior elevation is shown in this drawing. *What is the purpose of the foundation vents? What is the roof slope?*

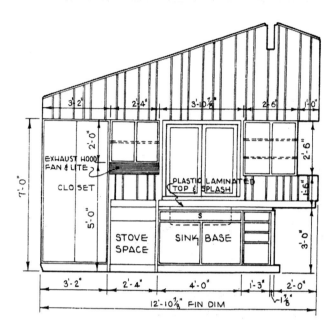

Figure 28-7. This interior elevation, #1, is of the kitchen's exterior wall. *What type of ceiling is in the kitchen? What fixture and appliance is in this elevation?*

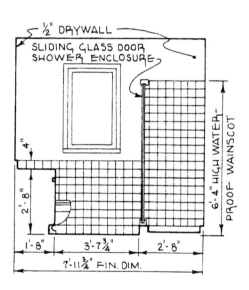

Figure 28-8. This interior elevation, #2, is of the bathroom's exterior wall. *Why is the shower's exterior finish waterproofed?*

Figure 28-9.

This is a sectional detail drawing, #3, through the fireplace and part of the kitchen. *What is the size of the flue and does it agree with the flue size in the floor plan?*

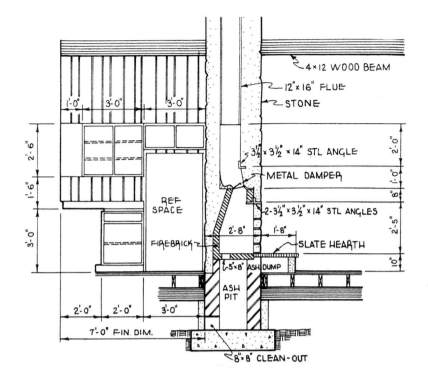

4×12 WOOD BEAM
12"×16" FLUE
STONE
3½"×3½"×14" STL ANGLE
METAL DAMPER
2-3½"×3½"×14" STL ANGLES
SLATE HEARTH
REF SPACE
FIREBRICK
2'-8"
1'-8"
1'-5"×8" ASH DUMP
ASH PIT
8"×8" CLEAN-OUT
1'-0"
3'-0"
3'-0"
2'-6"
1'-6"
3'-0"
2'-0"
2'-0"
3'-0"
7'-0" FIN. DIM.
2'-0"
1'-0"
8"
2'-5"
10"

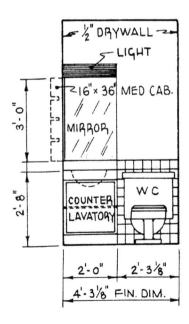

½" DRYWALL
LIGHT
16"×36" MED CAB.
MIRROR
COUNTER LAVATORY
W C
3'-0"
2'-8"
2'-0"
2'-3⅛"
4'-3⅛" FIN. DIM.

Figure 28-10. This interior elevation, #4, is of the bathroom. *What is the abbreviation WC?*

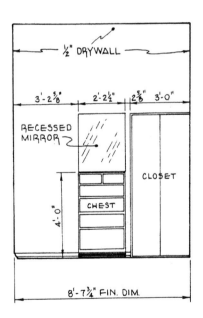

½" DRYWALL
3'-2⅝"
2'-2½"
2⅝"
3'-0"
RECESSED MIRROR
CHEST
CLOSET
4'-0"
8'-7¾" FIN. DIM.

Figure 28-11. This interior elevation, #5, is of the bedroom's storage wall. *What are the dimensions of the built-in chest?*

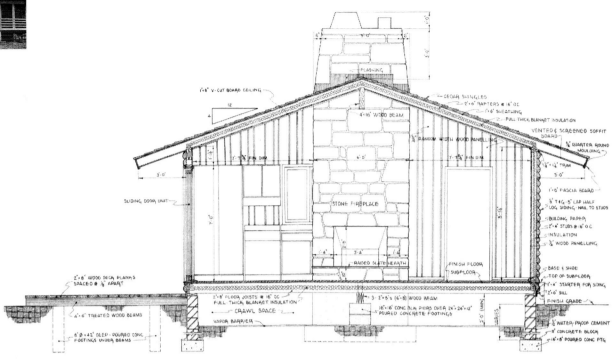

Figure 28-12. This is a full transverse sectional drawing through the cabin. It includes all the details from the foundation through the roof at the section line. A section through the length of the cabin would be a longitudinal section. *How is the transverse section indicated on the floor plan?*

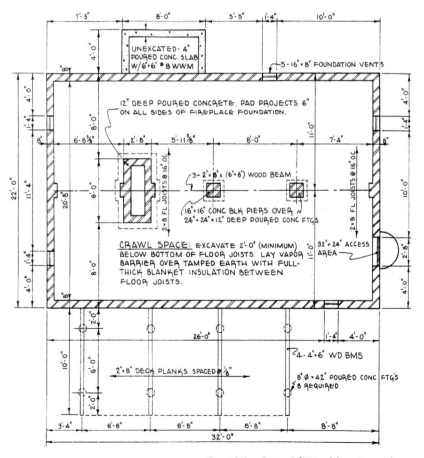

Figure 28-13. The foundation plan shows all the materials and sizes required to build the foundation. *What are the symbols for poured concrete and concrete blocks?*

Home Planners, Inc.

Figure 28-14. A perspective rendering and presentation floor plan is not required for the building department or builders. *Why would the architect or designer take the time to do these drawings?*

UNIT 28 ACTIVITIES

VOCABULARY CHECKLIST

1. working drawings
2. building permit
3. plot plan

4. elevations
5. construction details
6. sectional drawing

REVIEW QUESTIONS

1. What is the square footage of the cabin?
2. What are the dimensions of the deck?
3. Which elevation faces the lake?
4. What is the exterior siding material?
5. What is the roof style?

YOUR ARCHITECTURAL SCRAPBOOK

1. List the types of working drawings needed for a building permit and place it in your scrapbook.
2. Sketch the ideas for a perfect building site for your house and place the sketch in your scrapbook.

CAD ACTIVITIES

After reviewing Unit 28, copy the full set of working drawings for the cabin, or design your own set of working drawings using the cabin as a reference. The full set of working drawings consists of:

- Plot plan
- Floor plan
- Interior elevations

- Sectional drawings
- T- foundation and construction details
- Exterior perspective

UNIT 29
PLAN SET FOR A POTTING SHED

This set of working drawings for a potting shed is an excellent first architectural drawing project assignment. Although it is very small and simple in design, it covers all the required drawings needed for all sizes of residential design.

These blueprint reading questions for the set of drawings may be used as extra work, testing, or homework.

POTTING SHED
80 BLUEPRINT READING QUESTIONS

DRAWING 1
1. What are the overall dimensions of the potting shed?
2. What are the dimensions of the window?
3. What are the dimensions of the door?
4. What is the symbol for an electrical outlet?
5. What is the symbol for an electrical switch?
6. What is the symbol for the interior elevation callout?
7. What is the symbol for the light fixture outlet?
8. What do the dotted lines on the floor plan represent?
9. What type of drawing is the pictorial drawing of the potting shed?
10. How many vanishing points are used for the pictorial drawing of the potting shed?

DRAWING 2
11. What is the dimension of the front setback?
12. What do the circular, wavy line symbols indicate?
13. What are the two setbacks for the potting shed?
14. What is the dimension of the south side of the property?
15. What is the original drawing scale of the plot plan?

DRAWING 3
16. What type of siding material is used for the exterior cover?
17. What is the roof pitch? (Note: not the roof slope.)
18. What is the height of the door?
19. What is the height of the ceiling?
20. What type of wood covering is used for the roof?
21. What is the width of the footing?
22. What is the clearance of the plate from the soil?
23. What is used for the final roof cover?
24. What is the original drawing scale of the elevations?
25. What is the original drawing scale of the slab detail?

DRAWING 4

26. What is the size of the ceiling joists?
27. What is the spacing of the ceiling joists?
28. What is the size of the rafters?
29. What is the spacing of the rafters?
30. What is the lintel size for the door?
31. What is the ridge board size?
32. What makes up the top plate?
33. What is the height of the working counters?
34. What do the dotted lines on the interior elevation represent?
35. What is the distance of the roof overhang?
36. What is the ceiling height?

DRAWING 5

37. What is the scale of the stud layout drawing?
38. How many studs are used to frame a corner?
39. What is the spacing for most of the studs?
40. What is the difference in size of the rough frame opening and the door?
41. What is the difference in size of the rough frame opening and the window?
42. How many studs make up the framing for an intersection of an interior wall to an exterior wall?
43. What is the rough frame opening of the door?
44. What is the rough frame opening of the window?
45. What are the dimensions of a stud?
46. Will all studs fall on 400 mm centers?
47. Will a 1200 mm x 2400 mm piece of sheetrock always have a nailing edge with 400 mm stud spacing?
48. Do the studs in the wall-framing plan always align with the same studs in the stud layout plan?
49. What is the symbol for a spacer block?
50. What is the plan symbol for a stud?

DRAWING 6

51. What is the cross-sectional size of the ridge board?
52. What is the length of the ridge board?
53. What are the external rafters (on gable ends) called?
54. What is the cross-sectional size of the wall's double top plate?
55. What is the thickness of the subfloor?
56. What is the cross-sectional size of the mud sill?
57. What does the @ symbol represent?
58. What is the length of the anchor bolt?
59. What is the spacing for the anchor bolts?
60. What is the width of the T-foundation's footing?
61. What is the full height of the T-foundation?
62. What is the full height of crawl area? (Disregard the girder.)
63. What is the cross-sectional size of the girder?
64. What is the cross-sectional size of the floor joists?
65. When the girder is installed, with what structural member must its top side be level?
66. What is the clearance of the mud sill from the outside grade line?
67. What are the three overall dimensions of a foundation pier?
68. What is the width of the T-foundation's wall?
69. What is the rough opening width (RO) for the window?
70. What is the material used for the exterior wall cover?
71. What is the material used for the wall's vapor barrier?
72. How far is the roof's overhang?
73. What is the material used for the wall's interior cover?
74. What structural material is used directly on top of the wall studs?
75. What structural members are used to support the window's lintel?
76. What structural members are used between the rafters to seal the attic area?
77. What is the size of the attic's air-circulation vents?
78. What is the distance between the attic's vents?
79. What is the depth of the foundation's footing?
80. How many different architectural drawing scales are used for the construction details on Drawing 6?

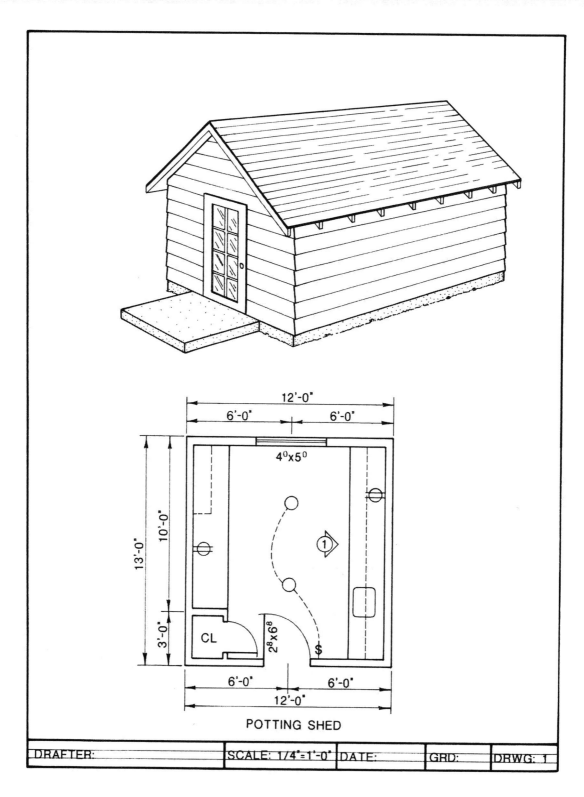

POTTING SHED

| DRAFTER: | SCALE: 1/4"=1'-0" | DATE: | GRD: | DRWG: 1 |

Drawing 1

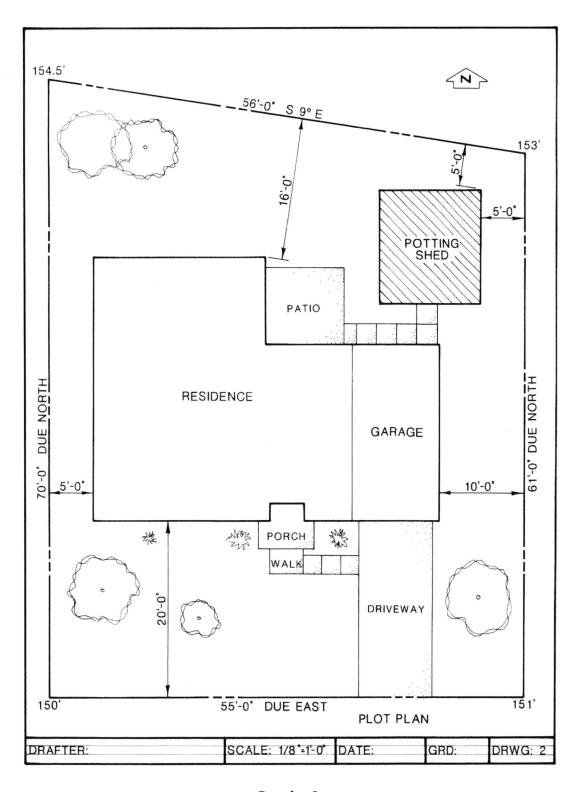

154.5'

56'-0" S 9° E

153'

5'-0"

5'-0"

16'-0"

POTTING
SHED

N

DUE NORTH

70'-0" DUE NORTH

61'-0" DUE NORTH

PATIO

RESIDENCE

GARAGE

5'-0"

10'-0"

PORCH

WALK

20'-0"

DRIVEWAY

150'

55'-0" DUE EAST

151'

PLOT PLAN

DRAFTER:	SCALE: 1/8"=1'-0"	DATE:	GRD:	DRWG: 2

Drawing 2

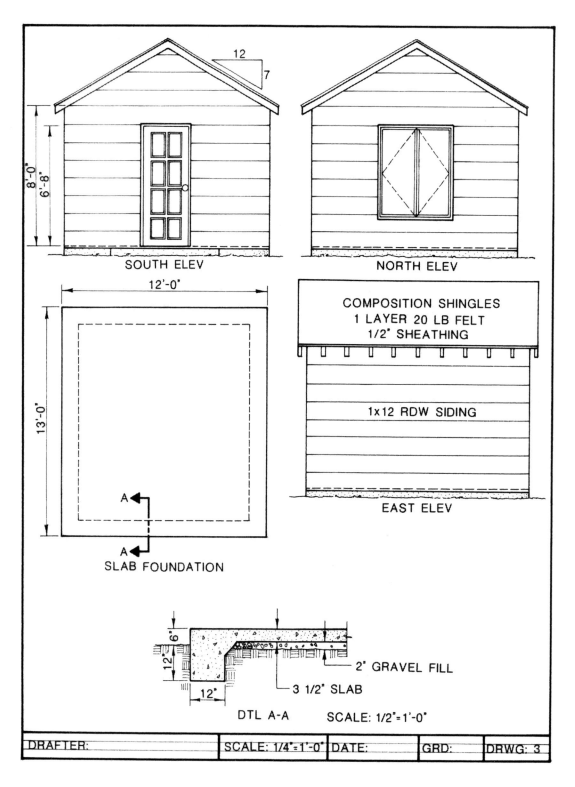

SOUTH ELEV

NORTH ELEV

12

7

8'-0"

6'-8"

12'-0"

13'-0"

A

A

SLAB FOUNDATION

COMPOSITION SHINGLES
1 LAYER 20 LB FELT
1/2" SHEATHING

1x12 RDW SIDING

EAST ELEV

6"

12"

12"

2" GRAVEL FILL

3 1/2" SLAB

DTL A-A   SCALE: 1/2"=1'-0"

| DRAFTER: | SCALE: 1/4"=1'-0" | DATE: | GRD: | DRWG: 3 |

Drawing 3

INTERIOR ELEVATION 1
SCALE: 1/4"=1'-0"

3'-6"
18"
3'-0"
8'-0"

6" CONT OH

ROOF PLAN
SCALE: 1/8"=1'-0"

2x6 RIDGE BRD

12
7

2x4 RAFTERS at 16" OC

2-2x4 TOP PLATE

2x4 CLG JST at 16" OC

4x6 LINTEL

SOUTH CONST DTLS

| DRAFTER: | SCALE: 1/2"=1'-0" | DATE: | GRD: | DRWG: 4 |

Drawing 4

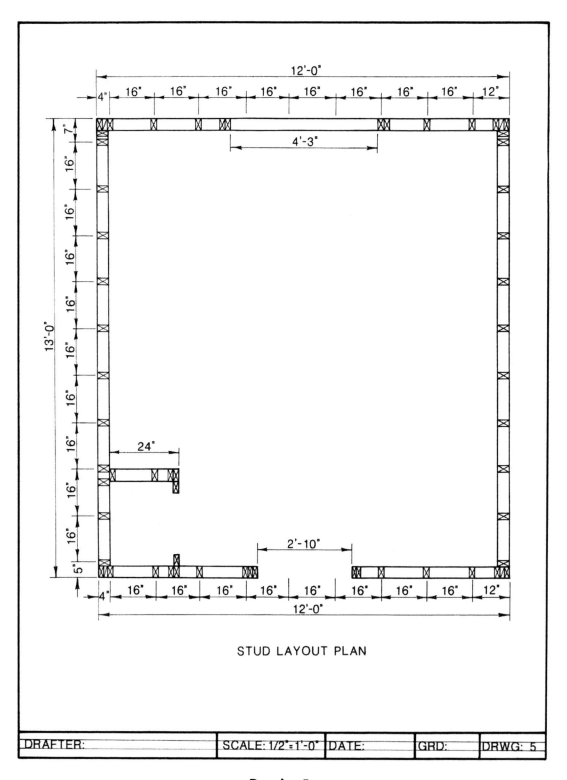

STUD LAYOUT PLAN

| DRAFTER: | | SCALE: 1/2"=1'-0" | DATE: | GRD: | DRWG: 5 |

Drawing 5

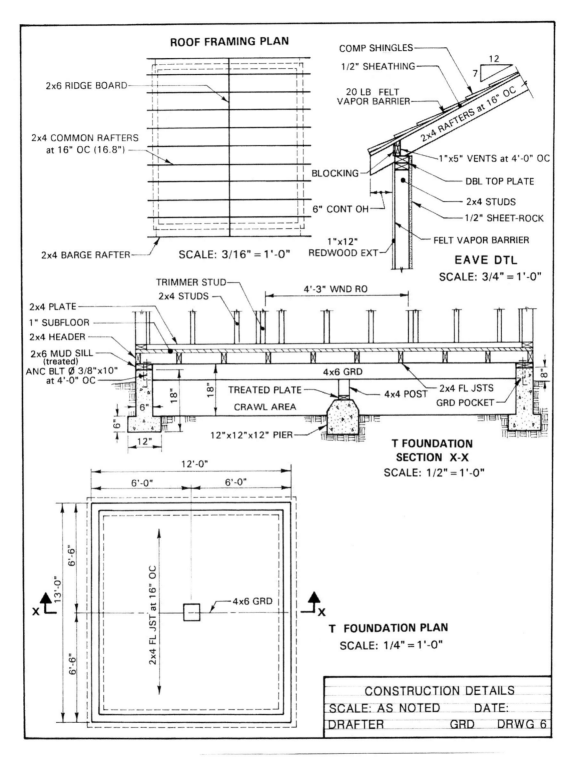

ROOF FRAMING PLAN

2x6 RIDGE BOARD

2x4 COMMON RAFTERS at 16" OC (16.8")

2x4 BARGE RAFTER

SCALE: 3/16" = 1'-0"

COMP SHINGLES

1/2" SHEATHING

20 LB FELT VAPOR BARRIER

2x4 RAFTERS at 16" OC

12 / 7

BLOCKING

6" CONT OH

1"x12" REDWOOD EXT

1"x5" VENTS at 4'-0" OC

DBL TOP PLATE

2x4 STUDS

1/2" SHEET-ROCK

FELT VAPOR BARRIER

EAVE DTL
SCALE: 3/4" = 1'-0"

TRIMMER STUD
2x4 STUDS

4'-3" WND RO

2x4 PLATE
1" SUBFLOOR
2x4 HEADER
2x6 MUD SILL (treated)
ANC BLT Ø 3/8"x10" at 4'-0" OC

18"
6"
6"
12"
18"

TREATED PLATE
CRAWL AREA

12"x12"x12" PIER

4x6 GRD

4x4 POST

2x4 FL JSTS
GRD POCKET

8"

T FOUNDATION SECTION X-X
SCALE: 1/2" = 1'-0"

12'-0"
6'-0"
6'-0"

13'-0"
6'-6"
6'-6"

2x4 FL JST at 16" OC

4x6 GRD

X
X

T FOUNDATION PLAN
SCALE: 1/4" = 1'-0"

CONSTRUCTION DETAILS		
SCALE: AS NOTED	DATE:	
DRAFTER	GRD	DRWG 6

Drawing 6

UNIT 30

ADVANCEMENTS IN DESIGN AND CONSTRUCTION

Advancements in architecture have been in flux since prehistoric times. Humans have constantly attempted to obtain safer and more comfortable living situations. We have advanced from caves to living in outer space (**Figure 30-1**).

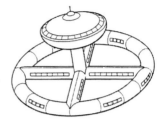

Figure 30-1 Humans have made great strides from living in caves to outer space. *What are the basic requirements that ancient and modern humans want?*

ARCHITECTURAL STYLES

The past 50 years have shown more advances in architecture than in past recorded history. The development of architectural design, tools, and construction materials has made advancement possible. *Traditional architectural styles* from the past (**Figure 30-2**) have developed into modern styles that have clean lines with large glass areas (**Figure 30-3**).

Figure 30-2 An example of traditional architecture. *What is the architectural style of this home?*

270   **Part VI—Sets Of Working Drawings**

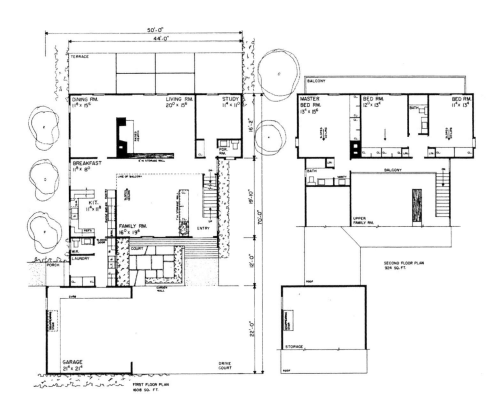

Figure 30-3 An example of a modern style of architecture. *What is the difference between traditional and modern architectural design?*

STEEL CONSTRUCTION

The majority of today's homes are wood-framed. With the recent development of steel framing members and the reduction of their costs, more steel-framed homes are being built (**Figure 30-4** and **Figure 30-5**). *Steel framing* members are used for floor joists, wall studs, ceiling joist, and roof rafters. Some of the many advantages of steel construction are:

- Steel is moisture resistant which eliminates dry rot and termites.
- Steel is uniformly straight, which means level floors and flat walls.
- Steel is one-third the weight of wood and much stronger.
- Steel is recyclable.
- Steel will not burn, which lowers homeowners insurance.

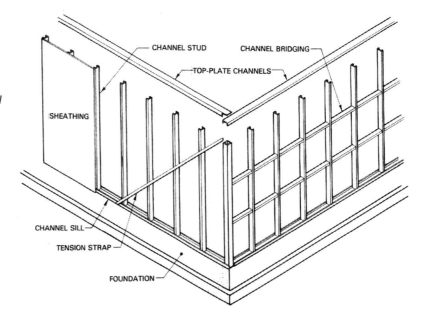

Figure 30-4 An example of steel framing for walls. *Name two advantages of steel framing over wood framing.*

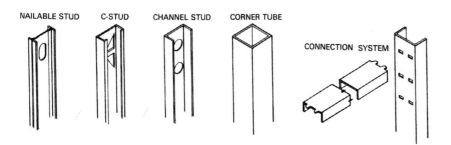

Figure 30-5 Examples of various types of steel framing studs. *Why are there more wood-framed houses than steel-framed houses?*

ADVANCES OF CONSTRUCTION MEMBERS

The conservation of our forests has caused the development of many new types of construction members. Following are some new products that the lumber industry has developed (**Figure 30-6**).

- The wood *I-beam* is constructed from a plywood web that is inserted and glued into wood flanges. They are used for joists and rafters, are lightweight, and very strong. They will not shrink, twist or warp.
- *Laminated veneer* construction members are made from strips of thin wood veneer that are glued together. These beams are very strong and can be made into very long lengths.
- Thin veneer strip beams are fabricated from thin veneer sheets that are cut in narrow strips. The strips are coated with a resin glue, placed into staggered positions and pressed to form. These beams are heavier than natural wood, but are much stronger.
- *Cellulose fiber* strands may be obtained from poor quality trees and other fiber plants such as rice, rye, and wheat straw. These plants are crushed into long cellulose strands, coated with glue, woven together, heated, and compressed to shape. They may be fabricated into very long lengths and easily sawed, nailed, screwed, and/or glued.
- Recycled thermoplastics may be finely ground, then glued, and pressed into form. These plastic members can be easily sawed, nailed, screwed, and/or glued.
- Light-weight masonry blocks may be produced by adding a sawdust base mix to concrete. Another method is to add *fly-ash,* a residue of coal from burned plants.

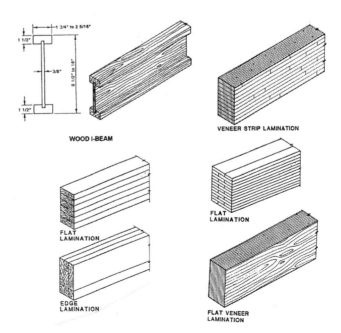

Figure 30-6 New types of wood construction members. *Why are wood laminates stronger than solid wood construction members?*

RENEWED CONSTRUCTION SYSTEMS

Many old construction systems have been revised and modernized. A few of these construction methods that are becoming common practice are:

1. *Rammed-earth construction* is when soil, clay, sand, and cement are mixed together in a semi-dry mix and then forced (rammed) into forms to create walls. Wood or steel lintels are used over the windows and doors. The foundation is made of concrete with horizontal and vertical rebars. The rammed-earth walls offer excellent insulation and will last a thousand years.

2. *Earth-sheltered homes* are designed to be fully or partially below the surface of the ground (**Figure 30-7**). There are many advantages to earth-sheltered homes.
   - The soil just below the surface stays at a comfortable temperature, reducing heating and cooling costs.
   - No problems with wind resistance of storms.
   - Low upkeep and repairs.

A major problem with earth-sheltered homes is water seepage. Care must be taken to use water repellant building materials, moisture barriers, and swails to keep water away from the house.

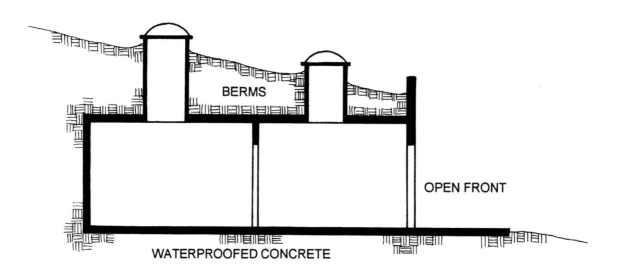

BERMS

OPEN FRONT

WATERPROOFED CONCRETE

Figure 30-7 An example of one type of earth-sheltered construction. *What is the purpose of the wells over the structure?*

3. Straw bale construction uses 24" thick straw bales **(Figure 30-8).** A concrete foundation with vertical steel rebars run through the bales to stabilize them. The bales are covered with moisture barriers, metal flashing, large overhang roofs, and plaster or stucco to seal the straw bales. This type of construction has five times the insulating value of insulated wood framed walls.

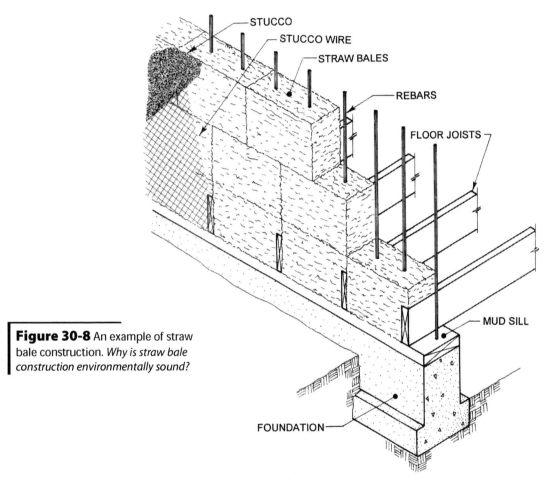

Figure 30-8 An example of straw bale construction. *Why is straw bale construction environmentally sound?*

ADVANCES IN INTERIOR DESIGN

With modern advances in design and construction many new types of rooms have evolved. Some of these rooms are:

- Computer room
- Entertainment/media room for movies and music
- Safe room from hurricanes, tornadoes, earthquakes, and break-ins
- Exercise room
- Meditation/quiet room
- Collection room
- Hobby room
- Wine cellar
- Smoker's room
- Solar green house

THE ELECTRONIC SMART HOUSE

The aim of *smart house* technology is to increase comfort, security, and save energy. Very small and powerful digital chips are embedded into the electrical systems and electronic appliances in the home and are controlled by linking them together in a single network system with sensing controls. They may now be controlled within the home with a computer, small sensing panels, and/or screens mounted flush to a wall in each room. The networking of the items in a home can be accomplished with hard wiring or by a wireless system.

Outside of the home, *sensing controls* may be controlled by telephone, cell phone, or a small hand control, similar to a key fob used for car alarms. They are coded to identify the user that will activate the sensors.

The various activities for a smart home are limitless. All the following activities are now available.

- A chip in door locks opens when it recognizes an ID fob.
- Controlling the temperature, humidity, and air quality.
- Fire alarm will automatically call fire department.
- Security alarms and cameras will automatically alert police department.
- Detects gas leaks and carbon monoxide levels.
- Opens and closes windows and curtains for comfort and safety.
- Starts shower or bath to your comfort level.
- Assist physically impaired persons by controlling the height for all working areas, fixtures, and appliances.
- If any appliances are not functioning properly, the smart house will call for the necessary repair or maintenance.

From work, or when you wake up in the morning, you can operate the lights, get coffee and breakfast started, turn on your shower or draw your bath, and have your favorite news broadcast or music turned on before you have to get out of bed or get home.

Computer chips will make toys smarter, foods in the refrigerator and pantry can be identified and inventoried. Picture frames on the walls can be scheduled with digital pictures at your command. With some imagination there is no limit of conveniences that can be had with an intelligent house.

UNIT 30 ACTIVITIES

VOCABULARY CHECKLIST

1. traditional architectural styles
2. steel framing
3. I-beam
4. laminated veneer
5. cellulose fibers

6. fly-ash
7. rammed-earth construction
8. earth-sheltered homes
9. smart house
10. sensing controls

REVIEW QUESTIONS

1. Name several things that help to develop modern architecture the past 50 years.
2. What are the major advantages of a steel-framed house?
3. Why is a wood beam I-beam so strong?
4. What makes veneered lumber so strong?
5. What part of a rice plant can be used for construction material?
6. What may be used to lighten concrete masonry blocks?
7. What is the material in rammed-earth construction that makes it so strong?
8. Why do earth-sheltered homes have small heating bills?
9. What is the major control for a smart house?
10. Name two ways that smart fixtures can be controlled.

YOUR ARCHITECTURAL SCRAPBOOK

1. From magazines or the Internet, obtain pictures of traditional and modern homes for your scrapbook.
2. Download information from the Internet on steel-frame construction for your scrapbook.
3. Using a CAD system, draw a floor plan and exterior elevations for an earth-sheltered home.
4. Design a floor plan with as many "new type" rooms as possible for your scrapbook.

CAD ACTIVITIES

After reading Unit 30, design and draw the following:

• Earth sheltered house
• Straw-bale house construction (24" walls)
• Design a home with the additional rooms:

Computer room	Entertainment room
Safe room	Exercise room
Solar green house	

GLOSSARY

active solar design A design procedure using mechanical devices to make use of the sun's energy to produce electricity, heat the house and heat water.

adobe A clay like soil found in the southwestern part of the United States. Sun-dried blocks or bricks of adobe soil are used for building walls.

air conditioner A device that heats, cools, and circulates air within an enclosed area.

air duct A pipe that carries air from a source, such as a heater or air conditioner, to rooms within a building. This pipe is usually made of sheet metal.

alcove A small or secluded space. This recessed, or set-back, space is connected to and opens out of a larger room.

anchor bolt A metal rod, threaded like a screw, that connects the foundation of a building to the sill.

appliance A free-standing service item such as a washer or dryer.

apron Finished wood trim under the window sill. This molding strip is used on the interior, or room, side of windows.

arch A curved structure that supports itself and any weight above its curved opening. This support is achieved by mutual pressure of the sides of the arch.

architect A person who plans and designs buildings. The architect also may oversee the construction of the building.

areaway A recessed, or set-back, space below ground next to the foundation. Its purpose is to allow light and ventilation into basement windows.

asbestos A mineral that does not burn or conduct heat. It can be made into cloth, paint, or roofing materials which are fireproof.

ashpit The area under a fireplace hearth where ashes collect.

atrium A central hall or an inside courtyard of a building. An atrium may be either open at the top or covered by a glass roof.

attic The space between the roof and the ceiling.

balcony A platform that projects from the wall of a building above ground level.

banister The handrail and supporting posts, or balusters, used alongside a stairway.

baseboard A horizonal finished board used to cover the interior wall where tbe wall and floor meet.

base course The lowest row of masonry construction.

basement The lowest story of a building. A basement may be either partly or entirely below ground level.

bay window A window or set of windows that project out from the wall of a building. The window forms a recess or alcove in the room.

beam A horizontal support. The load, or weight, of the building's floor system or ceiling is carried by this structural member.

bearing wall A wall that supports any vertical weight as well as its own weight.

bib An outdoor faucet which is threaded so a hose can be fastened to it.

bill of material A list of building materials.

blanket insulation Insulation that comes in rolled sheets. Insulation is used to keep cold, heat, or sound in or out of a building.

blocking Small horizontal pieces of wood framing that prevent studs from bowing. They are used to add stiffness to the studs.

blueprint A copy of an architectural drawing or building plan. The original drawing is transferred to a sensitized paper. When developed and printed, the paper turns blue with white lines. Or, the copy may print blue lines on white paper. These prints are used by workers as instructions for building construction.

board and batten A type of construction using wide vertical boards with the joints between the boards covered by narrow, vertical strips known as battens.

board foot Unit of measure for lumber that is 1"x 1'x 1'.

breezeway A covered walkway with open sides often connecting a house and garage.

Fundamentals of Architectural Design

GLOSSARY

building code A collection of local laws that regulate the building of homes and other structures. These legal requirements are in tended to protect the safety and health of the people who live and work in the buildings.

building load The total weight (mass) of all the live and loads in a structure.

building paper A heavy, waterproof paper that is used over sheathing and subfloors. Its purpose is to prevent the passage of air and water.

building permit A document issued by the local government which allows the construction of a building or structure.

buttress A protruding support added at the base of a wall for added strength.

cabinet work The finished interior woodwork of a building.

cantilever Projected construction that is fastened or supported at only one end. It is used for balconies and similar structures.

carport A roofed structure without walls used as a garage.

casement window A hinged window that opens outward. It is usually framed in metal.

casing The metal or wood molding used as a finishing trim around doors and window openings.

cathedral window A window which extends up in height to the pitched roof line.

caulking A soft waterproof material used to seal cracks.

cedar shingles Shingles made of cedar wood. These are used for roofs or siding.

cement A material made by burning a mixture of clay and limestone. This pulverized powder is mixed with water, sand, and gravel to make concrete. Poured in its soft state, this masonry material dries to a stonelike hardness.

central heating A system in which heat is distributed throughout a building from a single heat source The heat is distributed through pipes or ducts.

ceramics Clay articles which have been fired in a kiln. The firing produces a hard surface.

chimney An upright structure connected with a fireplace or a furnace that rises above the roof of a building. It enables smoke and gases to pass to the outside of the building.

chimney pot A pipe on the top of a chimney used to increase the draft.

cinder block A building block made of cement and cinder.

circuit The path of an electric current. This is the closed loop of wire in which an electric current flows.

circuit breaker A safety device which opens and closes electrical circuits.

civil engineer's scale A ruler that measures with feet and the decimal part of a foot.

clearance A space to allow passage.

clerestory A set or group of high windows above the roof line of a building.

closed plan A floor plan in which the rooms are separated by walls.

colonial A style of architecture, furniture, and accessories adapted from the American colonial period.

column A vertical supporting member.

common wall A single wall that serves two dwellings as in an apartment.

compass A drawing instrument used to draw arcs or circles.

column A vertical supporting member or structural piece, usually round.

concrete A substance made of cement, sand, gravel, and water. The mixture is poured in semi-liquid or soft form and hardens as it dries.

concrete block Blocks of concrete that are precast.

condensation The formation of water on a surface. For example, moisture forms on walls or windows inside a building when warm air or vapor comes in contact with a cold surface.

GLOSSARY

conductor In architecture, this is the drain pipe which leads from the roof. In electricity, it is any material that permits the passage of an electric current.

construction details When the construction of a specific part of a structure on a drawing is too small to clearly read, a blown-up drawing is made so there will not be any errors made in construction.

contemporary architectural design A design for a structure which reflects the area and customs of the period in which it is built. Generally, this reference is to present day structures, representing current customs.

contours In architecture, this refers to land formations (hills, valleys, etc.) that rise and fall.

contractor A person who assumes the responsibility for the building of a structure for a specific sum of money.

convenience outlet An electrical box or receptacle through which current is drawn from the electrical system for appliances.

cornice The part of a roof that projects out from the wall.

course A continuous row of stone or brick of the same height.

court An unroofed space entirely or partly surrounded by walls or buildings.

crawl space The area between the ground and the floor joists in a T-foundation building.

curtain wall An outside, or exterior, wall cover which provides no structural support.

data processing system Computer hardware and software used together to do specific jobs.

dead load All the weight of the building materials and permanently installed components in a structure.

designer A person who designs buildings but is not a registered architect.

detail To add instructions, such as dimensions, notes, or parts of the construction, to the drawing of a structure.

diameter The distance or measurement across the center of a circle.

digitizer A special input tool for computer-aided drafting (CAD) which can be used to draw on a flat surface. The device translates images to numbers for transmission to a computer.

disc file, magnetic disc file Computer storage units that resemble stacks of phonograph records. They are able to hold billions of units of information.

dimension The measurement of length, width, or thickness. A surface is two dimensional, having only two measurements: length and width (breadth). A three-dimensional drawing shows thickness, or depth, as well.

dimension line A line with arrowheads at both ends that is used to show the distance between two points.

dormer A structure which projects from a sloping roof to form another roof and wall into which a window may be built.

double-hung Refers to a window which has a top and bottom sash, each of which can be moved up and down.

downspout A pipe which carries rainwater from the roof to the ground.

drain A pipe used to carry waste water.

drafting divider An instrument used to compare sizes of drawing elements and measuring distances on drawings.

drafting triangle A precision instrument for drawing lines at specific angles.

drawing board A rectangular board with a straight, smooth edge that has a perfectly flat, smooth surface.

drawing charcoal A soft carbon material used for shading in drawings.

dry wall An interior wall covering material made of gypsum board. This is applied in large sheets or panels.

ducts The pipes through which warm or cool air is distributed through a building.

GLOSSARY
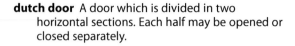

dutch door A door which is divided in two horizontal sections. Each half may be opened or closed separately.

easement The right-of-ways across private land for passage and utilities lines.'

eave The lower part of a roof that projects or hangs down over the wall.

ecological planning The planning for a structure to protect or improve the environment.

electrical fixture A lighting unit that is installed in a structure.

electrical switch A lever or other device for breaking or completing an electrical circuit. Mounted on the wall at an outlet point, it is used to turn lights on and off.

elevation A two-dimensional drawing that shows the exterior and interior walls.

elevation drawing A drawing of the exterior and interior walls of a building. It is a perpendicular, or upright, projection from the floor plan to show vertical architectural or design details.

facade The front elevation of a building. In construction, this may also refer to the exterior covering material of a building.

face brick A quality brick that is used on the outside of a wall.

facing Any material that is used to cover another as a finishing surface.

fascia A horizontal board attached to the ends of the rafters at the eave.

fiber board A building material made of fibrous materials and binders. It is used as an insulating board.

finished lumber Wood used for making furniture, inside trim, and cabinets.

firebrick Brick that is especially hard and heat-resistant. It is used for fireplaces.

fire cut The angular cut at the end of a joist that is designed to rest on a brick wall.

fire door A door that is fire resistant.

fixed light A permanently sealed window that cannot be opened.

fixture An electrical or plumbing unit that is a permanent part of the building.

flagstone A flat stone used for floors, steps, walks, or walls.

flashing A material used to make framing and roof intersections and other exposed places on the outside of a building watertight.

flat roof A roof with little or no pitch.

floor plan A drawing showing the top view of a building at a specific floor level.

flue The opening in a chimney through which smoke passes.

footing An extension at the bottom of a building foundation wall which distributes the load into the ground.

formal design Refers to an architectural design that follows a set or traditional pattern, featuring closed or separate rooms and a symmetrical floorplan.

foundation The basic structure on which a building rests.

framing The skeleton construction of a structure.

frost line The depth to which soil may freeze.

furring Narrow strips of wood nailed to a wall or ceiling to which wallboards, paneling, or ceiling tiles are attached.

gable A triangular end wall above the eaves of a building.

gable roof A roof which slopes on only two sides.

gambrel roof A roof having two slopes on each side. The lower slope is usually steeper than the upper one.

general lighting Lighting which is diffused, or spread, over a large area.

girder A horizontal beam which supports a floor system.

GLOSSARY

glazing Installing glass in windows or doors.

gothic An architectural style developed in Western Europe during the Middle Ages. Some of its features are pointed arches, high, steep roofs, and buttresses (projections beyond the outside wall which create additional strength and support).

grade The level of the ground.

graphic symbols A specific shape or design used on drawings to represent an object. The symbolic representation simplifies the drawing of a complex item.

green lumber Lumber that has not been dried and contains high levels of moisture.

grille An open work of wood, metal, or masonry that forms a screen-like wall. The open spaces allow passage of light, heat, and air.

ground line The level of the earth around a structure.

gusset A wood or metal plate used to strengthen joints.

gutter A horizontal trough at the eave for collecting water from a roof. The water flows into a downspout and is carried away from the building.

gypsum board A board composed of gypsum rock and fiberglass with a covering of paper. It is used for interior walls.

hardwood Wood from trees that grow slowly and have broad leaves as distinct from needles. Oak, maple, elm, birch, cherry, and mahogany are hardwoods as compared to pine and fir which are softwoods.

head The upper horizontal frame on a door or window.

header The horizontal construction member above wall openings.

headroom The space between the floor line and the ceiling.

hearth The fire-resistant floor inside a fireplace and the part of the floor that extends out into the room. It is usually made of fire-resistant brick or masonry.

hip rafter The diagonal rafter that extends from the top wall plate to the ridge board to form a hip.

hip roof A roof with four sloping sides.

humidity The moisture content in the air.

I-beam A steel beam with a cross section shaped like the letter I.

incandescent lighting Lighting produced by closed filament bulbs.

indirect lighting Artificial light which is reflected off ceilings and walls for general area lighting.

informal design Refers to an architectural style which is contemporary and fits into modern lifestyles, usually with open areas and a non-symmetrical floor plan.

insulation Material which obstructs the passage of sound, heat, or cold.

interior trim All interior finish molding, casing, and baseboards.

jack rafter A short rafter, usually used on hip roofs, that does not extend from the top plate to the ridge.

jalousie A window made up of many long, horizontal, thin, hinged panels.

jamb The upright piece which forms the sides of a doorway or window frame.

joints The points at which two separate materials meet or come together for a common bond.

joist A horizontal structural member which supports a floor or ceiling system.

keystone The middle stone at the top of an arch. This wedge-shaped piece holds the other stones or pieces in place.

lallycolumn A vertical steel column that supports girders and beams.

laminated timber Timber made from thin layers of wood glued together.

landscape architect A person who develops the land around a building to enhance and support the use of the structure.

lap joint The joint which is formed when two pieces of material are overlapped.

Fundamentals of Architectural Design

GLOSSARY

lath Sheet metal screening or wooden strips used as a base over which plaster is applied.

lattice A grille made by crossing strips of wood or metal.

leader A line on a drawing that connects an explanatory note to an area or symbol.

lites The multiple panes of glass which make up a window.

linear foot One foot measured in a straight line.

line conventions The series of lines in the drawing that have a special designations.

lintel A horizontal member across the top of door or window openings in a wall. It supports the load, or weight, of the wall, above the opening.

live load The weight in a structure from all the moveable objects that are not permanently installed.

loads Refers to weight. Live load is the total weight of all movable objects within a building. Dead load is the total weight of all permanent or stationary construction in a building.

load-bearing walls The walls that support weight from above as well as their own weight.

lot The area of land on which structures are built.

louver An opening with a series of horizontal slats which can be adjusted to provide ventilation and light but to keep out rain. They can also be adjusted to control the amount of sunlight entering and to provide privacy.

mansard roof A four-sided roof with two slopes on each side. The lower slopes are nearly vertical and the upper slopes, nearly flat. This allows for more headroom throughout the upper, or top, story.

marble A hard limestone that can be highly polished.

masonry Refers to anything built with stone, tiles, brick, or concrete.

material list A list of all the materials and their description that is needed to build the structure.

member A single piece of structural material in a building.

metal tie A strip of metal used to fasten members together.

millwork The finished woodwork in a building, such as cabinets and trim.

model A small size copy of a structure, often made to scale so the size or dimensions compare to the original being represented, which is created to show the appearance of the finished building.

moisture barrier The materials that stop the passage of moisture into the structure.

mortar A combination of cement, sand, and water used for bonding bricks and stone.

newel The end post that supports the handrail at the top and bottom of a stairway.

nonbearing wall A wall that does not support a roof.

nonferrous metal Metal that does not contain any iron.

nosing The rounded edge at the front of a stair tread.

on center (oc) The measurement made from the center of one structural member to the center of another.

open plan A floor plan in which there are few interior partitions or walls in the living area.

orientation Refers to the particular placement of a structure on a site in relation to the sun, wind, view, surrounding noise, and land contours.

outlet An electrical box, or receptacle, through which current is drawn from the electrical system for lighting or appliances.

overall dimensions The dimensions that give the total length, width, and height of an object.

overhang The distance a roof projects beyond a wall.

pane Small sheets of window glass.

panel A thin sheet of wood, plywood, or similar material used for a wall cover.

partition Any structure or wall that divides or separates spaces within a building.

passive solar design Capturing the heat from the sun into the building with no mechanical parts.

GLOSSARY

patio An open court used for outdoor living activities.

picture window A large single-pane window.

pilaster A reinforcing column set within or against a wall.

pitch The ratio of the roof's slope.

plan A horizontal drawing of a section of a building that shows walls, doors, windows, stairs, chimneys, etc., as viewed from above.

plaster A mortar-like mixture that hardens on drying, used for covering walls and ceilings.

plasterboard A rigid board made of a plaster-type material covered on both sides with heavy paper. It is often used instead of plaster.

plat A map of an area which shows the boundaries of lots.

plate The horizontal member at the top and bottom of a row of studs.

plate glass Thick, high quality sheets of glass used in large windows.

plot A parcel of land.

plot plan A drawing that is part of the working drawing set that shows the size and shape of the building site. included in the plan are all structures, walks, drives, decks, patios, pools, and large geologic features.

plywood A panelized wood product made from thin sheets of wood that are glued together at right angles to increase its strength.

porch A covered area attached to a building.

post A vertical supporting member.

post-and beam construction A construction of vertical columns supporting horizontal beams.

presentation drawing A drawing showing an artist's interpretation of the appearance of a structure.

protractor Drawing instrument with markings to measure angles in degrees.

quarter-round A small convex molding that is a quarter of a circle.

quoins Large, square stones set in the corners of a building.

rafters Structural members of the roof frame.

reinforced concrete Concrete in which steel bars are embedded for strength.

rendering Adding realism to a drawing by putting in shading and/or coloring.

ridge The top edge of a roof where the roof rafters meet.

rise The vertical height of a roof, of a step, or a flight of stairs.

riser The vertical board between two treads, or steps, of a stairway.

rough floor The subfloor over which the finished floor is placed.

rubble Irregular-shaped stone or brick used for masonry.

run The width of a step or the horizontal distance covered by a flight of stairs. This term is also used to describe the horizontal length of a rafter.

r-value The rating of the resistance of the heat flow through building materials. Insulation materials have R-values. The greater the number the better the insulation quality.

reinforcing bars Steel bars added to concrete for additional strength. Often called rebars.

sash The single frame in which window glass is set. This frame can be moved up or down.

scale, architect's Measuring instrument used in architectural drawing. Scale also refers to the dimension that represents the structure shown in a drawing.

schedule A listing of parts.

section A drawing of an object as though it were cut in order to expose the interior construction.

sectional drawing A sectional is made when it is necessary to reveal the interior of an item. The drawing is a "slice" to depict inside of the item.

Fundamentals of Architectural Design

GLOSSARY

septic tank A tank in which sewage is decomposed by bacterial action. Solids and liquids flow from the tank into the ground through a tile bed.

service connection The point at which the electric wires are connected to a building from utility company power lines.

set back The allowable building distance from the property line of a lot for a building. This distance determines the area of the lot on which a structure can be built. Local zoning regulations determine these distances.

sheathing The covering material placed over the exterior studding or rafters of a structure.

shed roof A roof that slants in one direction.

shingles Thin pieces of material that overlap each other in covering a roof or wall. Types of shingles include wood, tile, slate, and asphalt.

siding The outside surface or finish of an exterior wall.

sill The first wood member placed directly on top of the foundation wall. It is also the horizontal member that forms the bottom of a window or door opening.

site The lot on which a building is constructed.

site analysis The study of the building site to insure proper land use and good design.

skeleton framing Structures that are built stick-by-stick and are open framed.

skylight A glass or plastic covered opening in a roof that admits light.

slab foundation A concrete floor and foundation system poured directly on the ground.

sleepers Wood strips laid on a slab floor to which the finished flooring is attached.

slope diagram A drawing that indicates a comparison between the horizontal run and the rise of a roof.

soffit The underside surface of an overhang, such as under the roof overhang.

solar energy The heat generated by the sun. An active solar system collects the sun's heat outside the structure, stores it, and distributes the warmth through the building by means of air or liquid. A passive solar system has no mechanical parts. It is designed to take advantage of the positions of the sun, capturing heat when there is sunshine and keeping heat losses to a minimum when there is no sunlight.

spacing The distances between structural members.

span The horizontal distance between two supports for structural members such as walls, beams, and joists.

specifications The written descriptions, dimensions, or directions about parts or members of a structure.

splice To attach, or join, two similar members together in a straight line.

split-level house A one-story house with another level about half a floor above or below the main level.

stack A vertical plumbing pipe.

steel cage construction Skeleton framing using steel girders and beams.

steel framing Skeleton framing using structural steel.

stock Materials that are available in standard sizes.

stool The bottom horizontal strip on an inside windowsill.

stringer The side of a stairway. The supporting member holds the treads and risers of the stairs.

stucco The plaster used for covering exterior walls.

studs The evenly spaced upright members in the framework of a building's wall.

subcontractor A person or company providing specialized construction services.

subfloor The flooring surface which is laid directly on the floor joists and is covered with finished flooring.

surfaced lumber Lumber that has been smoothed, or dressed, by putting it through a planer.

survey A drawing showing the topographic, or surface features, of a lot.

GLOSSARY

symmetrical Refers to something that is balanced, or the same on both sides. In a symmetrical design, each side of a central dividing line is the same.

texture The roughness or smoothness of a surface.

thermostat A device for controlling the amount of heat automatically.

threshold The member on top of the finish floor and the sill of the exterior doors. The door swings over this piece of stone, wood, or metal.

tile A flat piece of baked clay, often glazed for a hard, smooth surface, that is used for covering floors, walls, and other surfaces.

timber Structural lumber which has a cross section larger than 4 by 6 inches (100 by 150 mm).

traditional architectural design A design that reflects the influence of the customs, habits (traditions), building, etc., of earlier periods.

traffic pattern The routes by which people move around and through a building.

tread The horizontal member of a stair.

truss A prefabricated triangular-shaped structure for framing a roof. It will support a roof load over a long span.

T-foundation A foundation in which the widest portion, the footing, is at the bottom. Built in the shape of an inverted T, it is used for structures requiring a basement or a floor raised above the ground.

T-square A drafting instrument shaped like the letter T used for straight, accurate drawing of horizontal lines.

valley The internal angle formed by the two sloping sides of a roof.

vapor barrier A watertight material that is used to block the passage of moisture or water vapor into or through walls.

vault A row of connected arches which creates an arched roof or ceiling.

vent An opening to allow the passage of air in or out of a structure, for ventilation.

ventilation The exchange of air throughout a structure.

vestibule A small entrance hall, or lobby.

video display terminal (VDT) An input device for a computer that has a keyboard similar to that of a typewriter, a light pen, and a screen for display of information entered and stored in the computer.

wallboard Large rigid sheets fastened to the frame of a building to provide a surface finish.

water closet The toilet fixture.

waterproof Material or construction that prevents the passage of water.

weatherstrip Strips of material which are attached along the edges of windows and doors to help keep out cold air and to reduce heat loss.

well opening An opening in a floor for a stairway.

work triangle A triangular space created by connecting the three basic areas in a kitchen: storage, cleaning and preparation, and cooking.

zoning ordinance Building code ordinances controlling land development and the location of structures.

APPENDIX

POTTING SHED
ANSWERS FOR BLUEPRINT READING QUESTIONS UNIT 29

1. 12' x 13'
2. 4' x 5'
3. 2'-8" x 6'-8"
4. ⊖
5. ◇
6. $
7. ○
8. wall cabinets
9. perspective
10. 2
11. 20'
12. 153'
13. 5'
14. 55'
15. 1/8" = 1'-0"
16. redwood
17. 7/24
18. 6'-8'
19. 8'-0"
20. ½" sheathing
21. 12"
22. 6"
23. composition shingles
24. ¼" = 1'-0"
25. ½"=1'-0"
26. 2 x 4
27. 16"

28. 2 x 4
29. 16"
30. 4 x 6
31. 2 x 6
32. 2-2 x 4s
33. 36"
34. door swings
35. 6"
36. 8'
37. ½" = 1'-0"
38. 3
39. 16"
40. 3"
41. 2"
42. 3
43. 2'-10"
44. 4'-3"
45. 2 x 4
46. 1 ½" x 3 ½"
47. yes
48. yes
49. ▱
50. ⧅
51. 2 x 6
52. 14 feet
53. barge rafters
54. 2 x 4

55. 1 inch
56. 2 x 6
57. diameter
58. 10 inches
59. 4 feet
60. 12 inches
61. 18 inches
62. 18 inches
63. 4 x 6
64. 16 inches
65. mud sill
66. 8 inches
67. 12" x 12" x 12"
68. 6 inches
69. 4'-3"
70. 1 x 12 redwood
71. felt building paper
72. 6 inches
73. ½" sheet-rock
74. double top plate
75. trimmer studs
76. blocking
77. 1" x 5"
78. 4 feet
79. 6 inches
80. 4 different scales

INDEX

Fundamentals of Architectural Design